BECTON

BECTON:
Autobiography of a
Soldier and Public Servant

★ ★ ★

By Lt. Gen. Julius W. Becton Jr.

NAVAL INSTITUTE PRESS
Annapolis, Maryland

Naval Institute Press
291 Wood Road
Annapolis, MD 21402

Library of Congress Cataloging-in-Publication Data

Becton, Julius W. (Julius Wesley), 1926–
  Becton : autobiography of a soldier and public servant / Julius W. Becton, Jr.
    p. cm.
  Includes bibliographical references and index.
  ISBN 978-1-59114-021-4 (alk. paper)
  1. Becton, Julius W. (Julius Wesley), 1926- 2. Generals—United States—Biography. 3. African American generals—Biography. 4. United States. Army—Biography. 5. United States—Officials and employees—Biography. I. Title.
E840.5.B43A3 2008
355.0092—dc22
[B]

                                                                        2007045298

Printed in the United States of America on acid-free paper ∞

14 13 12 11 10 09 08   9 8 7 6 5 4 3 2

Dedication

Louise and I dedicate this autobiography to our children, to their children, and to all the children yet to come. It is our gift to our descendants, and it is designed to leave them with a sense of who we are and how we spent our time on this earth. Even those not born by the time our physical remains are laid to rest in Arlington National Cemetery will have an opportunity to know us by this legacy. Blood will be able to speak to blood beyond the grave.

CONTENTS

ILLUSTRATIONS

FOREWORD

★　　★　　★

God's grace is so awesome and so wonderful! It is by His grace that I have been privileged to share my life with Julius Wesley Becton Jr. As of this writing, I have been married to him for almost sixty years. After that amount of time, you could say that I am biased in my opinions about him. And you would be absolutely right. Loving eyes are very forgiving. Our affection for loved ones compensates for their human failings.

Like the rest of us, Julius is just a human being. But, I should add, a great human being. He is a man of the highest integrity, and his word is his bond. He is a gentleman in every sense of the word. He does not know how to be any other way.

Julius is also a courageous man. He is confident but not cocky, and he moves through the world with poise and ease. He is secure in himself and his ability, and he nurtures the talents of others without fear of being over-shadowed. He is a team player, and he plays to win. I believe that he is a natural-born leader.

Julius loves our country, and he loved his life's work in defense of it. His extensive involvement in a wide array of professional and civic associations is just another labor of that same love he feels for America.

In a nutshell, I am proud of my husband. He has lived a full life, and he has risen to professional heights he and I never contemplated. But both of us know where the credit belongs. It has been only by the grace of God that he has accomplished what he has and that we have been able to enjoy the life we have had together.

Julius' life is a story worth sharing. I invite you to draw your own conclusions.

Louise Thornton Becton
April 2007

ACKNOWLEDGMENTS

★   ★   ★

T he seed for this autobiography was planted by my close friend Jafus Cavil while I was president of Prairie View A&M University in the early 1990s. Jafus was aided and abetted by Joseph Galloway, who spent several days with us discussing the feasibility of such a project. Joe's work on his own book *We Were Soldiers Once, and Young*, which he coauthored with Harold G. Moore, precluded his collaborating with me, but he has remained a close friend and adviser.[1]

My wife Louise has been the guiding force, as chief contributor and severest critic, in making this book a reality. Her superb intellect and unwavering vision helped to chart its direction. No man could ask for a better life partner.

I also thank our children Shirley, Karen, Joyce, Renee, and Wes for their love, inspiration, and constant encouragement. No one could imagine a better cheerleading squad. Although she is not our child by birth, Marquita Brooks, Esq., is among those we consider family, and we are grateful for her careful scrutiny of the text.

In the early 2000s Linda Louise Riley, Esq., joined the effort as the primary writer. Her breast cancer, diagnosed not long afterward, slowed the pace considerably. But her dogged determination, with collaboration from her son, Thomas Louis Spencer, made the difference.

A host of friends helped keep us on track with encouragement, suggestions, and information. Bob and Betty Williams, Betty Travaglini, and Bob Healey helped Louise and me re-create on paper the minutiae of our early lives. The research of Ted Goldsborough, a retired teacher with access to Lower Merion High School archives, was a godsend. Al and Jasper Horton, cousins on my father's side of the family, offered invaluable family history. Bill Robertson's unpublished memoirs provided an outstanding account of our Vietnam experiences.

Some people cannot read or hear about my thanks to them. Gen. Creighton Abrams, now deceased, is among them. He was a godfather of sorts, selecting me to command the 1st Cavalry Division. His replacement, Gen. Fred Weyand, read beyond a negative report that could have killed my career as a general officer.

There is no way I can acknowledge everyone who deserves mention. Countless people have touched my life, and the fact that their names are not mentioned here does not in any way diminish their influence and their lasting impact on my life.

In closing, I give honor and thanks to God. It is only by His grace that it has been possible for me to tell this story.

PROLOGUE

★ ★ ★

Pusan, 1950

"**L**ieutenant Becton, the old man wants to see you." So said the messenger from company headquarters.

I immediately stopped trying to get my platoon organized and reported to Capt. Bill Porter, the ordinarily gregarious company commander. This time Bill's words were few. His puzzled look said, "What in the hell is going on?" but all he said aloud was, "They want to see you at battalion." When I asked why, he said sharply, "Get your butt up there!"

The battalion operations officer, Maj. "Windy" Phillips, second senior black officer in the battalion and a World War II combat veteran, was almost as cryptic as Porter. "Becton, they want to see you at regiment. There is a jeep waiting to take you there and a truck for your men," Phillips said.

The company commander, I explained, had said nothing about my platoon. "You will only need about half a squad," Phillips replied. "What in the world is going on, sir?" I asked. "All I know is that regiment called and said have you report to regimental headquarters with your soldiers," he said. "You don't have much time to waste. Be sure to take all your gear."

When the messenger found me, we had been in Pusan, Korea, for less than twenty-four hours, so this was rather heady stuff. Rumors were flying that we were getting our butts kicked: The U.S. Forces were being pushed back by the North Koreans into something called the Pusan Perimeter. And now I was off to God knows where.

As we bounced along a very bumpy road to Taegu, the location of the 9th Infantry regimental headquarters, I was at a total loss. Try as I might, I could not think of any reason for what was happening. The fact that both my company commander and the battalion operations officer (S-3) were apparently in the dark added to my apprehension.

We reached Taegu and found the regimental command post and the operations center. Having commanded the 9th Infantry Regimental Drill Team back at Fort Lewis, I knew quite a few of the officers and noncommissioned officers (NCOs) in the S-3's shop. There was no time for conversation as I was rushed in. After a brief, "How are you doing?" the harried S-3 informed me that my battalion, the 3rd Battalion, would move out this evening, heading to Pohang. I was to proceed there with a large radio rig for task force command communications.

I had a lot of questions. Why me? Why is the only black infantry battalion in the division being moved out? What's our mission? Will the regiment follow? I only managed to ask about Pohang's location, to whom I would report, and the expected enemy situation en route.

Personnel in the S-3's office laid out maps and sketched the route. No enemy had been reported in the area, I was assured. The 3rd Battalion would be part of Task Force Bradley, so named because it was headed up by Assistant Division Commander Brig. Gen. Sladen Bradley. It would include elements of the division engineers, artillery, and other support units. Frankly, I did not give any thought to the fact that this task force would be integrated, made up of all white units except for my black infantry battalion and led by a white commander.

After a quick field meal, my unit and I headed east toward Pohang with a two-and-a-half-ton radio truck, a trailer, a three-quarters-ton truck, and a jeep. We moved through hills and valleys, which were fairly wooded with considerable underbrush. Certain points seemed to me to be ideal places for an ambush. I tried to banish the thought, recalling that regiment had said, "No sweat," because no enemy activity had been reported nearby.

We arrived at our destination, the Yonil Air Field, at about 0430 hours. Uneventful. Mission accomplished.

Little did I know how close we had come to death. While we waited at the airbase for the rest of the battalion to join us, we caught a few winks, then woke abruptly to the news that the battalion had been ambushed and sustained casualties in the same area we had passed through. Obviously, the ambushers let my squad through, not appreciating the significance of our cargo.

This was the first time I really appreciated my guardian angel—that unseen something that always seems to be present, aligning the stars and providing protection from near misses, that sixth sense that whispers, *"You don't want to do that."*

CHAPTER ONE

★ ★ ★

Growing up on the Main Line

I was born on Tuesday, 29 June 1926, to Julius Wesley and Rose Banks Becton in Bryn Mawr, Pennsylvania. For the most part, it was an uneventful day. The only notables were my birth weight—a sizeable nine and one-half pounds—and the fact that I was birthed in Bryn Mawr Hospital. At the time, many black mothers did not have access to medical facilities and gave birth at home. A year later my brother, Joseph William Becton, joined our family.

That unseen protective force I first truly recognized in Korea must have been watching over me from the start. Two years into my life, I contracted diphtheria, an acute bacterial disease that was common in the 1930s and claimed many lives, especially among children. I was at death's door. It was the grace of God and the efforts of Dr. Monroe Tunnell, a black physician, that made the difference. I survived.

During the Great Depression, my brother and I were joined by Barbara Godett, who for all practical purposes became our sister. John Godett and my father had been childhood friends back in North Carolina and had reconnected as adults in Philadelphia. They were both married, and each had two sons. When Barbara was born on 2 June 1934, her mother, Violet, became very ill and was hospitalized for seven months. My parents offered to care for Barbara. As she described the situation in a letter to me, "Mom and Daddy Becton became my godparents, and Julius and Joe became my brothers. [Suddenly, I had] four brothers and two sets of parents."

Home was a two-bedroom basement apartment in the Bryn Mawr Courts Apartments on the northwest corner of Morris and Montgomery Avenues. This was a twenty-four-unit, horseshoe-shaped building whose tenants included railroad magnates, lawyers, bankers, and the like. At the very least, an apartment unit sold for about $10,000, which was a lot of money in the 1920s and 1930s.

The former Bryn Mawr Courts Apartments, now called College Hall Apartments, at 801 Montgomery Avenue and Morris Road, Bryn Mawr, Pennsylvania. (Taken by Ted Goldsborough October 1996; courtesy of the Lower Merion Historical Society)

Left to right: Me, Mom, Dad, and Joe. (Author collection)

Bryn Mawr is in a wealthy area of Pennsylvania known as the Main Line. As I remember, it lacked much of the racial tension that plagued many parts of the United States, probably because few blacks could afford to live there and most of those who did held nonthreatening positions serving the white community. Perhaps the fact that we were rare explains something I remember clearly from when Joe and I were three and four years old. We would be playing outside, and white teenage girls and young women en route to one of the nearby private schools or Bryn Mawr College would often pat us on the head and touch us under the chin. Maybe they thought we were novelties, with our black skin and nappy hair!

I perceived no derisive or derogatory intent. As a child, you can often tell when a touch does not feel right, and that was not the case with these girls and women. I think it was just innocent curiosity.

My father was the head janitor for our apartment building. Five or six black women who worked as maids in the units upstairs also lived in the basement, along with a male assistant janitor. We developed into a very close-knit group, a little "village" of very hardworking, religious people. In such an environment, Joe and I found it exceedingly difficult to get away with any mischief. There was always someone to tell on us when we misbehaved.

As a janitor my father earned about thirty-five dollars every two weeks with "benefits." For one, our apartment was rent-free. We also received free milk and ice. This was because the iceman and milkman perceived my father to be the building's gatekeeper. Whether this was true, I do not know. But you could say my father controlled access to the market of residents upstairs and accepted small gratuities from various tradesmen.

My father's position also allowed him to help our relatives. Twelve of the apartment units upstairs had maid's quarters in the basement that my father controlled. This translated into a place to stay, and one less worry, for a relative from the South who was trying to get a fresh start up North. From age eight or nine, I do not recall a time that a relative or close friend was not "visiting." The visitors included James Robert "Bob" Williams, whom I tagged as my mother's third son and who later became my best man. His family lived in Haverford Township, but he aspired to be a medical doctor and wanted to attend Lower Merion Senior High School, so he came to live with us during his last two years of high school.

All in all, we lived very well. My father's job, coupled with my mother's work as a housekeeper and laundress, amply provided for us. I cannot remember a day when we went hungry—something many blacks of that era could not say.

My parents were quite frugal when it came to money. Things we could do for ourselves without spending, we did. I was almost a teenager before I had my first barbershop haircut. Every two weeks, Dad sat Joe and me on a stool and cut our hair. He got to be pretty good at it.

There were no personal telephones in any of the basement units, just a pay phone shared by all. I believe we could have afforded phone service in our apartment. My mother was against this, however. Her view was that if we had a phone, all the neighbors would be knocking down our door to use it.

All the residents in the basement complex were churchgoers. There were two black churches in Bryn Mawr and on Sundays, we split. Half went to the Bethel African Methodist Episcopal Church and the other half, including my family, attended Saints Memorial Baptist Church. At the age of five, I decided to be baptized. I cannot honestly say that I had some magnificent rapture or sudden longing to cleanse my original sin. It just seemed like the thing to do at the time.

For my mother and us children, Sundays were completely dedicated to church. A typical Sunday began with the weekly family reading of the Bible, followed by the blessing and breakfast. At 10:30 AM, it was off to Junior Church. The regular service—the only part my father attended—lasted from 11:00 AM to sometime between 12:30 PM and 1:00 PM, and that was followed by an hour and a half of Sunday school. Sunday communion lasted from 3:00 PM to about 4:00 PM or 4:30 PM. I then attended the Baptist Youth Protestant Union from 6:45 PM to 8:00 PM, and concluded the day with the evening service. More than twelve hours of church!

I doubt that you could find a preacher who would say that you could get "too much Jesus" in one day. I would not say that myself. Nowadays, however, my wife Louise and I attend only the one-hour 10:30 AM service at the Fort Myer Memorial Chapel. That has been our practice for more than fifty years.

To say that my parents valued education would be an understatement. My father had a third-grade education. My mother had attended school until tenth grade, which was the highest level available during her school days. However, it was not even questioned that my brother and I would go to school and do our best. We attended the Bryn Mawr Grammar School from kindergarten through grade seven, and I missed only two days of class.

In third grade, my teacher was Miss Florence A. Rees. I remember her genuine concern when I got into trouble to this day. I was fortunate to have a teacher who actually cared about my well-being and growth. In fact, our school district always had some of the best, most loyal, dedicated, and caring teachers available. I don't think any were crusading to bring equal educational opportunities or rights to blacks or other minority groups. They were not activists or saints, simply very good teachers. I never had a minority teacher during my entire K–12 years.

Beyond kindergarten, my school utilized a tracking system that divided students into tracks A—the higher level—and B. I started out in the A track and remained there through the third grade. In fourth grade, however, I was demoted to 4B—not for bad grades, but for bad behavior. What happened was that one day, a white boy and I took a white girl into the boys' bathroom. I say "took" because I do not think she went willingly. Why I did it, I do not know. But after a thorough sentence of corporal punishment executed upon my rear end, I never considered doing such a thing again. I eventually returned to the A track in fifth grade.

All students in our school were required to play a musical instrument. I took up the clarinet, quickly dashing any dreams of my being the next Benny Goodman. My brother, who chose the violin, stuck it out a little longer but eventually realized he was never going to be a virtuoso. It is worth noting, though, that years later, Joe's sons Jerry and Joseph turned out to be fine musicians.

Following grammar school, I attended Lower Merion Junior High School (renamed Ardmore Junior High School in 1939) for the eighth and ninth grades, then graduated to Lower Merion Senior High School, which was right next door. Lower Merion was and still is ranked in the top high schools in the nation, with a long and impressive list of distinguished alumni and all the trappings of a first-rate prep school.[1] When I attended, it offered every activity imaginable, including Riding Club. The student body totaled approximately 1,400. There were about 420 in my graduating class, and they represented three basic ethnic groups: white Anglo-Saxon Protestants (primarily the wealthy children of the Main Line), Italians, and blacks. There were also a few Asians. One of my good friends, Don Okada, had a German mother and a Japanese father, which was a noteworthy mix of ethnicities once World War II starting raging during our high school years.

Lower Merion's excellent academic reputation was well deserved, and my high school curriculum was quite rigorous. I learned pretty fast, and I particularly liked any class that required mechanical activities, such as shop. I also enjoyed social studies and Portuguese, which was taught by Miss Nora Thompson, my homeroom teacher.

I struggled through biology and chemistry. Ironically, my parents had always expected me to become a physician—the epitome of success in black society at the time. In truth, I did have some interest in medicine, stemming from when I developed a series of boils under my right arm and Dr. Atkinson, then the only black doctor in Bryn Mawr, lanced them for me. I found the procedure fascinating. But my difficulties with the core courses of medical studies made it pretty clear that I was not meant to become a doctor.

When Joe and I got home from school, homework came first. No arguments. After we finished our schoolwork and Mom had conducted a cursory review, we were free to go outside and play or run errands for our family and for apartment tenants. I enjoyed running errands for the residents because doing so often meant generous tips.

There were also lots of chores to be done. During the heating season, Joe and I shoveled coal into the basement furnace and shoveled snow off the walks. In warm weather, we cut grass, although more often than not we got in the way of the serious grass cutter—our father. The onset of fall meant raking leaves around the property. We helped pick up trash all around the year.

A typical evening after dinner was spent listening to radio programs such as *Amos 'n Andy* or *The Jack Benny Show*. Some of those programs are now considered demeaning to black people, but such racial sensitivities came later.

There were no other black children in the apartment complex where we lived, and my brother and I did not play with the white children from upstairs. Throughout my school years, most of my close friends were black. My best friends in grammar school were Charles Harper and Charles Callahan.

Charles Callahan's parents were servants on a wealthy estate in Bryn Mawr, and they had four sons who attended the grammar school. Often, the Callahan brothers, my brother, and I had to band together to protect ourselves from the bullies.

There is, of course, nothing unusual about bullies in school. What was troubling about our situation was that the bullies in question were black like us. They called us the "white folks' niggers," and they did not use that noun in an endearing sense, the way some blacks do today. We were white folks' niggers because we were literally from the other side of the tracks—the white side of the Pennsylvania Railroad line that divided Bryn Mawr physically, economically, and ethnically.

Looking back on it, I would say those bullies demonstrated a "crab" mentality, a "Willie Lynch" syndrome in which blacks try to keep other blacks down rather than help to lift them up.[2] Fortunately, we left the bullying behind in grammar school. There was little, if any, of that at the junior and senior high schools.

My own family stressed constant, habitual respect for other people, especially for women and the elderly. From my earliest recollection, Dad hammered that lesson into our heads, and it goes without saying that he practiced what he preached. We were expected to open doors and hold them for women and older people. We were expected to offer up our seats on public transportation. When walking down the sidewalk with a female, we were expected to walk on the street side. I presume this was meant to shield them from the traffic in the event a vehicle ran off the road, although I have heard that before the widespread adoption of indoor plumbing, men walked on the street side to protect women from being hit by the contents of slop jars emptied from windows above.

Needless to say, the rules of respect extended to family members, living and dead, which was a reality that caused me considerable discomfort on at least one occasion. In January 1941, my father's brother died. In keeping with the long-standing black custom of burying loved ones where they had been born, Uncle Will was to be buried in North Harlowe, North Carolina. I was appointed to accompany his casket on the journey from Philadelphia. I was fourteen, which made me old enough to understand death, but I was not all that keen about being around dead people. In recognition of the solemn nature of the occasion, I wore my Boy Scout uniform on the trip.

We had to change trains in Washington, D.C., and trains in the South were still very much segregated in 1941. Blacks sat in the passenger cars toward the front of the train, which placed them closest to the smoke and soot of the coal-fed engine, and whites sat farther back. The races shared eating facilities, but segregation was enforced by the clock: Blacks ate after the whites had finished, and if the black passengers were still eating when the train pulled into a station, crew members pulled the shades of the dining car so that white folks outside would not see the black diners. Rather than put up with this indignity, blacks often brought their own food on board and ate in their Jim Crow cars.

Needless to say, when I boarded the train in Washington, I sat up front in the colored section. But it was not the rules of segregation that disturbed me on that particular journey. Uncle Will's remains were in the baggage car right in front of our coach. As far as I was concerned, that was much too close for comfort.

We arrived in New Bern, North Carolina, late in the evening, and ours was the very last train to stop that night. The station master had the casket moved into the baggage room, then he showed me to the station's colored section next door, where there was a bench where I could sleep. Then he went home, telling me the undertaker would arrive in the morning. The station was empty except for me and Uncle Will. I had a very sleepless night.

I did not know for sure what I wanted to be when I grew up for much of my childhood. But I knew from an early age that I did not want to become a farmer.

Every year, from the time I was six or seven, Mom, Joe, and I spent two weeks visiting my mother's birthplace in Caroline County, Virginia. My maternal grandfather, Randall Banks—"Round" Banks, as he was known— owned about twenty acres of land there, and he raised cucumbers, tobacco, corn, pigs, cows, and chickens. His house was on a dirt road, and it lacked certain comforts to which I had become accustomed. Sometime in the late 1930s or early 1940, my grandfather installed a pump in the kitchen, which meant we no longer had to carry buckets of water from the well outside. But the bathroom facilities continued to be an outhouse, and pages from the Sears & Roebuck catalog served as toilet paper. The house had no electricity, just a kerosene lantern for light.

I did enjoy much of the time I spent at my grandfather's house. We fished for catfish and eel in nearby streams, and it was always thrilling to feel a tug on the line. Also, since religion was integral to my grandfather's life, we usually attended two or three revivals during our stay. These were always memorable events. The preaching was spirited, and the singing was good.

What I most enjoyed, though, were the food and the attention I got from the girls who liked black guys from up North.

Field work was another matter. I picked cucumbers, pulled "suckers" off tobacco, and cut corn. I slopped the hogs and milked a cow—once. I was, for the most part, a city boy. Out in the fields, I was ready to quit after three or four hours. It was really hard work! The only thing that kept me going was a determination not to be outdone by the others working in the fields.

After our time with my mother's family, Dad would join us and we would drive to Craven County, North Carolina, to spend his fifteen days of vacation with his folks. My paternal grandfather lived in Harlowe and was also a farmer. We normally stayed with Dad's sister, Aunt Ada, in Morehead City. Her husband, Curtis Horton, ran an oyster house in the winter, worked as a gardener during the summer, and served as a sexton at a white Methodist church.

I learned to swim in Morehead City, and I also spent a lot of time there fishing and crabbing. Morehead City was also where I got shot at for the first time.

I was five or six years old and playing down by the waters with my cousins Cecil, Hank, and Alphonzo Horton. Somebody had the bright idea of liberating a small rowboat that belonged to someone else. We were enjoying the ride until shots from a .22-caliber rifle rang out. Our assailant turned out to be a distant cousin who had decided to teach us a lesson. We learned it well. You never saw young boys get out of a boat so fast.

I always had a good time in Morehead City. I had a lot of relatives there. Aunt Ada had nine children, and Dad's other sister, Sarah Sadie George, had seventeen. Aunt Sadie's husband, Napoleon George, had a bad heart and almost never worked. I do not know how they made it from Aunt Sadie's earnings as a domestic worker, but they did.

In 1934, when I was eight, we were in Morehead City for our annual visit. My cousin Al Horton was ten, and he was always bugging my father to let him drive our two-year-old Ford. One day, he persuaded my father to let him drive the car down the alley to wash it. As Al drove off, his older brothers Cecil and Hank showed up, along with Lonnie George, another cousin. "Move over," Lonnie said to Al. "You don't know how to drive this car." The drive through the alley became what the law calls a "frolic and detour." And not far from my Uncle Curtis's house, Lonnie lost control. The car flipped over several times and landed on its top.

Some white passersby took the group to the hospital, but, luckily, no one was badly hurt. The car was totaled.

Hank was the first to leave the hospital, so he had a head start on explaining the accident at home. Even then he had the gift of gab, and this may have been his audition for his later career as a preacher and politician. He served three four-year terms as mayor of Morehead City.

My father took the news about his car in stride. He was not easily riled. But I think he also figured that since he had given the car keys to Al, he had to accept whatever happened. He wired the manager of the Bryn Mawr Courts Apartments that his car had been totaled, requesting money to buy a new one. The money was immediately sent, and the next day Dad went to the Ford dealership. Dad had always driven a Ford.

I am sure he thought he would be able to buy a new car without a hassle. After all, money was no object. But the people at the dealership did not know that. All they saw was a black man—somebody to be ignored at will—so they ignored him. Dad was extremely patient, but anybody can get tired of waiting. Finally, he left.

He went to the Chevrolet dealership the next day and bought a new car. He drove back to the Ford dealer, parked the Chevrolet out front, and walked over to the salesmen. He calmly told them he had been there yesterday to buy a new Ford but because everybody ignored him, he had been forced to buy that Chevrolet.

I think they got the message. Dad drove Chevrolets from that time on.

Sports, particularly football and track, were where I stood out as I got older. Lower Merion excelled at sports due to a skilled and consistent coaching system, quality trainers, and the best fans in Pennsylvania. We were expected to win, and win we did. During my three years of high school football, the Bulldogs of Lower Merion won all but two games and tied one. I had to maintain a B average in order to play football. Because I naturally enjoyed the sport and also wanted to do well academically, I had a double incentive to excel.

I was pretty good at football. In my sophomore year, I played on the second-string team, then moved up to first string. In those days, there were no separate offensive and defensive teams, so I played center on offense and linebacker on defense.

During my senior year, Red Blaik, football coach at Dartmouth, sent me a card, asking whether I would be interested in playing football there. That same year, I was selected as a runner-up to Chuck Bednarik as center on the Pennsylvania All-State Team. Bednarik went on to play for the Philadelphia Eagles. I also had the privilege to play against the great Emlen Tunnell, who attended Radnor High School and was, to the best of my knowledge, the only black team captain for a school on the Main Line. Tunnell ended up playing for the New York Giants and the Green Bay Packers. Both he and Bednarik were named to the Pro Football Hall of Fame in 1967.

I remember both bad and good days on the football field. One of the worst was in 1942, when Lower Merion was playing West Philadelphia High School. I missed intercepting a pass and was so furious that I lay on the ground, childishly pounding my fist into the grass. I did not realize it, but the guy filming the game kept the camera on me for what seemed like an eternity, particularly during the postgame critique. I never did that again.

One of my best days came a year later, when Lower Merion was playing Upper Darby, an archrival. Gus Dielens was the Upper Darby passer, and I was one of the Lower Merion linebackers. As the newspaper reported, Gus was throwing and I was catching. I intercepted five passes.

Although Lower Merion had never had a black captain of a major sports team, I was good enough to be seriously considered as a candidate, and at the start of the 1943–44 school year, I did something that may have set my azimuth for the future. All varsity-lettered players voted for the captain, and the vote resulted in a tie between Dick Whiting and me, with Dan Poore one vote behind us. I had voted for Dick. Rather than simply name Dick and me cocaptains, the coaches called for a new vote, in which we would choose two cocaptains. The top two vote-getters the second time around were Dick and Dan. In all honesty, losing out had no impact on me. But when I share this story, people often ask why I didn't vote for myself. The answer is that I had some vague notion about the impropriety of voting for myself, and becoming captain of the football team was not important enough to me to do that.

I also excelled in track and field. My events were the short dashes—50 yards, 100 yards, and an occasional 220 yards. I also competed in the long jump, which was then called the broad jump, and became state champion of the Pennsylvania Interscholastic Athletic Association during my senior year. As a matter of fact, the first time I was inside Franklin Field at the University of Pennsylvania was to participate in the Penn Relays twice for Lower Merion High School. I had previously been to Franklin Field when Mom took Joe and me to watch the parade of cadets and midshipmen for

The "winning" Lower Merion High School football team, ca. 1943. Left to right: (line) Dick Whiting, Bill Ellmaker, Jules Arronson, Stewart Young, me, George Morgan, Luiz Mortenson; (backfield) Frank Junker, Dan Poore, Ted Hepke, Frank Basile. (Author collection)

the annual Army and Navy football game. We did not go inside the stadium then, so it was a big deal for me to compete inside the stadium.

My mother was the big sports buff of the family, and she made it out to every one of my football games. She was an avid fan of baseball, basketball, and football. During baseball season, she listened to the Phillies and Athletics games on the radio while she ironed clothes. Later in life she held season tickets for the Philadelphia Eagles. She also closely followed the career of one of her cousin Ora Washington, who was a singles tennis champion in the 1930s.

Although my father took Joe and me to see both of the Philadelphia Major League Baseball teams and also the Philadelphia Stars of the Negro League, he was rather lukewarm to football and basketball. And he saw me perform in track only one time. In early June 1944, after I had graduated from high school, my father came to a track meet at Franklin Field that featured high school champions from the various branches of the regional school districts. I was the reigning broad jump champion, and I really wanted to impress Dad. It was a disaster. I ended up with a severe knee bruise and had to be carried off the field.

Looking back, I can truly say that my participation in the Lower Merion sports program was extremely beneficial not only for my physical and mental well-being, but also for the life skills it imparted. For one, I learned true sportsmanship. Sports also taught me much about people in general. For example, there were few blacks on the football team, and during my senior year, I was the only black on the first string. On the football field, however, everyone was equal. During the game, the only issue was winning, which was embraced by the team.

I think that there are certain concerns all humans share and goals they will work together to achieve, no matter how different their backgrounds. The desire to win is one of those.

It would not be long before I witnessed another: the desire to survive.

CHAPTER TWO

★ ★ ★

My Call to Service

December 7, 1941, was a typical Sunday for my family. We spent the bulk of the day in church, so we did not hear about the Japanese attack on Pearl Harbor until late that evening when we were listening to the radio. The next day in school, students and teachers discussed the attack and the U.S. declaration of war against Japan. I was fifteen years old, however, and it was some time before I really grasped the enormity of what had happened.

By this time it was my ambition to become a pilot—a desire enhanced by a visit to the school by Gen. Henry "Hap" Arnold, who was then chief of staff of the Army Air Corps and a Lower Merion graduate. I had even joined the Civil Air Patrol (CAP) in my junior year in high school as a prelude to learning how to fly. CAP members took classes in aeronautics, navigation, meteorology, and aviation regulations, and we routinely participated in close order drill. I became quite proficient in that, and I often found myself in charge of the drilling, which gave me an opportunity to demonstrate leadership skills and gain experience giving orders to a racially mixed group.

In December 1943, at the age of seventeen, I joined the Army Air Corps Enlisted Reserves. I took the oath of enlistment along with four other members of the Lower Merion football team, which meant that I would be joining the active Army after I graduated from high school in June 1944. I was very eager to join. Bob Williams, who had lived with my family while attending high school, was already in flight school at Tuskegee and had fueled my eagerness with stories about his experiences there.

My parents showed no anxiety about my joining the service. All able-bodied Americans were contributing to the war effort. In fact, my brother Joe was already in the Navy. When he was fifteen, he had run away from home a couple of times. I never knew why, but he wanted to join the Navy.

Since Mom was convinced he would keep running away until something drastic happened, she signed papers stating that he was seventeen, permitting him to enlist.

The vast majority of Americans supported the war. There were conscientious objectors, of course, but they acted out of their deeply held religious belief that war is wrong no matter what. Generally, total mobilization was the order of the day.

At home, most people accepted severe restrictions without any grumbling. Sugar, silk, cigarettes, and gasoline were rationed—although black market gas was readily available at 25 cents a gallon—and hoarding was frowned upon. People saved empty bottles, tin cans, and the foil from cigarette packages and turned all these items in at collection points to be used for other purposes. I had not yet heard the term, but this was "recycling" in the truest sense. Families planted victory gardens of vegetables and fruit in their backyards. Those who had no backyard had flower boxes seeded with tomatoes and carrots. People figured that if they grew food at home, more would be available for the troops overseas.

On July 22, 1944, my mother drove me to a recruiting station in downtown Philadelphia, where I was inducted. I had made a conscious decision to volunteer instead of waiting for the inevitable draft. I thought that as a volunteer I would have more control over the direction of my military career. After being inducted, I went, along with five high school classmates, to the Army depot in New Cumberland, Pennsylvania, the area reception station for inductees and new recruits.

That was the last time I saw any of my classmates for several years. Based strictly on race, I was sent in one direction and they were sent in another. The U.S. Armed Forces were segregated in those days, and there were separate militaries for blacks and whites.

From New Cumberland, I was sent to Keesler Field in Mississippi to prepare for aviation school. There, my dream of becoming a pilot was shattered.

Even though I have astigmatism, I had always been able to pass eye examinations before the one at Keesler with a little help from my memory. In the old days, the examinee was asked to read a chart that hung on the wall that had a great big E on top and rows of progressively smaller and smaller letters beneath the E. Knowing the limitations of my eyesight, I would quickly memorize the chart—top to bottom, left to right, right to left. Then when the examiner told me to read a specified line in a specified direction, I was able to recall what I was unable to see.

But at Keesler they had new technology to detect people like me. Much to my dismay, we were taken into a darkened room one by one, seated on a stool, then asked to read a chart that was projected from a machine at the touch of a button. I did not have a chance to memorize anything. I received a score of 20/25, and I needed a 20/20 to become a pilot. I was disqualified from flight school before I even had a chance to start.

I experienced two incidents while I was stationed at Keesler that would today be called hate crimes. One occurred at a small club for black enlisted men. Quite a few young soldiers were having a beer and a good time when a white security guard decided it was time to close the place even though it was half an hour before the club's official closing time. The guard apparently had something else he wanted to do.

As the guard was hustling us out, he unshouldered his carbine, presumably to make us move faster. We did. Obviously enjoying his authority, he pulled back on the receiver arm, clearly placing a round into the chamber. We moved even faster. Then he got carried away, and pulled back the receiver arm a second time. And guess what? Nothing happened. There were no rounds in the chamber or the magazine. He had been bluffing. All of a sudden, recognizing his bluff, everyone stopped moving. He was descended upon. Lesson learned: Be careful of bluffing.

The second incident occurred while I was on a pass to downtown Biloxi. I went into town one Saturday afternoon with George Barbour of Pittsburgh, who was another washout would-be aviator. While walking down one of the main streets, we heard a commotion. We turned around just in time to see some white guys in a beat-up pickup truck hurtling down the pavement right at us. "There are two of them!" they yelled. As the truck approached, we flattened ourselves against the storefront window and the truck zoomed by, barely missing us. We literally ran back to the base, returning to the safety of our black unit.

I did not visit Biloxi again until thirty-eight years later. As deputy commander of the Army's Training and Doctrine Command and the Army inspector of training, I was invited to address a reserve component convention there. I flew into the Biloxi International Airport in my designated Army aircraft. The deputy adjutant general for the Mississippi National Guard met me, and we had a motorcycle escort to the hotel. I received a standing ovation when I was introduced. I could not resist making my opening comment, "My, how things have changed!"

From Keesler, I was sent to an all-black aviation engineer training facility at MacDill Airfield in Tampa, Florida. Most of the time, the black soldiers lived in a separate part of the cantonment area and occupied the least desirable facilities. Such was the case at MacDill, where black units were on the far side of the airfield in single-story tarpaper buildings with corrugated roofing. The white units were housed on the main base in two-story wooden buildings. Each area had its own facilities such as mess halls, clubs, and small post exchanges. All units were generally supplied from the master menu, and the quality of the food was similar for each group. The black airmen could not eat with the whites, but at least we ate the same food.

The training I received at MacDill consisted primarily of backbreaking engineering work. However, it was there that I found out that membership in my high school typing club would yield astronomical benefits. On one very rainy Friday afternoon, the first sergeant came out and addressed the assembled company of soldiers. He asked, "Any of you boys can type?" My hand shot up, and I said, "Yes, sir. I can type First Sergeant." He said, "Come in here," and I followed him into his office. I became his company clerk.

My first sergeant was from the old school, and I soon found that one of my duties was to read the roster to him. He could not read. So I read the roster to him until he memorized all 120 or so names and could hold it in front of him and call them out as if he were reading.

The company commander was a white officer from Arkansas, and he had a couple of first and second lieutenants as junior officers. Even though they were responsible for training the black soldiers, these lieutenants made it clear that they did not want to be around us. Despite the facts that there was a war on and we were contributing to the war effort, they could not overcome their racist attitudes about the perceived inferiority of black soldiers.

At MacDill I observed firsthand how American whites generally treated black soldiers worse than the Italian prisoners of war (POWs) housed at MacDill. The POWs were white, after all, and thus accorded more dignity and respect on the base than black soldiers. The Italian POWs treated blacks with a disdain like that of the American whites'.

The Italian prisoners ran the shoe repair and laundry operations on base. One day I took a pair of shoes to the repair shop and took my place in line. There were other soldiers in line, all white, both ahead of me and behind me. But as it turned out, the place I held in line was of no matter. The POW behind the counter made a point of ignoring me until there was no one else in the shop. His eyes and body language conveyed contempt, an unquestioned belief that he was superior to me.

None of the black soldiers who received such personal slights liked it. These POWs treated us just as any typical white would treat a black in the South in the 1940s. They discriminated against us, but there was nothing we could do about it. We had sustained no wrong that could be vindicated because the American whites in charge felt the same way about us as the POWs did.

After I had worked as the company clerk for several weeks, the first sergeant told me that an officer candidate board was going to be convened. He said it might be a good idea for me to apply for officer candidate school (OCS) since I had been in pre-aviation cadet training. Also, he added, he thought I had the "smarts" to get by the board of officers.

In the first round of examinations of the officer candidate test, I received a score of 124. The minimum qualifying score was 110, so the next step was to appear before the board of officers. To my pleasant surprise, the major serving as president of the board was well acquainted with the Main Line of Philadelphia and knew of Lower Merion High School. It was very comforting to appear before someone who seemed to know something about me, about where I had come from and what I had been doing. I think that positively influenced my appearance before the board and helped me win a favorable recommendation from its members. In any case, shortly before Christmas in 1944, I was sent to officer candidate school in Fort Benning, Georgia.

The job of Fort Benning's OCS was to turn out second lieutenants of infantry who were able to lead their men into battle. Because several of the office candidates—including me—had not received infantry basic training, the decision was made that we be retrained in order to have a halfway decent chance to succeed. So a handful of us spent five weeks at Fort McClellan in Anniston, Alabama, to learn infantry tactics and infantry weapons. Then we returned to Fort Benning.

Although the Army was segregated in 1944, the officer training program was not. The seventeen black candidates in my OCS class lived in the barracks with everyone else.[1] Bunk assignments were made alphabetically, which meant that a black could end up sleeping next to a white or a member of any other racial or ethnic group.

Officer candidate Julius W. Becton Jr. (Author collection)

The black officer candidates collectively decided early on that we *all* were going to make it. Still, because we wanted to be judged on our individual merit, we agreed that we would hang together privately, but not publicly. We decided that all seventeen of us would never assemble as a group in formations or during breaks. This could probably be attributed to a hangover from tactics blacks employed during slavery, but it was definitely a sign that we understood the critical importance of being able to each stand on our own as an individual.

I did not find the academics in OCS all that difficult even though I was an eighteen-year-old kid who had never been inside a college. Also, I was in great physical shape, which meant that if I had a shortcoming in the classroom, I could more than make up for that with my physical performance.

My OCS company was divided into four platoons that were all overseen by tactical officers who were white lieutenants. The tactical officers were in charge of all of the officer candidates' activities. On one occasion, we were out in a bivouac when the time came to eat lunch. Our tactical officer said to me, "I want to get a picture of you eating watermelon." I said, "Sir, I don't like watermelon." Obviously either not believing me or thinking I was kidding, the lieutenant prodded, "Come on, Candidate. You eat watermelon. All you people eat watermelon." Again I said, "Sir, I don't like watermelon." After a third request—and my third insistence that I did not like watermelon—the lieutenant finally left me alone.

He then went to every one of the other sixteen black candidates and repeated the same request: "I want a picture of you eating watermelon." The other black cadets had witnessed my exchange with the lieutenant and, as if on cue, each one said, "Sir, I don't eat watermelon."

Over the weekend while we were on pass, some of the black officer candidates got together and the watermelon incident was a topic of conversation. In a congratulatory manner, they said to me, "Man, you did the right thing! You refused to be a stereotype." I said, "Guys, really, I don't eat watermelon." They said, "You don't?"

It was true. Once when I was very young, I insisted upon having more and more watermelon, and my father went along. As he probably suspected, my eyes were bigger than my belly. Finally I said, "That's it," thinking I would not have to eat the last piece I had asked for. But my father said, "Didn't you say you wanted it? You're gonna eat it." So I did, and I got sick as my father knew I would. It was a painful but effective lesson in greed and gluttony.

Like my father, the lieutenant could have had the last word on my eating the watermelon. When I wouldn't cooperate with him, he could very well have said, "You are insubordinate, and you're out of here." Fortunately, he did not.

April and May 1945 were momentous months. President Franklin Delano Roosevelt died of a massive cerebral hemorrhage on 12 April, and the war in Europe ended on 8 May. Rumors were rampant at Fort Benning that the officer training program was going to be curtailed because now we only had to beat the Japanese and, presumably, would not need quite so many second lieutenants. But as it turned out, we did not defeat the Japanese as quickly as expected.

So 15 August was my last day as a private. On 16 August 1945, at the age of nineteen and having just been awarded a good conduct medal, I became 2nd Lt. Julius W. Becton Jr.

2nd Lt. Julius W. Becton Jr. (Author collection)

Back on the Main Line, before I joined the Army, I had met the love of my life. The irresistibly charming Louise Thornton had been born 1 March 1927, in Chester, Pennsylvania, to Louis Edward and Adelaide Thornton. Her father was a laborer and her mother was a domestic worker. When Louise was in her senior year of high school, her family moved to Wayne, which is about four miles from Bryn Mawr. Louise then attended Radnor High School, (where she became a classmate of Gwendolyn Connor, who was my steady girlfriend at the time.) Even though Louise and I were both dating other people, our interest in one another soon became apparent. Louise Thornton was special, and I knew it. On my part, at least, it was love at first sight.

Louise had been interested in nursing since she was eight years old and had her tonsils removed. After surgery, when her throat was extremely sore, the hospital served tomato soup for lunch. She took one swallow and started crying from the pain. One nurse—a real witch—ranted and raved at her, insisting that she eat the soup. Then another nurse, just as sweet as the first one was mean, offered to get Louise some ice cream, which would feel better on her throat. From that moment, greatly influenced by the second woman's kindness, Louise wanted to be a nurse just like her. So after graduating from Radnor in 1944, Louise enrolled in Mercy Hospital School for Nurses in Philadelphia.

I had a period of leave after I graduated from OCS and before I had to report to Fort McClellan, where I was being reassigned, and my thoughts were firmly fixed on Philadelphia and a certain young nursing student. So four of us newly commissioned second lieutenants hired a cab to drive us from Fort Benning to Atlanta so we could catch the first train heading north.

On the leg of that train ride from Atlanta to Washington, D.C., we bumped smack into Jim Crow. The four of us sat in the rear of the colored section on the one set of seats that faced each other. We did not know it, but this was where the conductor normally sat because he could put his feet up there and spread out his papers in comfort. When he came into the car to collect tickets, he said, "Boys, that's my seat." I said, "I don't see four other seats where we can talk to one another." More impatiently, the conductor repeated, "That's my seat." With equal resolve, we said, "We're not moving," prompting him to reply, "I'll get the MPs." In those days, military police rode the trains to maintain order and provide protection.

Shortly after the conductor left, two burly white MPs raced through the door. They took one look at us and told the conductor, "There's nothing we can do," then went back in the direction from which they had come. We were second lieutenants—officers—doing what we had a right to do, and we were not violating any rules. Off post, the MPs were subject to the Uniform Code of Military Justice.

I think nearly all the conductor's blood rushed to his face. He hurled a couple of racial epithets, and then he walked away in shock and disbelief.

Immediately after I arrived in Philadelphia and had a chance to say hello to my parents, I contacted Louise, and we proceeded to have the best time we possibly could. We went to the Savoy Ballroom in New York City, where most people danced. But I have no prowess whatsoever on the dance floor, so Louise and I sat and enjoyed the incredible music from artists such as Cab Calloway, Duke Ellington, and Ella Fitzgerald. We also went to the Apollo Theatre in Harlem. It was a wonderful time, but my leave lasted less than ten days.

I returned to Fort McClellan as a second lieutenant and was assigned to the same company I had joined as a private several months earlier. But it was a very short assignment. Within just a couple of days, I was on orders heading overseas to the Pacific.

My first ride overseas on a transport ship was unpleasant in every sense of the word. The aroma alone was a memorable mixture of stenches, from the body odor of people who had not taken showers to seasickness-induced vomit and seemingly every other conceivable unpleasant scent that could foul the air.

To pass the time, I learned how to shoot craps. My teacher was Henry Minton Francis, a West Pointer and future official at Howard University. I also ran into some old acquaintances. A couple of the nurses on the boat had trained at Bryn Mawr Hospital back in my high school days when I was working there as a short order cook. Seeing me talk to these white women in 1945 raised a lot of eyebrows among the other soldiers and ship's crew, and probably a lot of hackles as well.

The ship stopped first in the Philippines, then went down to Morotai, a small Indonesian island southeast of Mindanao and northwest of New Guinea. On Morotai I joined the black 93rd Infantry Division.

I was assigned to Company C of the 369th Infantry Regiment. Other than our rank, I had little in common with the other officers. The average age of First Lieutenant Brownwell Payne, the company commander, and the three or four other lieutenants was thirty-two or thirty-three. I was nineteen. I did not drink, I did not smoke, and I was not interested in chasing any of the native women. I naturally gravitated to soldiers my own age and started hanging out with some of the enlisted men.

One day the first sergeant approached me. "Lieutenant, you are an officer, and those are enlisted," he said. "You can't do what you're doing, and if you continue, you will get in trouble." I heeded his advice. The first sergeant wanted me to clearly understand that I was compromising my position as an officer. It is difficult to lead effectively if friendships may influence your judgment. Also, I think the old adage that familiarity breeds contempt applied.

There had been reports that Japanese soldiers were holed up in the center of Morotai. They posed no real threat to anyone, and thought had been given to leaving them alone and letting them either "go native" or starve. On one assignment, I was sent on patrol with a squad to inform the Japanese hiding out there that the war was over. Armed with M1 rifles and carbines, we went out into the woods with a bullhorn and a Japanese translator. The Japanese responded with gunfire. Although the Japanese were too far away to hit their targets, the ringing of the bullets let me know that this was not a make-believe game of cops and robbers or cowboys and Indians. It was real. They wanted to kill us.

The island housed two divisions: the 93rd Infantry Division, which was all black except for the senior officers, and the 31st Infantry Division, which was also known as the "Dixie Division." The Dixie Division was an all-white National Guard unit from the South, meaning that most of its soldiers came from the same hometowns. As you can well imagine, the two divisions mixed like oil and water. In fact, a lieutenant from each division had to ride around the island in a jeep patrol driven by an MP to make sure the soldiers from these divisions did not fight each other.

It was during this time that I learned that some white Americans had rather weird ideas about black people. White soldiers told the indigenous peoples that the black soldiers had tails. Some of the natives believed this nonsense, and when they came around, you would actually see them looking for your tail.

The 93rd Infantry Division was deactivated in December 1945, and I was assigned to the 542nd Heavy Construction Company in Manila as a platoon leader. The 542nd was a signal unit charged with installing poles on which to hang communications cable and open wires. Of course, as an infantry officer, I knew absolutely nothing about signal construction.

Not to worry. Company commander Capt. John C. Harlan, who was also an infantry officer, gave me some good advice: "Do what I tell you to do, and do what the sergeants say."

My platoon consisted of about thirty soldiers. Their work normally consisted of setting braces and hanging and tying wire and cable. Most of it took place at the top of the poles, twenty to thirty feet above the ground. To get to the top of a pole, you had to climb it.

I dislike heights intensely. Nevertheless, I was determined that my men were not going to do something that I could not and that I needed to set an example. I went out each evening and practiced climbing poles, and I became quite proficient at scurrying up and down after several weeks. I took a great deal of pleasure in being able to chat with my soldiers at the top of a pole.

Eventually, my platoon was selected to install several one-hundred-foot poles to be used for radio antennae. Installing a pole of that size is not a trivial matter. About ten feet is buried, and the remainder is above the ground. Of course, my soldiers were basically fearless, and the sergeants quickly got them to work putting up the poles. Then they started affixing the hardware attachments. And, of course, my soldiers expected me to join them at the top. I had no choice.

I climbed one of the poles. The higher I got, the greater the pucker factor, and the more I wanted to hug the pole, which is the absolute worst thing you can do when you are climbing a pole. In pole line climbing, you must wear climbers with gaffs. If you get too close to the pole, you can "gaff out" and lose your hold altogether. Suddenly, there is nothing but air between you and the ground, which in my case would have been some ninety feet below.

Did I mention that I dislike heights intensely?

My determination was greater than my fear, though, and I mastered both the stress and the climb to the top. My men were proud that I had climbed the pole because the other platoon leaders did not climb. Of course, I was still a teenager, and the other leaders were not. But the men also knew, when I got back down on the ground, that I was not going to do it again. I had proved my point.

My philosophy of leadership has not changed much in the last fifty years. A leader is a leader. He must set the example and lead his soldiers in whatever they are doing.

The first time I came face to face with death during my military career was during that time in Manila, even though we were in a noncombat situation. A soldier drowned in our swimming pool, and I was the one who found him. It was the first time I had ever used artificial respiration, and my attempts to revive the drowning victim were unsuccessful. I still remember the sense of powerlessness I felt.

I also had a brief skirmish with political violence. On one occasion, a local Communist guerrilla group approached our supply sergeant, wanting to buy explosives. The sergeant told me about the approach, and I reported the incident to the Criminal Investigation Division (CID). The CID officers wanted to set up a sting. They instructed the supply sergeant to inform the guerrillas that he and I would sell them the explosives. The contact point was arranged. We gave the guerrillas the marked demolitions, and they gave us the money. Then the CID, Philippine police, and MPs moved in. At the time, the thought never crossed my mind that the guerrillas might come back, wanting revenge for the betrayal. But apparently, the matter was resolved, since I heard nothing further.

The rest of my stay in the Philippines was mostly uneventful. Toward the end of 1946 my overseas tour was completed, and I was shipped home. I was transferred from the infantry to the signal corps, and on 30 November 1946, I was separated from the service at Fort Dix, New Jersey. Because terminal leave promotions were the practice then, I was simultaneously promoted. I could now wear the silver bar of a first lieutenant.

For the next two and a half months, my good friend Bob Williams and I managed to spend a lot of money. Bob had been separated from the Army Air Corps a month or so earlier than I, and each of us received nearly $1,000 in separation pay. That was a lot of money in those days.

Bob had several young ladies interested in him, and I, of course, spent as much time with Louise Thornton as I could manage. As a foursome, we frequented Baltimore, Philadelphia, and New York, wherever there was outstanding music, and we often tipped much higher than necessary. I am sure that Bob's and my largesse had a lot to do with our desire to impress the ladies with whom we traveled.

Despite my struggles with high school biology and chemistry, I still had some desire to become a medical doctor. On the recommendation of Matthew Gordon, who had been my first sergeant in Manila, I applied to his alma mater, Lincoln College in Oxford, Pennsylvania, and was immediately accepted. But the week before I was to start school, I received a telephone call from Dick Mattis, my high school football coach, who asked if I would be interested in going to Muhlenberg College to play football. He knew I wanted to become a physician, and reminded me that Muhlenberg had an outstanding premed program. I told him I would be interested. Then he said, "Oh, by the way. You're going to be the first Negro to go there."

I appreciated his candor, but I was not troubled about being the first black to attend Muhlenberg. I had decided a long time before then that I was not going to let such situations prevent me from accomplishing my goals. Somebody had to be first, so it might as well be me.

During our conversation, Dick asked a question that had nothing to do with school: Had I registered to vote? I said I had not. He then suggested, "Why don't you register, and register Republican." I agreed to do so. I could not possibly appreciate its significance at the time, but that one action had much to do with what happened to me for the next many years.

My political preference was probably set early on by my father, who held the view, along with many other blacks, that since the Republican president

Abraham Lincoln had freed the slaves, his own political affiliation should be Republican. I am sure the fact that his employers in Bryn Mawr were all staunch Republicans also influenced his thinking. (In hindsight, of course, this view ignored some significant developments since Lincoln's time, especially the fact that Democrat Franklin Roosevelt was becoming a hero for the working class.)

I was accepted at Muhlenberg just days before I was supposed to enroll at Lincoln College. My education was mostly paid for by benefits I received under the GI Bill of Rights. In addition football players at Muhlenberg received a stipend of $35 per month. All told, I was in good shape financially.

Muhlenberg is in Allentown, Pennsylvania, which was about an hour and a half drive from where my family lived in Bryn Mawr. I enrolled as a second-semester sophomore because I had taken a series of college-level classes and examinations sponsored by the Veterans Administration while I was stationed in Manila and I had also received advanced credit based on aptitude and experience. I was assigned to a single room even though all the other dormitory rooms housed two or more students. I was black, and no one else was.

During the check-in process I was given football gear that was too small, but I thought I could deal with it. Foolish me. The shoulder pads were so tight that I suffered a pinched nerve after my first contact in practice.

The football coach at Muhlenberg was Ben Schwarzwalder, who had been an Army major during World War II. He had coached at a prep school before he came to Muhlenberg and had recruited heavily among his prior players. His idea of spring practice was two hours in the afternoon and then another two hours at night under the lights. Four hours of football practice a day! The other players went along, but I could not. I wanted to be a serious premed student, and I knew I could not keep up with both that rigorous practice schedule and my studies. I used my pinched nerve as reason to stop playing football. That ended my football scholarship, but the veteran's benefits covered my education expenses with some pocket change left over.

With football off my plate, I settled in on my studies. To the amusement of my classmates—my linguistic ability is severely limited—I became president of the German American Club. My German instructor, who served as the club's faculty sponsor, did not expect his students to speak the language. All we had to do was to read and write it, which is much easier.

Meanwhile, I spent a lot of time on the highway between Allentown and Philadelphia. Louise had earned the second highest grade average in her nursing school class and graduated as salutatorian. She had initially enrolled in the wartime Cadet Nursing Program, but because the war was over by the time she graduated, she was under no obligation to join the military. Instead, she went to work in the psychiatric ward at Philadelphia General Hospital, becoming the first black nurse the hospital had ever hired.

I proposed to Louise in August 1947. Getting down on my knees was not my style, so I invented my own way to ask the question. For some reason, I had borrowed some money from her, and one day, while we were driving through Philadelphia, I paid her back. I placed the wadded paper money on her lap. Wrapped inside it was a solitaire diamond engagement ring. Louise took the money and put the ring on her finger.

We set 29 January 1948 as the date for our wedding. I took a final examination in analytical geometry the day before our wedding. What an experience! I had made the serious mistake of trying to memorize the geometry, but in math, memorization works only up to a certain point. I reached it during that exam. I drew a blank, and I could not solve a single problem. Later, my professor told me that he knew exactly what I had done. He gave me a C for the course because my grade up to that point was pretty good. I blamed my poor performance on pre–wedding day jitters.

The wedding itself was extraordinary. Louise's grandmother had died a short time before, and her Aunt Hattie wanted us to postpone the ceremony. We did not, so Aunt Hattie came to the wedding dressed all in black, still visibly in mourning, something that was definitely taboo back then.

The father of the bride thought the wedding should be completely called off for a different reason. In Louise's words, her father was a "strange bird" who did not think any man was good enough for his daughter. As a result, he refused to attend, and Louise's Uncle Albert, Aunt Hattie's husband, gave Louise away.

By contrast, my parents were extremely happy for us. They loved Louise and thought I had made an excellent choice for my partner in life. So despite my father-in-law's lack of cooperation and the pall cast by the death of Louise's grandmother, the occasion was joyous.

We were married at the church my family attended, Bryn Mawr Saints Memorial Baptist Church with the Rev. J. Arthur Younger officiating.[2] Bob

Presenting Mr. and Mrs. Julius Wesley Becton. Our flower girl was Betty Jane Robinson. (Author collection)

Williams was my best man. He had a terrible time liberating the rings from the pillow borne by the ring bearer. He even uttered an exasperated oath, drawing a stern look from Reverend Younger, but eventually he succeeded. The ceremony concluded without incident, and the reception was wonderful. We felt the love and good wishes of all who were there.

Our honeymoon was a bit unusual: a driving trip to take my brother Joe to Shaw University in Raleigh, North Carolina. My mother was with us the whole way, and Joe was along for half the trip.

Louise's and my ability to purchase our first home was due, in large part, to my mother's foresight and my confidence in her judgment. When I became a second lieutenant, my mother had asked, "How much money are you going to make now?" I told her $150 a month.

"How much were you making before?" she asked. After I told her it had been $50 a month, she came up with a plan for the extra earnings: I should allocate $75 per month to go into a savings bond. By the time Louise and I got married, I had put aside enough money to make a down payment on 1024 North 46th Street in West Philadelphia, a two-story house with three bedrooms, one bath, and an unfinished basement with an alley on the side, a driveway in the rear, and a garage beneath the kitchen. The Rudolph Blankenburg Elementary School was immediately behind our row of houses.

In March 1948 Louise and I learned that we were expecting a little one. We did not know how we were going to make ends meet. The mortgage on our home was only $48.10 a month, but to make the payments, we needed income—something a premed student and a pregnant nurse do not have.

We were determined to make it, and we just knew we would. So we did everything we could think of to earn some money. We returned empty bottles for the deposits, pawned certain nonessential items, and took out small loans. When school ended that summer, I found temporary jobs as a laborer for a roofing company and as a helper in a rug-cleaning firm.

It was not enough. I guess you might say my back was up against the wall.

By this time, President Harry S. Truman had issued his executive order aimed at ending segregation in the military. And frankly, I had really liked the work I had done in the Army. Finally, in all honesty, I was not convinced that I wanted to become a doctor.

So I applied to be recalled to active duty in August of 1948, intending to become a professional soldier.

CHAPTER THREE

★ ★ ★

Active Duty Again

I reported back to active duty on 1 November 1948, reverting to the rank of second lieutenant since my recall was voluntary. My first duty station was supposed to be Fort Bliss, in El Paso, Texas, which was a long way from my expectant wife. I asked to be assigned, instead, to a temporary duty station near Philadelphia, at least until our child was born.

As a result, I was temporarily assigned to the 229th Signal Operations Company at Fort Monmouth, New Jersey. I was the only black person in the unit, and I knew nothing about signal operations. But they were willing to put up with me because they knew I would be leaving after my child was born. Shirley Inez Becton was born on 5 December 1948, and I was en route to Fort Bliss within a week. I spent Christmas in El Paso, assigned to Company A of the 29th Signal Battalion.

Once again, I was a member of a unit whose mission was pole line construction. All of the enlisted men were black. So was one hard-charging young captain by the name of Albert Johnson, who immediately befriended me. And during the short time I lived on the south post at Bliss, Louise was able to visit because her mother was at home taking care of Shirley.

Near the end of January my company received orders to participate in Exercise Southern Pines in Fort Bragg, North Carolina. We were to be part of an umpire group as two larger forces conducted war games. Our responsibilities were to lay and maintain new and existing cables for the communication network and open wire.

Our first challenge, of course, was to drive from Bliss to Bragg. As a signal heavy construction company, we had more than twenty vehicles—a variety of jeeps, two-and-a-half-ton trucks, and unique signal vehicles. I was the only black officer in the company, and my job was to be the mess officer, a perennially menial task. I had to feed the soldiers and then leapfrog ahead of the company and pick the next site where they would camp and eat for the night. That meant cooking out in the field, serving my men, and moving on.

Our first stop was in Van Horn, Texas, which is about 135 miles from Fort Bliss, and we spent the night in a field outside town. When soldiers have a chance to stop, they want to eat. They also usually want junk food rather than what is on the Army menu. This was true that night. Being the junior officer, my job was to collect money and orders from all 110 men. Then two sergeants and I went into Van Horn to make the purchases.

We went to the local drugstore with a very long list, and the store manager was getting very happy. What a windfall.

I ordered an ice cream cone and sat at the soda fountain as my sergeants went down the list. I heard the door to the store open behind me. The faces of the two clerks behind the counter turned pure white. I felt a tap on my shoulder and heard a voice: "Boy, get away from that counter." I responded, "Who said so?" The voice answered, "I did." I turned around to behold a great big badge and an even bigger weapon on the hip of a slightly built, ruddy man.

"I'm the sheriff," he said. "Get away from that counter." I muttered, "Okay," and moved away. I then asked a sergeant, "Have we paid for anything yet?" He said, "No, sir." I paid for my ice cream, and we walked out.

The sheriff wasn't through with me. He beat me back to the field where we were bivouacked to talk with the company commander.

"Major, you've got a boy back there who don't understand how people act down here," the sheriff said.

"Maybe he doesn't understand you people," the major responded. "He's not from down here."

As he walked away, the sheriff said, "Well, you better teach him something!" End of conversation.

The next morning we fed the troops and got on the road early. My jeep, followed by two trucks, headed east on Route 10. Suddenly, I saw a Studebaker heading toward us at very high speed on our side of the road. My driver was able to swerve out of the way, but the truck behind me could not, and the Studebaker plowed into it. The car was no match for the truck, which almost sheared it in half.

We rushed to the car and found two white women covered in blood. We cleared out the undamaged truck and laid the women on blankets in the back so one of my sergeants could drive them back to Van Horn. I kept going because I had to reconnoiter our next bivouac and supervise preparation of the meals. When the sergeant rejoined us, he told me that the sheriff had come to the hospital to find out what had happened. The attending physician told him that the quick action of the soldiers probably saved the two women's lives. The sergeant then told the sheriff that the officer in charge was the same lieutenant he had chased out of town.

We continued east. Where we could, we stayed on or near military bases. But while the other officers were able to stay in hotels or at bachelor officers' quarters, I always had to stay with the troops. Keep in mind that the Armed Forces had just in theory been integrated. Desegregation of public accommodations would not come for many more years.

At Barksdale Air Field in Shreveport, Louisiana, a white colonel in the newly formed U.S. Air Force had an opportunity to observe our formations, maintenance drills, and just plain soldiering. He was so impressed that he asked whether I would be interested in transferring to the Air Force. While my answer was no, I was flattered.

We finally arrived at Fort Bragg ten days after we left El Paso. After our eventful trip, the maneuvers went just fine. We did a good job making sure the umpires could communicate by telephone.

I returned to active duty to become an officer in the Regular Army, which is roughly analogous to being a tenured professor at a university. Once chosen, you pretty much have a job for life unless you really screw up. To be selected, I had to compete with a pool of about one thousand candidates in what was called a "competitive tour."

The first step for me was the Infantry Officer Basic Course (IOBC) at Fort Benning. My superiors thought I needed to attend because I had been out of the service for several years. Things had changed a lot between 1946 and 1949, and they wanted to give me a decent chance to compete. So in June 1949 I reported back to Georgia. Louise and Shirley joined me, and we rented a couple of rooms in a house with my classmate Lt. Houston Melvin and his wife. On the whole, the basic course went smoothly. I did well, finishing in the top 10 percent of my class.

The next stop for Houston Melvin and me was Fort Lewis in Washington state, which was the home of the 2nd Infantry Division. We were both assigned to the 9th Infantry Regiment, which was nicknamed "The Manchu." Although President Truman had ordered the military desegregated, the 2nd Infantry Division still had one all-black infantry

3rd Battalion, 9th Infantry Regiment on parade. (Author collection))

battalion, the 3rd Battalion of the 9th Infantry, and one all-black artillery battalion, the 503rd.

Louise and Shirley joined me at Fort Lewis in late September. Although Fort Lewis officially prohibited segregated housing, our initial quarters were not all that integrated. For the winter of 1949–50, we lived in a unit off post called American Lake Gardens. It was substandard in every sense of the word. The stove was wood-fired. The bathroom had no tub, just a shower stall, and the apartment was warmed by an oil-fueled space heater. Snow could blow right under the front door. But we determined that we were going to make it. We bought a hot plate for cooking and chinked the space beneath the front door to block out the cold. When we were able to move on post, we welcomed the opportunity.

On post, we lived on the second floor of the billet. One sunny spring day when Shirley was about eighteen months old, Louise was doing chores around the apartment. Shirley was riding her tricycle around the living room. Louise came out of the kitchen area just in time to see Shirley disappear into mid-air as she rode her tricycle out the open door onto the porch and under the banister.

Louise raced down the stairs, expecting the worst. A neighbor saw Shirley fall to the ground and dashed over to her. He got there at about the same time Louise reached the ground floor, shaking like a leaf. She was thinking like a mother, not like a nurse. The neighbor took charge, bundled up both Louise and Shirley, and hurriedly drove them to the hospital.

Luckily, the only damage Shirley sustained was to her clothing, which was soiled by the moist dirt. More damage was done to Louise's nerves.

In October 1949 Lt. Col. Hyman Y. Chase assumed command of the 3rd Battalion. I met many memorable people during my Army career, and Chase stands prominently among them.

The Army had fewer than six black lieutenant colonels in 1949 and only one black Ph.D.—Hyman Chase. He was convinced that there were some people in the Army who had no business being there, and he felt his job was to get rid of them. Woe unto the soldiers who merited that assessment.

He used to intimidate people deliberately, and he was good at what he did. He could be brutal. He could be demeaning. He could be hard-ass. It was all in the name of whipping his soldiers into mint fighting condition. He was the only black battalion commander in the division, and he was determined that his battalion would be better trained than any other battalion in the division.

I had tremendous respect for Chase's rank and academic achievement. But I also knew I was a good lieutenant, so we got along just fine.

To say that my wife was not intimidated by Chase would be putting it mildly. At one point during our time at Fort Lewis, Louise and I were attending a social function, and Chase came up to Louise. We were expecting our second child, and she was starting to show. Chase patted her on the stomach and said, "You're getting a little fat, aren't you, Mrs. Becton?" Louise did not miss a beat. She patted his stomach, too, smiling. "So are you, Colonel," she said.

I almost died. Chase was, in fact, a fairly portly fellow, and I just knew I would have hell to pay. A couple of people who witnessed the exchange said, "Oh my God! There goes Becton's career." But Chase loved it.

The other first lieutenants on the competitive tour, which started on 15 January 1950, were Houston Melvin and Marvin Adams. Since I was the tallest of the three of us and I excelled in dismounted drill, I was selected to be the leader of the battalion's drill team, a hand-picked group of thirty soldiers trained to do precision/fancy drill. We were very, very good at what we did. In fact, the drill team became so good that the regimental commander decided we ought to become the regimental drill team.

The regiment had one black infantry battalion and two white infantry battalions, and white soldiers from the other battalions kept bugging me to let them join the drill team. I went to the regimental executive officer, a white lieutenant colonel, in April or May 1950 and told him that we needed some replacements and that soldiers from the other battalions wanted to join the team. "No," said the colonel. Somewhat taken aback, I asked why. "Very simple," he said. "You put a white face out there, and it breaks up the symmetry." I asked, "Sir, have you seen my drill team?" He said, "Sure, I've seem them." I said, "Well, take a really good look the next time you see them. I've got some soldiers out there who look almost as white as you but they're black." But the colonel was adamant. "Lieutenant," he said, "we're not going to bring anyone else in."

My team drilled at football games, baseball games, and other events, demonstrating formations and silent drill (counting steps to ourselves). The team was so good at silent drill that they could perform for fifteen to eighteen minutes without any commands whatsoever, going through a series of intricate movements with their weapons. Their precision was something to behold! It was hard to believe that so many human bodies could move in such perfect harmony.

Ironically, it was as leader of the drill team that I experienced one of the most embarrassing moments of my military career. The experience stung, but it taught me the importance of what I call the "Seven Ps": Proper Prior Planning Prevents Piss-Poor Performance.

The drill team had an engagement to perform in Olympia, Washington. Perhaps I had gotten too cocky. Whatever the reason, I did not have my team make a reconnaissance of the area where we were to drill, nor did I have the team practice there beforehand. My failures to observe these standard procedures led to disastrous results.

We were to perform in a square area formed by the blocking off of an intersection of several streets. The area was just a wee bit too small. To make matters worse, we started in the evening. My men could not see the unfamiliar area as well as they could have during broad daylight. Things did go well initially, but they soon began to fall apart. The count did not make sense. The men reached a boundary, could not go any farther, and started bumping into each other. As some members of the audience laughed, others stared in stark disbelief. I finally commanded, "Platoon halt! Assemble on me." We returned to Fort Lewis disgraced, and determined never to do that again.

The North Koreans attacked South Korea on 25 June 1950. I was at the officers' club for a battalion social function when the word came to us. Shortly thereafter, our division was alerted to go to Korea.

Not long before Lieutenant Colonel Chase had received orders reassigning him to Prairie View A&M College as a professor of military science and tactics. Some people in the battalion were happy about that. But his replacement was not due to arrive until later in the summer. In view of the pending deployment, some of us—myself included—assumed that the Department of the Army would change Chase's orders and let him take the battalion to Korea. After all, it was his battalion, and he had trained us. To our chagrin, the answer was no. The Army brought back the previous battalion commander, Lt. Col. D. M. McMains. We thought at the time that this was an instance of the powers that be not wanting to have a black lieutenant colonel in command of the battalion in combat.

We were entirely wrong. Years later, I learned that there was an ongoing investigation into complaints against Chase stemming from when he was commander of a battalion in Germany that was charged with providing transportation support for the Berlin Airlift. His hard-nosed approach was the same there as at Fort Lewis, and he had not been at all reluctant to use Article 15 of the Uniform Code of Military Justice, nonjudicial punishment, against anyone who was not performing to his satisfaction. I guess some of the people who had been punished decided not to take it lying down, and while the investigation proceeded, Chase had to remain in the United States.

Meanwhile, candidates on competitive tour were supposed to be transferred every three months. Our next transfer was scheduled for 15 July. But Marvin Adams, Houston Melvin, and I did not want to be transferred. We wanted to deploy with the soldiers we had trained. Nothing beats a failure but a try, so the three of us went to the regimental commander to request permission to remain with our current units. Our commander, Col. Charles C. Sloan, responded without a second thought. "I don't know what the regulations say, but we're not going to transfer you guys," he said. "You have been training your unit. You're the ones. You're going to take the soldiers you trained into combat."

By this time, Louise was about seven months pregnant; Karen Louise Becton would be born in September, when I was far from home. There was no way Louise could drive from Fort Lewis to Philadelphia. So I called my mother and told her I was on my way to Korea and that we needed her help. She flew out to Washington, and drove cross-country with Louise, Shirley, and Yuki Porter, my company commander's wife, plus our dog Bonehead and Yuki's dog. Yuki and her dog were dropped off in Ohio.

Mom did all the driving. The woman had nerve.

★ ★ ★

CHAPTER FOUR

Back to the Pacific

My unit, Company L, had about 125 soldiers at the time of the alert. We had the full complement of 186 by the time we deployed. The additional men came from replacement training centers, the stockade, and other units. Some were trained, some were not, but we all shipped out anyway.

Training for combat takes time. Just as with a football team, Army units have certain "plays," and knowing them is a prerequisite for success. The best we were able to do aboard the transport was allow the untrained men to get familiar with firing their weapons. It was not a good deal.

The 9th Infantry Regimental Combat Team was the first major unit from the United States to land in South Korea. Soon after we landed at Pusan I was told to report to regimental headquarters at Taegu. Now, it was highly unusual for a lieutenant to be pulled out of the unit where he was supposed to be leading his own men. When I reported at Taegu, I was told that I would provide security for a radio truck on the way to Pohang that would provide the communications link for a task force under the command of Brig. Gen. Sladen Bradley. Of course, I said, "Yes, sir!" when I got the order.

That was also the moment when I discovered the 3rd Battalion would not move with the rest of the regiment, but would be sent to Pohang. What a strange way to go into combat.

The regiment was losing a third of its fighting power right off the bat. I later learned that decision was made because Gen. Walton "Johnnie" Walker's Eighth Army headquarters was not sure how the black battalion would do in combat. Essentially, someone thought the battalion should be eased in.

That was the night my unit so narrowly avoided ambush and learned later that the rest of the battalion had been attacked along the same route we had taken. The North Koreans let my group go through unscathed, not realizing that if they had taken us out, they could have inflicted far greater damage on the unit than they did by killing a couple of infantrymen.

From the latter part of July to early August, my company mainly provided protection for the Far East Air Force's Yonil Airfield. Even if you are trained combat is a very interesting environment, and one-third of the men in Company L were not. The first night after my men and I rejoined the company we were on the perimeter line, facing toward where the bad guys would be. We probably used enough ammunition that one night for three days of fighting. My men fired at every twig, blade of grass, and anything else they thought moved.

The other officers, NCOs, and I realized that our men were scared. We knew they needed to get the fear out of their system, so we decided to let them go ahead and have at it. They did not kill anybody or anything, but they sure shot up a lot of grass and trees.

We held long conversations and training sessions with the soldiers the next morning, discussing what had happened. We talked in depth about what the men did and did not do. This was the start of the unit's settling down and becoming acclimated to combat.

In early September Task Force Bradley dissolved and the Third Battalion was ordered to rejoin the regiment. The regiment was south of the Naktong River, which divided the Pusan Perimeter between the good guys and the bad guys, and the division was preparing to break out of the perimeter.

We had experienced a couple of good firefights by this time, but the unit was still far from perfect. On one very memorable occasion I was on a hill and my platoon was rather heavily engaged. We had close air support with fighter aircraft firing in support of our units. But during the initial attack, instead of hitting the enemy's position, our planes hit us instead of the enemy. It was a classic case of friendly fire.

There is not much you can do when the planes moving three hundred miles per hour are shooting at you. We just hugged the ground as they strafed us, but some of my soldiers got up and started running when the pilots swung their planes around for a second pass.

I had warned my men in no uncertain terms not to run during our training back at Fort Lewis. I had said, "Guys, I'll kill you if you run away from the enemy. You're putting our entire unit in jeopardy. You're helping the enemy. I want to make sure that every soldier is out there doing what he is supposed to be doing."

Wounded soldier being evacuated from Hill 201 in the background. (Author collection)

Now, my men were doing exactly what I had cautioned them not to do, and the new soldiers were in the lead. Of course, the fighter pilots thought they had the enemy on the run.

I saw red. I had a carbine with thirty rounds in the magazine. I jumped up and unloaded that carbine in front of the running soldiers as they were moving off the hill. Startled, they stopped. They looked at me, looked at the aircraft, and looked back at me: the devil or the deep blue sea. They got back down on the ground.

When the aircraft were on their second pass, my messenger, ignoring the enemy fire still coming from the next hill over, jumped up and ran forward, frantically waving the chartreuse panels that were used to mark our positions. Finally, the pilots realized they were attacking the wrong hill and, after dipping their wings in recognition and apology, they hit the next hill instead. My messenger received a medal for his heroic action.

When things calmed down and we held what is now called an after action review, my men asked whether I really would have shot them if they had not stopped running. "What did I tell you?" I asked. "I was serious. We're alive today, aren't we?"

It was a very important lesson and part of the bonding between the leaders and the soldiers that takes place in a unit.

Around 17 September, we concluded our preparations to break out of the Pusan Perimeter. Hill 201, just south of the Naktong, was the key terrain feature in our area of operations. Company commander Capt. Bill Porter laid out the plan of attack: "This is the formation we're going to use. I want somebody to lead the attack. I want somebody on the flank. And I want somebody in the rear. I want the mortars providing overhead fire and artillery on call."

Then he looked at me and said, "Becton, I want your platoon to lead." I said, "I've been lead platoon now ever since we've been over here. You've got two other guys who are far senior to me, older than I am, and more experienced." Porter said, "I know that Becton. You're gonna be the lead platoon." I said, "Yes, sir."

Deep down inside I knew why my platoon was picked. Bill basically did not trust the other platoon leaders to get the job done.

Company L kicked off the next day with my platoon in the lead going up Hill 201. The following excerpt from a citation for the Silver Star describes what happened:

[Lieutenant Becton] led his men in a courageous attack upon the enemy positions. Although subjected to intense mortar, automatic weapons and small arms fire, he speared his men on through the heavy hostile fire in a spirited charge up the forward slope of the hill. In the initial charge he was struck and wounded by enemy fire; but, completely ignoring his painful wound, he continued determinedly on through the withering fire, encouraging his men on as they killed and wounded many of the enemy and forced the remainder to seek supplementary positions. At this time the remainder of his company was pinned down by intense enemy automatic weapon fire from an adjacent ridge. Realizing that his platoon was cut off from the main body of friendly troops, he pressed forward, inflicting severe casualties on the enemy, until he reached an advantageous position from which he could repel any enemy counterattacks until he could rejoin his unit. Skillfully deploying his platoon, he established a defensive perimeter and threw back enemy attempts to overrun the position. For a period of approximately 10 hours his small force directed effective fire upon the enemy, inflicting many casualties, until, under cover of darkness, they were able to move back and link-up with the main elements of the battalion. The initiative and tactical skill displayed by Lieutenant Becton prevented the enemy from launching a counterattack and enabled his battalion to occupy an advantageous position from which they later launched a successful attack which drove the enemy from the entire area.

The wound in my thigh was considered "light," but I still needed time to heal once the shrapnel was removed. I had a short stay at the 8976th Mobile Army Surgical Hospital, which was made famous by the long-running television show *M.A.S.H.* Then I was flown to the Tokyo Army Hospital. I ended up at the 172nd Station Hospital in Sendai, Japan, for recuperation.

I was eager to get back to Korea because the United Nations (UN) forces had crossed the 38th parallel, which was the boundary between North and South Korea, and were heading through North Korea to the Yalu River, which marked the North's border with China. I wanted to be in on the final push and the victorious return home before Christmas that General Douglas MacArthur had promised us.

When I did return to the regiment, I joined Company I as the executive officer, second in command. The commander, Capt. Ed Phillips, also appointed me 1st Platoon leader.

At the higher levels of command there were several major worries about the move into North Korea. The first concern was the terrain. North Korea is substantially more mountainous than South Korea, and there were few good east–west roads. The second difficulty was logistics. UN forces were being supplied through two seaports, Pusan and Inchon, and both were overtaxed. Finally, as reported by Clay Blair Jr. in *The Forgotten War*, there were tensions in the chain of command.[1] History has shown that there were major differences of opinion at the highest levels, including disagreements about how Communist China, which was backing the North Koreans, might respond.

The 9th Infantry Regiment at first had little enemy contact as we moved through North Korea. But units started reporting sporadic encounters around 11 November. Occasionally, the battalion received heavy mortar fire. As the units pressed onward, they ran into sniper fire and greater patrol activity.

On Thursday, 23 November 1950, we celebrated Thanksgiving Day dinner with roast turkey and all the fixings. The weather was quite cold, and since we were served outside, so was much of the food. But that did not dampen our spirits. We were on the short end of General MacArthur's pledge to have us home by Christmas.

The Eighth Army's offensive began the very next day. The forces were deployed so that the 24th Infantry Regiment, the only all-black regiment to fight in Korea, was on its division's right flank, and my unit, the 3rd Battalion of the 9th Infantry, was on the left flank of the 2nd Division. This meant that all four of the Eighth Army's black battalions were on line and abreast.

Blair has suggested an explanation for this: "While the 24th Regiment had a questionable record and it was still not fully trusted, a stampede in the 24th could have a 'contagious' effect on its neighbor, the 3/9. D. M. McMains had led and fought the 3/9 well in its two prior battles, but hitherto it had been sandwiched between white battalions. Why Gen. Walker deployed the blacks in formation is not known—possibly to keep them 'segregated.'"[2]

Early in the afternoon that Friday, I was leading the 1st Platoon in reconnoitering the high ground in our sector when we drew small arms fire from a distance. When I reported this to the company commander, I met the white commander of the adjacent 24th Infantry's battalion, who was coordinating with his right flank unit. He basically ridiculed my report, saying there were no enemy forces in the area. My platoon was sent back up the hill to check it out further.

As we reached the crest of the hill, we again drew fire. This time I was hit in the left ankle. The 24th's battalion commander was still in the area when I reached the bottom of the hill headed to the aid station. As I passed him, I said, "Are you satisfied now?"

That wound in all probability saved my life. Within a few hours, the 9th Infantry began the worst day in its illustrious history.

Blair reported it this way: "At about 8:00 PM the Chinese Communists attacked in massive force. They swarmed over the hills, blowing bugles and horns, shaking rattles and other noisemakers, and shooting flares into the sky. They came on foot, firing rifles and burp guns, hurling grenades, and shouting and chanting shrilly. The total surprise of this awesome ground attack shocked and paralyzed most Americans and panicked not a few."[3]

I had no idea. By then I was back in the chain of medical care and en route to Japan. I had sustained a wound from a small arms round that went through my ankle between the Achilles tendon and the bone without touching either. This is another reason why I often say, "Thank you, Father."

There are numerous books on what happened next and I will not review the disastrous defeat of the UN command, except to say that the 9th Infantry was devastated. Fewer than six of the battalion officers succeeded in getting out; the rest were either captured or killed. Readers interested in pursuing the details are encouraged to read Clay Blair's aforementioned *The Forgotten War* and S. L. A. Marshall's *The River and the Gauntlet*.[4]

My recuperation was almost complete by early March, and I was sent to a rest camp near Sapporo in northern Japan with instructions to rebuild my strength by learning how to ski. Unlike today's skis, which are clamped to the boots in a manner that enhances control, those 1950 skis were precariously strapped on. Skiing, it turned out, was not my strong suit. But eventually I was ready for duty.

Back in Korea, Operation Ripper had kicked off on 7 March 1951. The offensive was designed to drive the Communists back to the 38th parallel and to recapture Seoul. The regiment was faced with a stubborn enemy, mountainous terrain, no supply roads and almost inaccessible lines of communications. It took unceasing work, day and night, before the engineers managed to construct passable routes for moving supplies to the front-line troops.

When I reached the regiment, I met the new regimental executive officer, Lt. Col. O. M. Barsanti. He was a battle-wise World War II veteran with a host of awards for valor, and he had been sent to fix the perceived problem that black officers lacked the ability to command effectively. The regimental adjutant introduced me to Barsanti, commenting that I was one of the original members of the 3rd Battalion and deserved to be assistant operations officer. "Like hell!" Barsanti screamed. "Becton, get your ass down to L Company. They have lost all of their officers." That was how I got my first combat command.

I found Company L at little more than half strength, with few NCOs and no officers except me. It had led one too many of the battalion attacks and had simply been decimated. I later discovered that there was a peculiar sensitivity about the number of battle casualties within the regiment. Some thought this could be explained by the fact that the regiment was, as they put it, "40 percent colored."

Now, for the first time since landing in Korea, the regiment was slowly building up to full strength. As we rebuilt, we were initially kept in battalion reserve, participating in extensive patrolling. Col. Edwin Messinger, the regimental commander, described that March this way in the unit journal: "It had been a tough month. Weather, terrain, and enemy did their best, but with the lessons that had been taught and learned the hard way, the officers and men of the regiment could look back with pride and forward with confidence."

In April the regiment had no significant enemy contact for 30 consecutive days. There were key changes in personnel, however. The regiment received many replacements and lost some combat-tested leaders who were rotated out. Headquarters even brought in a white captain to command Company L. However, he recognized that I was more battle-tested than any other company officer, and he basically left me in charge.

We planned and executed realistic training. Under the close supervision of regimental headquarters, the officers perfected discipline, which had necessarily been left almost entirely to small unit leaders during combat. Morale, which had been very low in early December, soared. During that April, my fellow officers and I instilled a proud and aggressive esprit de corps into our soldiers.

Eight months in combat was the prerequisite for rotation, but I presented a problem. Even though I had more front-line duty that anyone else in the battalion, I had been hospitalized for nearly six months. For the purposes of the competitive tour, this was difficult; it meant six months when my performance could not be observed.

All of my peers had been killed, captured, or maimed in combat. I myself had been wounded twice, and the old adage "three strikes and you're out" was heavy on my mind. I am human. I was tired. I declined an opportunity to extend my tour of duty, even though staying in the field would have nearly guaranteed me a promotion to captain.

I left Korea and headed for home in May of 1951.

Since the early years of the Korean conflict were the first real test of the desegregated military following President Truman's executive order, it is fair to ask what we learned. First, the widely held view that "Negroes won't fight" was destroyed. Blair wrote that as a result of the performance of some black units in World War II, it became fashionable in the Army to analyze battle factors scientifically. Army boards and committees studied "the Negro Problem" endlessly and exhaustively. The Army Service Manual titled *Leadership and the Negro Soldier*, issued in October 1944, was the result of such efforts.[5]

Blair further wrote, "There were still some generals, Lt. General Ned Almound being one, who came into Korea with their opinions that blacks, stereotypically Sambo and Uncle Tom were cowardly and lazy; prone to panic and hysteria; indifferent to or contemptuous of military discipline, customs, and traditions; and mentally inferior for modern warfare."[6] History reflects that General Almound in World War II commanded the 92nd Infantry Division, which was the only black division sent to North Africa and Europe and was, therefore, the expert on the black soldier.

Other senior officers were far more objective, however. As an example, both of the 9th Infantry regimental commanders during my period in the division, Col. C. C. Sloane and Colonel Messinger, as well as the two Manchu battalion commanders, Lt. Col. John E. Londahl and Lt. Col. Cesidio "Butch" Barberis, immediately recognized the value of integration because of what they saw on the ground—blacks, whites, and Hispanics fighting well together. And our battalion commander, Colonel McMains, was singing my praise until the day he died two decades later.

Of course, even in the face of evidence to the contrary, some people consciously and willingly hold onto racist and prejudicial viewpoints. But the bottom line is this: Regardless of the rightness of a mission, American soldiers generally will not do well when they are ill-trained, ill-equipped, ill-led, and uninformed. Properly trained, the American soldier is unmatched, no matter what his race or background. There is no substitute for preparedness.

CHAPTER FIVE

★ ★ ★

Peacetime Duty

When I returned home I was assigned to Fort Dix as a unit training officer. One evening when I was at home in Philadelphia, I got a telephone call from someone who said he was with the Federal Bureau of Investigation (FBI) and wanted to see me. The caller was knocking at my door a few minutes later.

I answered the door attired in a robe with a .45-caliber pistol in the pocket, and we sat down in the living room after he showed me his identification. Louise was at my side.

The FBI agent knew our entire history: where we had been born, where we attended school, my service in Korea, our parents' names—everything. He went on to say that the person living diagonally across the street from our house was suspected of being a Communist agent and that the agency wanted to use our house to observe him. This started an association with the FBI that lasted for almost five years.

The members of the surveillance team always used the basement door to enter and leave our house. When we had guests, the agents used the basement. When we were upstairs in the bedroom, they used the living room. Early on we rejected any type of compensation, but they always presented gifts on family birthdays, at Christmas, and on other special occasion. Since I was away a great deal of time, it was very comforting to know that my family was under the protection of the FBI.

My stay at Fort Dix was brief. Within thirty days I was reassigned to an all-black service battalion at Camp Edwards, Massachusetts, that had the sole missions of feeding the white troops and policing the post (i.e., pick up the trash). I lasted in that do-nothing assignment for three weeks. I made a trip to the Pentagon and requested another assignment—anyplace. I was first put on temporary duty at Fort Bragg as an umpire for a major maneuver.

I then received orders to report to the 5th Infantry Division at Indiantown Gap Military Reservation in Pennsylvania as a training officer.

I was integrated into the Regular Army in 1952. The move was clearly the result of my service in Korea, and, in effect, I was no longer "Christmas help," but a permanent member of the U.S. Army. Later that year I became a training center company commander. And in March 1953 I was promoted to captain.

My new job was to provide basic training to the enlisted men who had recently joined the Army, helping them adjust to being soldiers and giving them fundamental soldiering skills. I was responsible for overseeing the individual training for every enlisted soldier, for taking the new recruits out to the field training areas, for the head count, for their feeding and billeting, and for the cleanliness of the area.

Whether the company commander actually participated in the training was up to him. He could lead the way, or he could lie back and let the NCOs do it. Although I did not routinely participate, I did lead the training from time to time. That is part of my leadership style. I wanted my soldiers to know that nothing was being asked of them that I could not do.

At the time there were about two hundred trainees in a training company, and they spent eight to ten weeks in basic training. A two-hundred-person company would be divided into four platoons. Each generally had four NCOs as trainers. We did not use the term back then, but those NCOs were equivalent to drill sergeants.

In a typical movie scene you often see a drill sergeant yelling mercilessly at a miserable trainee as he participates in some form of training. In practice, however, a drill sergeant is not brutal or abusive. His job is to turn a trainee into a soldier by developing the trainee's discipline, mental toughness, and physical fitness.

If you were to ask the vast majority of soldiers who went through basic training many years ago if they recalled the name of their company commander, they probably would not have the foggiest idea. If you were to ask the name of their drill sergeant, they would know it without any question whatsoever. I think that is because they eventually understand what the drill sergeant was trying to do. Something the drill sergeant taught might well save one's life, and it is hard to forget a person who has done that for you.

My sergeants and I took the mission of preparing trainees to be soldiers very seriously. When an enlisted man left us, we wanted him to feel completely confident that he could do the job. We could issue our stamp of approval, and say, "Go forth and soldier!" If we did not think a young man was adequately prepared—and they were all men in those days, since women did not enter the training base until the early 1970s—he would be recycled through basic training or discharged. If we graduated someone who was not ready, we were essentially dooming him or one of his buddies to death.

Perhaps the most important lesson to be learned in basic training is unquestioned subordinate response, which is a fancy way of describing learning to follow instructions from someone who is responsible for your life. This is the glue that holds it all together. Close order drill, for example, is not designed to teach soldiers how to march around wielding weapons. It is designed to teach them to follow instructions immediately and without question. In combat, unquestioned subordinate response is essential. The Army does not operate on individualism. What are needed are soldiers who are following the orders of the person in charge.

Well aware of how meaningful the work was, I enjoyed my assignment as training center company commander. But at the end of my one-year tour, I relinquished responsibility to a replacement officer.

When I did so I discovered that the unit was a few hundred pillow-cases short. It was one of my responsibilities to ensure that the inventory was complete. So I appealed to the ingenuity of my wife. It was hardly the first time. Back at Fort Lewis, for example, Louise, who hated home economics in high school, had, at my request, made curtains for more than forty windows in my platoon's barracks building. Now, using extra sheets from the Indiantown reservation's stores, she created the requisite number of pillowcases just in time to bail me out.

Is it any wonder that most successful Army officers recognize that our spouses deserve much of the credit?

Now I had commanded a company for the second time. I also had completed several courses at Pennsylvania State University in Harrisburg while at Indiantown, and I returned to Fort Benning for further schooling in September 1953. This time I was assigned to take the seven-month Infantry Officer Advanced Course (IOAC). Once again, my family lived off post. Louise was expecting again, and Joyce Wesley Becton was born that December.

There were six black officers in the advanced school out of a class of 180 students. Capt. Marshall Bass, whom I had known at Fort Lewis and in

Korea, was one of the three who lived on post. There were no black officers on the faculty of the infantry school at that time, but there were several people who would be important later in my career. Lt. Col. George Blanchard was one. He had been military assistant to Gen. Omar Bradley and had been kept out of the school system to stay with Bradley. When he left Benning Blanchard went directly to the Command and General Staff College at Fort Leavenworth, which was a very unusual move.

The curriculum of the IOAC was pretty much based on fighting the last war. In the armored divisions we still had combat commands, not regiments; we did not have brigades. We were moving into the "Pentomic" division, which is a division with five battle groups that each have five line companies and no battalions. In effect, the battle group commander, a colonel, supervised and rated five company commanders. This proved to be a disaster because there was a break in the normal chain of command, and the experiment was short-lived. Organization is the heart and soul of the Army, and tampering with it causes problems. A chain of command from a colonel to a captain, without a lieutenant colonel and major to interpret, was a recipe for disaster. The Army, in effect, was fighting for its soul.

My IOAC class graduated in March 1954. After graduation, I did what I had done every time I left a school at Benning: I applied for airborne training. The first time was in 1945, when I graduated from OCS. I was told then that there was no unit to which I could be assigned because the single black airborne unit, the 555th Parachute Infantry Battalion, already had too many officers. I tried again in 1949 when I was graduating from the IOBC. That time I was told I was on competitive tour and had to get out and join a unit, so it was off to Fort Lewis for me. This time I was told, "No, you're on orders to Europe." I was reassigned to the 2nd Armored Division in West Germany.

After a short leave in Philadelphia I departed for my first trip to Europe. I left my family at home with Mom Thornton, which is what I had come to call my mother-in-law, because there was a housing shortage. Louise, Shirley, Karen, and Joyce joined me in Germany three months later.

I was assigned to Combat Command B (CCB) of the 2nd Armored Division, "Hell on Wheels," in Mainz-Gonsenheim, as a communications officer (COMMO). I was the COMMO for one year, and during that time I learned that communications depends as much on common sense as it does on technical knowledge.

On one occasion I almost lost my cool with the executive officer. We were out on maneuvers late at night, and he was having telephone problems. He was screaming, which he did not normally do, and they kept calling for the COMMO. I climbed out of my pup tent, put on my clothes, went over to his trailer, and listened to his telephone. It was not working. I looked at it, pushed two loose batteries back into the telephone, and cranked it. Then I said, "Sir, would you like to talk to someone now?" I wanted to say, "You dumb S.O.B.; all you had to do is put the batteries back in!" But I did not.

The 2nd Division headquarters was at Bad Kreuznach, and combat command (i.e., brigades) were posted in Mainz, Baumholder, and Manheim. Every week, we participated in division-wide communication exercises.

As the COMMO I won all kinds of brownie points with the commanders by obtaining a Military Affiliate Radio System (MARS) station for the command. The MARS station was staffed with five command radio operators, and it was able to provide free communications for our soldiers back to the states. I took and passed the examination to get my own radio license (DL4MG). Although I really was not that technically qualified, key bosses were impressed.

I also became an aerial observer, which gave me greater freedom, particularly during operational exercises, and also extra pay. All I had to do was maintain a minimum of four hours a month in either a light observation helicopter or a single engine, fixed-wing airplane. One of my classmates from the advanced course at Benning, Capt. Harry Townsend, was in Bad Nauheim, north of Frankfurt. He would fly into the CCB airfield in his helicopter, and we would fly over the countryside. As an official aerial observer I was able to justify the trip as training and, naturally, Harry was required to have a certain number of flight hours for proficiency. These trips made for some very pleasant weekends.

There were two infantry captains in headquarters CCB, Willard Latham and me. We both had made it very clear that we wanted to command companies, and we both got our wish within several weeks of each other. Will assumed command of Company B, 67th Armor Battalion, which was quite unusual: Infantry officers did not normally command tank companies. I assumed command of Company D, 42nd Armored Infantry Battalion from another Benning classmate, Capt. Tom Adams.

Tom was a good guy, but he had one idiosyncrasy: Unless forced to, he never wore the fatigue duty uniform. The soldiers obviously did not think much of that. So one of the first things I did when reporting in was put on fatigues.

In the 1950s Army officers had much more freedom of operation than in subsequent years. If I wanted to get my company out on a range for target practice, all I had to do was order the ammunition and, if the ranges were unoccupied, load up my soldiers in personnel carriers, go out the back gate, and start firing on the range. If I wanted to go on a road march, I just lined up the vehicles and drove to a starting point for the march. As a company commander, I was fairly independent, and I did not have to worry much about paperwork.

The battalion commander was Lt. Col. Francis Lang, and the other officers and I convinced him to let the company commanders run the companies. We said, "If you take care of your staff, we'll take care of the rest of the battalion." So that was his approach.

We did have some challenges. This was early in the Cold War, and we were west of the Rhine River. CCB's initial battle mission was to guard the bridges over the Rhine, thereby ensuring the orderly evacuation to the west of noncombatants and the early eastward flow of reinforcements in case of a Communist invasion. Bridge guard duty was rotated among the companies of the battalions. There were monthly alerts designed to exercise various portions of the overall defense plans. The senior U.S. Army Europe (USAREUR) command headquarters was located in Heidelberg. The high-level headquarters, V Corps, was in Frankfurt. Each headquarters was responsible for one exercise a quarter. During the USAREUR exercise, the bridge security force was also exercised.

It just so happened that my company had responsibility for bridge security during the period when we were scheduled for the battalion's annual general inspection. As the date of the inspection approached I asked the battalion commander what would happen if the inspection coincided with the unannounced-ahead-of-time USAREUR alert. At first my commander said that would not happen. I persisted: What if it did? What should we do? He said, "Well, you'll go. If it's a USAREUR alert, you'll go."

The night before the spit-and-polish inspection we carefully prepared for this demonstration of attention to details, scrubbing the floors, laying out our equipment on blankets so tight you could bounce a dime off of them. No one slept on a bed that night. The rooms were spotless.

At 5:30 the next morning the gong went off, signaling a full USAREUR alert. I was livid. Company D was the only unit affected because we were the bridge security.

I called battalion headquarters and asked, "Well, guys, what do I do?" The response was, "You go!"

"Roger that," I replied and told the company to load up.

We ripped up all the carefully laid displays of clothing and equipment and jammed everything into our A and B duffle bags; the A bag was carried by the soldier as he moved out for battle, and the B bag was sent to the supply room for storage. We whipped down to the motor pool, threw our bags in the back of the armored personnel carriers and half-tracks and started out the gate.

At the gate stood Maj. Ed Stewart, the battalion executive officer.

"Halt," said Major Stewart.

"What's wrong, Major?" I asked.

I sat in utter disbelief as I heard him say, "Becton, we just got word from division that you will stand the inspection." I used some very profane words. The major said, "I understand, but I was sent down by the battalion commander to tell you you're going to stand the inspection." I said, "Yes, sir."

We headed back to our billets. We turned the vehicles over to the platoon sergeants and returned the duffel bags to our rooms. I assembled the four platoon lieutenants, the company executive officer, and my first sergeant. I said, "Okay, guys, we've got a real challenge. We'll be the last to be visited, but that doesn't give a great deal of solace. I want you to do one thing. I want you to go from room to room, and this is the message: You think you're good; let's prove it. We're good. Let's prove it. Nothing else. Just charge them up with that."

Our guys passed the inspection. We were not the best company based on overall scoring, but no one else had to do what we did.

The inspection incident sent two messages about Company D: first, that ours was not an outfit to mess with, and, second, that we would do our best at all times.

I was the first black company commander in the command, and my soldiers were initially a little antsy about that. We had less than 15 percent black soldiers, but we had good NCOs who wanted to prove a point, and all my soldiers developed a pretty hard-assed attitude. If you said something bad about the black company commander, you had a fight on your hands. After a couple of my soldiers beat up on some people, the message went out, "Don't mess with D Company because they'll fight."

The second message was that I was determined that we were going to perform to our utmost abilities regardless of the task. I required all the company officers and all the NCOs to be able to drive every vehicle we had, fire every weapon we had, and operate every piece of communications equipment we had. I felt it was important that the leadership set the example.

I also expected my soldiers to excel in physical fitness. Will Latham had a similar expectation for his tank company, and it was natural for us to challenge each other. At the annual physical fitness evaluations Will tested my company, and I tested his. To motivate my soldiers, I told them that anyone with a higher score than mine would have the rest of the day off. I was the first to perform each of the five exercises on the morning of the test, and the entire company stood around to make sure I did each exercise according to the book. Needless to say, I was physically beat when I finished and returned to the orderly room to rest. That afternoon the battalion operations officer was inspecting unit training. He came storming into my office demanding to know where my people were. I must have had a good seventy soldiers on pass. When he heard what had happened, he burst out laughing and said, "That will teach you to challenge soldiers!" He was right, of course, but my company ended up with the highest score in the command.

At the end of my one-year command tour I was reassigned and became assistant operations officer for CCB. I was able to have Lt. Ray Huntington, my company executive officer, reassigned with me, and he became one of our liaison officers within the operations shop. Shortly after my arrival, the command operations officer (S-3) transferred, and he wanted to prepare an evaluation report for me even though I had not been there the requisite rating time. His main comment still rings in my ears: "Captain Becton is the best Negro officer I have ever worked with." His replacement was Maj. George Gradwell, a really decent guy who let Ray and me do what had to be done. I had excellent relationships with the senior officers in the command.

My first CCB commander was Col. Andrew Jackson Boyle, who went on to become a lieutenant general. The second was Col. Paul Lavern Bates.

Bates, an outstanding soldier, had been the commander—and the only white officer—of the 761st Tank Battalion, which was the first African-American armored unit to enter combat in World War II. Baseball legend Jackie Robinson had been an officer with the battalion nicknamed the "Black Panthers" during training in Texas, but on one occasion he had refused to sit in the back of a bus. Even though Colonel Bates refused to court-martial him for that refusal, Robinson was prevented from accompanying his unit to Europe.

Gen. George Patton, Third Army commander, was known for selecting only the best, and he hand-picked the 761st Battalion to participate in the Battle of the Bulge. The battalion proved its mettle during 183 days of continual fighting. After years of delays due primarily to the deep racial prejudices of the time, the 761st Tank Battalion was awarded the Presidential Unit Citation by President Jimmy Carter, and SSgt. Ruben Rivers received the Medal of Honor for his extraordinary heroism posthumously in 1997.[1] Some, including me, think that Colonel Bates should have become a general officer. It is likely that his connection to an all-black battalion helped thwart his promotion.

Through my involvement with CCB operations, I learned how to do many new things. Developing, drafting, and finalizing operations orders became second nature to me, for instance. I particularly appreciated the way that armored units did things. It took infantry units a considerable amount of time to change task organizations, but a single radio call could reorganize armored formations. My admiration for this flexibility, along with the encouragement of Colonel Bates, eventually convinced me that my future was in the armor branch. I requested a transfer from infantry to armor in February 1957, and my branch transfer became effective that April.

To the purist, I may not have seemed qualified to switch to armor. Had I ever engaged in tank operations? No. Had I ever even driven a tank? No. But armor is a frame of mind as much as it is technical know-how. And I had received a very strong recommendation from the 2nd Armored Division, including its commander, Gen. C. Stanton Babcock. When I was the assistant S-3, and CCB was participating in a command post exercise in the field, I heard that on several occasions the general said, "If Becton is out there, things will be okay." Apparently his confidence in me persisted. More than that, I felt comfortable with operating formations, whether they involved a battalion or brigade or even a division, which is, after all, just a larger unit.

Of course there were occasions when I did some dumb things. For example, early on, we needed lots of overhead firepower in an exercise, and we did not have enough available artillery. I made the dumb statement, "Hell, just line up all the tanks, elevate the tubes, and shoot." I thought Colonel Bates was going to die. He screamed, "Becton, don't you ever do that! That's not what we're made for!"

In situations like that, I learn quickly. "Yes, sir!" I said. "I understand."

Since there were not many black officers in the immediate community, my advice was sought on disciplinary cases that were related to race. I also got involved in many area activities, not always voluntarily.

We started a Big Brothers Club in Mainz, and I became the president because the combat command commander said, "You ought to do that." I said, "Yes, sir." We also started Protestant Men of the Chapel (PMOC), a group that met for prayer and fellowship. I became PMOC's president for the same reason as I took leadership of the Big Brothers Club.

Of course I also had family-related obligations, most of which gave me great pleasure. But every now and then, I was not entirely happy about them. An incident that still sort of rankles is that during the fifth game of the 1956 World Series, when Don Larsen of the Yankees was pitching a perfect game against the Brooklyn Dodgers and Louise insisted that I accompany her to a meeting of the local Parent Teacher Association. Needless to say, I was glued to the radio for the early part of the game, but with just two innings left to go, I went to the school function. I was not in a good humor as I left the radio and a history-making, once-in-a-lifetime event, however.

Domestic relations also played a role in one of my adventures as an authorized aerial observer. I was riding in the back seat of a single-engine plane en route from Mainz to Baumholder. The pilot was a captain, and we had reached our halfway point near Bad Krueznach, where we routinely changed heading. All of a sudden the plane's engine coughed, and the pilot decided to make an emergency landing. By the time we were coming in over the high tension wire at the end of the airfield for the landing, the pilot had a dead stick—the propeller was frozen. As we approached the ground the pilot remembered to say, "May Day."

Later, I learned what had happened. At the halfway point it was the practice to switch fuel tanks, but the pilot had failed to check the tanks before the flight. One had fuel; the other was empty. And much later, I discovered something else. That morning, the pilot had argued with his wife. The last thing she said as he left the house was, "I hope you go out there and kill yourself!" When I found that out I told her, "Don't you ever tell him that again when I am flying with him. Tell me." The pilot received an Article 15 and reverted shortly thereafter from captain to his permanent warrant officer because of that one dumb instance of failing to take a wooden stick and push it down in the tank.

On 30 October 1954, the military effectively declared that the last segregated unit had been abolished. And it is true that through the years I was in Europe from 1954 to 1957, the Army was gradually trying to comply with Truman's executive order. But segregation was definitely not a thing of the past.

To have true integration it is absolutely essential to have qualified personnel at every level who can make it happen. Within our division we had a relatively small number of black junior officers and a rather significant number of fairly senior black NCOs, whose presence tended to have a calming effect on potentially explosive situations involving racial prejudice. Such was not the case at places like Nuremberg, where racial conflicts among soldiers were fairly routine and unenlightened leadership played a big role in the problem.

The absence of senior black officers was a direct result of past policies. Quite simply, very few candidates for such positions were in the pipeline. We did have one black senior field grade officer, Lt. Col. Edward C. Johnson, infantry, who was located in Bad Kruenach and served as the executive officer of the Division Trains.

Toward the end of my tour in Europe some of us really wanted to push for integration within the division. So four black captains, including me, went to see Lieutenant Colonel Johnson. We wanted to encourage him to assume command of the 42nd Armored Infantry Battalion in Mainz. We basically said, "Sir, come on down and take over. We'll make you. You can't go wrong. It's a good battalion—we can make it happen."

But he never did. Eventually Johnson, whose wife was the sister of the great Brooklyn Dodgers catcher Roy Campanella, returned to the states and became a professor of military science and tactics at Morgan State University in Baltimore.

CHAPTER SIX

★ ★ ★

Higher Education

W hen it was time for me to return to the United States in the spring of 1957, I had several options. At this point, Lt. Col. John "Tommy" Martin entered the picture. Tommy worked with the deputy assistant secretary of defense for equal opportunity. I had met him in the early 1950s, and he had taken a liking to me. He recognized that my career would be stunted so long as I lacked a college degree. In Tommy's view, Reserve Officer Training Corps (ROTC) duty would help me get my degree in the quickest time, and the Army had implemented a plan to financially support full-time attendance for Regular Army officers who could complete their college work within one semester.

Tommy initially had my personnel file sent to Morgan State. Since I thought we had a pretty good rapport, I was shocked to learn that Lieutenant Colonel Johnson rejected my assignment, saying he could not use an officer on the faculty who did not have a degree. Tommy then had my name sent to Prairie View in Texas, where I was accepted by both the president, Dr. E. B. Evans, and Lt. Col. Tommy Wright.

I reported to PVAMC in June 1957, family in tow, and we rented a house off campus from "Pops" Randall, who was a legend in the math department. I then started settling into my job as the Military Science Department adjutant. I was the junior officer; the department faculty consisted of one lieutenant colonel, four majors, and me—a captain. The department's summer camp detail had already departed for the ROTC advanced camp at Fort Hood, and since my military science department orientation was not all that difficult and summer school was just starting, I decided to sign up for at least one class. When my new boss, Lieutenant Colonel Wright, found out, he blew up, saying, "You can't work for me and go to school at the same time."

I was dumbfounded. I had assumed that it was clear that I was sent to Prairie View to obtain my degree. I called Tommy Martin that evening. He told me not to worry; he would take care of it. Since my office was only about ten feet from the boss's office, I had no problem the next morning hearing him scream, "Becton, get in here!" After a few well-chosen words, Lieutenant Colonel Wright said, "All right. You can go to school, but you had best never let any of your work in this office slip. Is that clear?" Apparently, he had received a call from Martin.

When I reported to PVAMC, I already had taken more than one hundred semester hours of college classes. Some of the courses I'd taken at Muhlenberg such as religion and history of civilization were disallowed for purposes of degree credit. I first asked to pursue a degree in natural science because my premed work seemed to be applicable, but Prairie View did not offer a natural science degree. After checking my transcript, the dean of instruction felt my best course of action was to pursue a degree in math. Shades of analytical geometry!

Being the junior officer in rank and age meant that I was assigned all the additional duties the five field graders did not want. It was hard enough to go to school and work at the same time, and this compounded my problems. I was the only Regular Army officer on the military science faculty and the only officer with combat wounds, Purple Hearts, and a Silver Star. I did not belong to a Greek fraternity, and they all did. The camaraderie that I had hoped to find just was not there.

I became the instructor for the junior students who had just entered the ROTC advanced program. Up until this time, the students had participated in the two years of mandatory ROTC training that was then required of male students at all land-grant institutions. Failure to complete the two years of advanced ROTC, for which the students received a stipend, could result in either being required to repay all of the funds expended on the student's education or being called to active duty as an enlisted man. (We did not have women in the ROTC in those days.) Repayment was seldom required.

It was my job to select and motivate students who had the potential to do well and to eliminate marginal performers in their junior year. I was responsible for teaching leadership, small unit tactics, and physical fitness, which were all things in which I excelled.

During my first year I also officiated football and basketball for the Southwestern Athletic Conference (SWAC). The SWAC was the all-black conference that included PVAMC; Sam Houston State University;

Texas College; Wiley College; Southern University; Arkansas Agricultural, Military & Normal College; Texas Southern University; Grambling College; and Jackson State College. One of the other SWAC officials was Maj. Seth Finley, with whom I had served in Mainz Gonsenheim. During my three years officiating both high school and intercollegiate games, Seth and I developed quite a reputation for being both objective and fair since neither of us had any allegiance to local schools.

While I was teaching and pushing my students very hard, I also attended classes with some of them. This created an interesting domestic situation. Louise had gone to work as a registered nurse in the college hospital and was also pursuing a degree in nursing education. So Shirley, Karen, and Joyce were full-time students. Louise and I were part-time students, and Mom Thornton took care of the house. To say that we were busy is somewhat of an understatement.

We got a lot out of our three years at Prairie View. The girls had their first true black experience since the community was entirely African American. I had the opportunity to select some truly outstanding future Army officers, including two, Calvin A. H. Waller and Marvin D. Brailsford, who went on to become lieutenant generals. And Louise received her BS in nursing education in 1959.

In January 1960 I became a full-time student under the Army's new Final Semester Program. The very next month Renee Marie Becton was born. My new boss, Col. Arthur Booth, actually saw her before I did, primarily because I was a full-time student and could not get out of class and he was not so constrained. Booth later became Renee's godfather.

During this last year of undergraduate studies, I also received word that I had been selected to attend the Army Command & General Staff College in Fort Leavenworth, Kansas. Clearly, our two-door sedan would not suffice for Mom Thornton, Louise, me, Shirley, Karen, Joyce, and Renee. It was time for a new car.

I went to the local Ford dealer and was quickly reminded that I was in East Texas, with its lingering racial animosities. I was in uniform. As I walked around the small showroom, the salesmen ignored me and stood over in the corner talking. After about ten minutes, one of them wandered over and said, "Hey, boy, what can I do for you?" I said, "Not a damned thing," and stormed out. I went back to the campus in a fury, remembering the similar indignity my father had been subjected to back in Morehead City.

The manager of the Ford dealership found out what had happened and called the school. He had no difficulty finding out who I was. There were not that many black officers at Prairie View.

I refused to talk to the manager. He kept calling, and I kept refusing his calls. On the few occasions when he did catch me on the phone, I was very sarcastic. During one of these conversations I said, "I'm not going to spend my money where I am going to be insulted." He said, "Sir, why don't you come back and see if we can work a deal?" I finally agreed. That nine-passenger station wagon was listed at about $4,500, and when he sold it to me for $4,000, I laughed all the way to the bank.

The manager had known that I could do a lot of damage. Since PVAMC was the principal employer in the area, all I had to do was to spread the word not to do business with that dealership. That was why he tried to make amends. Even so, of course, I did spread the word about the way I had been treated and about the deal I had cut with the manager, particularly if I heard that someone was interested in buying a car. I said, "Go down there and let them insult you. You've got it made."

In mid-May, more than fourteen years after I had taken my first college course while stationed in the Philippines, I received my BS in mathematics. Although Louise had received straight As, I was quite pleased with my 3.5 grade point average. As I crossed the stage with my degree in hand, the college registrar announced that I was the 5,000th undergraduate from PVAMC. Everyone congratulated me, but I could not help but suspect that the whole thing was rigged. I am sure the 5,000th graduate was somewhere in that class of 1960, but was I the one? Really! Of course, it did not hurt the college that I was a successful Army officer with a certain amount of proven potential, as witnessed by my selection to general staff training at Leavenworth.

Our move to Kansas was uneventful, and we took up residence on post. Without the salary Louise had been earning in Texas, we felt a bit financially strapped. But the burden of supporting our large family eased a bit after I was promoted to major in February 1961.

In those days about 50 percent of the officer corps was selected to attend the CGSC based on their past performance and demonstrated potential. There were 670 officers in my class, and the class included the largest number of blacks in the history of the college. There were eight of us–William Bullard, Harvey Dickerson, Grover Dubose, Tim Howard, Mel

Hurtt, Harold Neal, Lloyd Stark, and me. Since that time the number of black students has grown to more than seven times as many.

The new commandant at the CGSC when I arrived was Maj. Gen. Harold K. Johnson, who had spent forty-one months as a prisoner of war of the Japanese during World War II and who later became Army chief of staff. We had heard that he was charged with bringing about a new day and eliminating the custom that "everybody passes." General Johnson definitely did put the clamps down and demanded that the faculty get tough. The end result was that several officers in my class did not graduate. To the best of my knowledge, none of them were ever promoted beyond the grade they held when they left Leavenworth.

In an attempt to ensure that we would make it, seven of the eight black officers formed a study group for each examination. The one holdout was the senior black in our class, a lieutenant colonel. It seemed he wanted very little to do with us, period. Near the end of the course, when it became apparent that he was having difficulty, four of us went to him and offered to help. He refused, and he did not pass the course. Personally, I think his refusal to accept our assistance led to his undoing. We could have pulled him through.

As an armor officer, I had every expectation that when I left the CGSC I would go to an assignment where I could use my training as an operations planner for combat forces. When I was at CGSC, however, the commander of the communications zone in France complained to the Department of the Army that he was not getting his fair share of talented officers coming out of the college. As a result, twelve combat arms officers from my class, including me, were sent to France, which was the site of communications and logistical support for the combatant forces in Germany during the 1960s. Four of us went to Bordeaux, which is in the western part of the communications zone (COMZ), four went to headquarters in Orléans, and four went to the Advance Logistical Command at Verdun. I was assigned to Verdun as the plans officer.

An armor officer classmate, Maj. Paul Crosby, was also there, assigned to the personnel staff officer (G-1). Neither one of us was thrilled about our assignments. Verdun was the site of a World War I battlefield and was the site of a mausoleum containing the skeletons of thousands of soldiers. Many have described the city as having a pall hanging over it. I found little comfort in the fact that the black lieutenant colonel who had failed the course at the CGSC was also sent to Verdun. The death knell had already been tolled on his career, and I began to wonder if a similar dirge was being played for mine. Part of the trouble was the perception back then that the real hotshots are sent to the combat units. If a combat arms officer was given a logistics assignment, the common wisdom held, he must not be qualified for a combat-related assignment.

What was more troubling was that the work I was being asked to do was completely foreign to me. Instead of planning operations for combat units, I would now be planning operations for logistical units. I did not find this an exciting prospect. Logisticians are people who stockpile, deliver, or build things. I was used to dealing with people—specifically preparing them to go into battle. I was not used to warehousing supplies and equipment.

It turned out that I was to learn a great deal from my time in Verdun and from the people with whom I worked. There were four of us in our little office, and we became very close. Sgt. Jay Rickman was the NCO in charge, and Peggy Shelton was the secretary. My immediate boss was Maj. Aldo Bettelli, a diminutive airborne reserve officer who was, I quickly learned, a superb soldier.

Aldo was a paratrooper and had fought in World War II and Korea. He was Italian, and spoke that language fluently, along with English, French, and German. He had been in Verdun for some time and got along very well with the civilians. He was not self-effacing, but he had a way with people. In the local community, my group was able to get a lot of things done that some other "ugly Americans" could not have accomplished, largely because of Aldo's demeanor and the fact that he could speak the language.

I was in Verdun during the chilliest period of the Cold War. Shortly before I arrived in August 1961, the Soviets built the Berlin Wall, the most tangible evidence of the enmity between East and West. Twice a year USAREUR rehearsed the removal of family members and nonessential civilian support personnel from the forward areas, which encompassed all of Germany. If the Communist forces attacked, our command had plans—we called them noncombatant evacuation orders, or NEOs—to remove noncombatants from Germany. Our job was to pick them up at the Franco-German border and expedite their movement to the west coast of France or down into what we called the safe haven, which was Spain.

To execute the NEOs we had to know where the potential evacuees were at all times. Families were required to have their passports and birth certificates in a specified package and be ready to travel at a moment's notice. They were also required to keep a full five-gallon can of gasoline in their homes at all times, as well as a certain amount of food they could take with them. We conducted periodic inspections to make sure they were in compliance.

When my family arrived in Verdun, we were moved into "guaranteed rental housing," which were very small housing units built and run by the French. We had three bedrooms, one bathroom, a combined living and dining room, and that was it. Again, I need to stress that at that time, our family consisted of seven people—Louise and myself, our four daughters, and Mom Thornton, my mother-in-law. Trying to get ready for anything with six females and one bathroom was a challenge. I used that argument to persuade the post commander that our living conditions were just not working out.

After about a year we were moved to "surplus commodity housing," which had been built by the French to American specifications. Our new house was freestanding, not a row house like the previous one, and it was much larger. We now had two bathrooms, a larger living room, and much larger bedrooms.

Louise and I both took French classes while we were in Verdun, but she was a more dedicated student than I was. I am not a natural when it comes to languages, and I have always had to really discipline myself to learn them. Throughout all my overseas assignments I preferred to help the host nation's personnel and local workers improve their English skills rather than taking advantage of opportunities to learn the host nation's language. Fifteen years later my shortcomings in spoken French came back to haunt me.

Since the TV programming was in French, we did not have a television set in our home. Our oldest daughter, Shirley, was thirteen at the time, and our youngest, Renee, was two. With no television that they could readily understand, our children did a lot of reading.

Our older daughters also attended the American dependents' school, which was excellent. It was relatively small, with an enrollment of no more than three hundred students. The teachers came from the United States on contract, and they were really superb. Joyce entered the third grade in 1963, and she did so well that her teacher suggested she be promoted to fourth grade at mid-year. We agreed, but had to live with some traumatic effects. For the first time Joyce was not always bringing home straight As, and her self-esteem suffered. It took some real work to convince her that she was not a failure if she earned a grade lower than an A. Louise was the nurse at the school, and this proved to be an ideal situation because she was able to use her professional training and also be near our children during the day.

The lives of all Americans were deeply affected by the assassination of President John F. Kennedy on 22 November 1963. Louise and I were playing bridge at the home of friends when we heard the horrific news. The French radio stations began playing very somber music. The Kennedys were highly esteemed by the French, and I suspect that the French people were more deeply saddened by the assassination than anyone other than Americans. I still remember the sincerity of their reaction. It was heartfelt.

In our new quarters, we were next door to a man who would become a professional mentor and a close personal friend. Col. Joe Heiser and his wife Edie took a liking to us. Colonel Heiser was the logistics officer at the time, and he went on to become the chief of staff of the Fourth Logistical Command. When he was promoted to brigadier general in 1963, he moved from Verdun to Orléans. But we remained in contact until he died in the late 1980s.

Heiser was a former semiprofessional baseball player and a sports nut. He was also an outspoken critic of officiating, and he critiqued me no end about my own extracurricular officiating of basketball games in the COMZ.

As a mentor Heiser made sure I received visibility in as many official tasks as possible. Inadvertently, he once also got me some visibility in an unofficial activity. One Sunday in Verdun, the COMZ football team played a game against a team of Americans stationed in Germany, and the home team lost. It was a pretty ugly loss, and emotions ran high. There was a lot of pushing and shoving between players and spectators after the game, and the pushing and shoving quickly escalated to blows.

Colonel Heiser was at the game, dressed in uniform. A large man, he waded into the middle of the melee, throwing people this way and that way, trying to break up the mob. I was sitting way up in the stands, and I saw what Heiser was trying to do. I was not in uniform, but concerned that someone would try to jump his backside, I went down to the field to help him. I had my ID card in my hand, and I flashed it to everyone. We eventually restored some order.

The next morning at a staff meeting, Colonel Heiser let everyone know how he felt about what had happened at the game. I have since been told that he cussed and swore at his staff, calling them cowards, weak-kneed, and chicken-livered. He said, "Men, only one person had enough backbone to come out there where I was to help to restore order, and that was Major Becton. And you guys watched him and did nothing about it!"

The result was that my stock went up pretty high.

All in all in fact, my time in Verdun was probably the most significant learning experience of my life. That assignment helped me to be better prepared for all of my future commands. The knowledge I gained in logistics helped me immeasurably later. In the 1970s, when I became a division and a corps commander, I had a much better appreciation for logistics because I had been there. I think the logisticians who worked with me and for me appreciated the fact that I knew what they were doing. They knew I respected and understood their work and valued what they did.

We receive many blessings in disguise.

My family and I left Verdun in December 1963 on a troop transport ship bound for New York. We arrived in New York Harbor on Christmas Eve, and my Mom and Dad had come up from Bryn Mawr to pick us up. They had to turn around and go back without us, however, because the longshoremen were not about to unload that ship on Christmas Eve or Christmas Day. So we stayed on board and had a great time. The crew broke out everything they had on the boat, including booze.

My orders were to attend what was then known as the Armed Forces Staff College (AFSC) in Norfolk, Virginia. This is the first school at the level of joint operations, a fact reflected by its later name change to the Joint Forces Staff College. One-third of the student body came from the Army, one-third from the Air Force, one-third from the Navy and Marines, and each student held a rank equivalent to Army major or lieutenant colonel. Maj. Chet Woods and I were the first two black armor officers to attend the institution.

The five-month program was designed to provide officers from the different services a better understanding of how the others operate. The curriculum included seventy-two hours of instruction in counterinsurgency and subjects directly related to counterinsurgency.

On a personal level, my family's stay in Norfolk was memorable because of the challenge—the second major challenge of her educational career—it posed for Joyce when she was put in the position of integrating her elementary school. There were about twenty students in her class and between two hundred and three hundred students in the school, and Joyce was the first black ever to attend.

The principal was a rather elderly professional who was determined not to let anyone or anything hurt his school. So almost each day during the five months we were in Norfolk, he personally met the bus that brought Joyce from the AFSC campus. He also frequently visited her classroom and routinely was present to see her board the bus back to our home. Perhaps as a result of his vigilance, Joyce did not encounter any ugly racial incidents.

But even in 1964 the nation was far from colorblind, as I would soon discover. While I was attending the AFSC, I received orders for my next assignment at the Pentagon in Washington, D.C., Louise and I had to find a place to live in the D.C. area, and at first we were interested in Northern Virginia. My first stop was the AFSC office, which maintained a list of available housing for Pentagon-bound students. Then I headed off to Washington.

I visited about a half dozen realtors that had postings on properties for sale. My approach was always to call first, identify myself as Major Becton en route from the AFSC with an assignment to the Pentagon. I said my family and I were looking for four bedrooms and two or more baths, etc. The answer always came back, "Why sure, come on by." But it was always a different story when I showed up at the realtor's office. The house was no longer available. It was off the market. The seller had changed his mind. After explaining why the house was no longer available, the realtors would continue: "Now, we do have some other property over in another area that you may be interested in. It is in the colored section of town." One look told me that I would not bring my family to such a place.

After a second trip with basically the same results, I reported the matter to the AFSC commander, who essentially did not believe me. He directed his adjutant to check it out. We looked at the bulletin board of "available" housing and started calling. Each phone call went something like this: "I am Colonel so-and-so calling from the Armed Forces Staff College about the house you have posted here as available. We have a major being reassigned to your area, and he is looking for such a home. Is the house still available? Good. Oh, there is one other minor matter: He is a Negro. I thought you just said that the house was available. I see. I am sorry to hear that. Goodbye."

After several such rejections the adjutant advised the commander, who basically said, "Go back up to the Washington area, take as much time as you need, and find yourself a home." Of course, by this time, we were prepared to live anyplace, not just in Virginia. Through word of mouth, we found a beautiful home in the District of Columbia, one block north of Walter Reed—1312 Floral Street, NW.

I was able to delay our move to Washington long enough to satisfy an old ambition of attending the airborne course at Fort Benning. After four unsuccessful attempts to get there, it was finally my turn.

The family returned to the Philadelphia area, and I headed to Columbus, Georgia. Even in 1964 it did not seem to me that much had changed during that trip through the Southland. I was very aware of my status as a "colored" man.

Once I was safely at Benning, two more things became clear. First, almost twenty years out of OCS my body was not in as great shape as it used to be. Second, attending a physically demanding course in Georgia in July is not very smart.

I discovered on the first day in basic parachute training that I was the senior officer and, therefore, the student company commander. I had five junior officers. The three weeks were hard but uneventful. Until the last day, that was.

Due to weather delays the graduation ceremony was moved from the cantonment area to the drop zone. Louise had flown in the night before, and she was bused out, along with other students' family members, to witness our last jump.

As luck would have it I ended up with a malfunction of the type known as a "Mae West." As my main parachute deployed, the risers—the heavy straps that connect the lines to the parachute's container—got caught over the canopy, creating two partially filled half chutes instead of a single, fully-filled one. I immediately did everything according to the drill. I got into a tight body position and released my reserve chute, prepared to float down with no control. The popping of the reserve chute freed the risers from the main chute. Now I was under two chutes that were fully deployed. I then became aware of the instructor on the ground saying over the public address system, "Man with a Mae West, pull your reserve." All of this took place in a very short time.

When I got onto the ground I recovered both chutes and turned them in. I then went looking for Louise. "Did you see that guy with the Mae West?" I asked her. "That was me!" Ever since then, Louise has not been keen on parachuting.

CHAPTER SEVEN

★ ★ ★

The Washington Rat Race

I reported to the Pentagon in August 1964, and my official assignment was to the Office of the Deputy Chief of Staff for Personnel, Reserve Affairs and Discipline Branch, Promotion and Retention Division. Essentially, I became the point of contact on personnel matters between the reserve component and the active Army.

One of my first duties was to develop a position paper for the Army that addressed the question of whether ROTC fell under the aegis of personnel or whether it should fall under the Office of Plans and Operations. My office thought the purpose of ROTC was to select college students who had the potential to become officers. This mission of "hiring" officers would clearly make running ROTC a personnel matter. Plans and operations held the opposing view, arguing that ROTC's main purpose was training students who would almost all become officers in any event.

The Army's comptroller office was the arbiter, and it ruled against my personnel office. ROTC became the business of plans and operations, but the dispute gave me the opportunity to renew a friendship. The action officer for the comptroller's office was Col. Henry Minton Francis—the same Henry Francis who had been aboard my first troop transport en route to the Pacific. Seeing him again brought back fond memories of how he had taught me how to shoot craps, and not so fond memories of the amount of money I had lost to him.

I was promoted to lieutenant colonel on 18 November 1964, and, as far as I was concerned, all was right with the Becton world. I had no idea I was about to get involved in another world—the active struggle for the right to vote.

Blacks in the deep south had traditionally been denied the right to vote through unfair (and now illegal) literacy tests and threats of physical violence. Late in 1964 the Southern Christian Leadership Conference, led by the Rev. Martin Luther King Jr., initiated a major campaign focusing on voting rights. Nonviolent protest was the primary strategy. Notable among these demonstrations was a planned march in Alabama from Selma to Montgomery in the spring of 1965.

Like millions of other Americans, I saw on television the vicious racial hatred that was demonstrated in Selma on 7 March. Early that afternoon some six hundred marchers headed for a bridge spanning the Alabama River. They were told to disassemble because their march was an unlawful assembly and not conducive to the public safety. When the marchers refused to disperse more than five dozen Alabama state troopers descended on the marchers on foot and on horseback, chasing them back into downtown Selma using nightsticks and whips. The marchers were also fired upon with tear gas even though they were retreating and offered no physical resistance. Fittingly, the day went down in the history books as "Bloody Sunday."

The actions of the Alabama law enforcement authorities elicited widespread public condemnation and outrage, and a court challenge to the police's actions resulted in a federal judge ruling that the demonstrators had the right to march from Selma to Montgomery. Not to be outdone, Alabama Governor George C. Wallace, who was an avowed segregationist, wired President Lyndon B. Johnson that the state did not have sufficient funds to call up the National Guard to protect the march. President Johnson immediately signed an executive order and a presidential proclamation calling 1,800 Alabama national guardsmen into federal service.[1]

That raised a pressing question: To whom would the Alabama National Guard show its loyalty? Deputy U.S. Attorney General Ramsey Clark, who coordinated federal efforts to protect the marchers, would not leave things to chance, and the military became very heavily involved in efforts to ensure the safety of the marchers.

As a staff officer attached to the normally skeletal staff of the Pentagon's Army Operations Center, I became part of those efforts. In those days, duty in the Op Center was performed by personnel from the various staffs on an augmentation basis, as required.

My specific job was to track the location of the marchers as they moved from Selma to Montgomery. Because of its high visibility and the extremely volatile circumstances, the work was intense, requiring twelve-hour shifts. Our team chief was a brigadier general who reported to the lieutenant generals.

Army Chief of Staff Gen. Harold K. Johnson took a direct and personal interest in what was happening. It was clear that he was genuinely concerned about the marchers' safety, and he wanted to make sure that the Alabama National Guard knew that it was working for the federal government rather than for Governor Wallace. During the evening briefings General Johnson asked probing questions that were highly unusual in their specificity: How many national guardsmen were protecting the marchers? What kinds of weapons did they have at their disposal? Where did they bivouac in the evening?

I was tasked with getting answers. When I called Alabama, I was put in contact with a brigadier general of the federalized National Guard. He took offense at my barrage of questions. If he had known what I looked like, I suspect he would have taken even greater offense.

I asked, for example, where the machine guns and other weapons were emplaced when the marchers and guardsmen bivouacked at night. Such questions were met with icy silence. I then explained that we really needed to have the information. He said, "Well, Colonel, I don't intend to give it to you because I don't think you need it." I said, "I will be more than happy to pass your comment on to the chief of staff of the Army, General Harold K. Johnson. He's the one who asked for it." With a much-changed attitude, he said, "Why didn't you say so in the first place?" I replied, "I really didn't think it was necessary to invoke the name of the chief of staff." Needless to say, I got the information.

Tracking the movement of the marchers was my closest physical contact with the civil rights activists. The fact that I, like many of my black colleagues in the military, did not participate in the protests or demonstrations did not go unnoticed and engendered strong feelings against us in some quarters.

We were often asked whether we would march in formation with the protestors or carry placards. My answer, the same given by many of my friends in uniform, was, "Hey, look. Everything we do every day is helping the cause for civil rights because we are demonstrating that black Americans are qualified." But that answer fell on deaf ears. We were considered not to be sympathetic to the cause. I felt then, and I still do, that those of us in uniform who did not participate in the demonstrations were unfairly judged. We contributed to the civil rights cause in ways that may have not been as visible or vocal, but, in my estimation, were just as effective.

Every year, generally in the summer and early fall, the Army selects officers for promotion to the next grade and also chooses those who will attend the senior service colleges such as the Army War College. (Selection for the senior service colleges is much more competitive than the pool of candidates for promotion because the former indicates an officer has demonstrated the most potential to succeed at the next grade and beyond.)

On one occasion the two selection boards reached some inconsistent and untenable conclusions. Six officers who were attending the Army War College failed to be selected for promotion to the grade of colonel. How could this possibly happen? The answer had to be that there had been information in the officers' records that was not reviewed by the board that selected them to attend the war college but was seen by the board that recommended promotions.

The incident caught the attention of the Army chief of staff. General Johnson wanted an explanation, and I happened to be the junior officer in the group summoned to provide it.

The official reason determined by the personnel office was that the two boards had met independently and did not exchange information because regulations did not permit such an exchange. General Johnson asked, "Well, why can't they? Why didn't they?" The answer was simple: "It's against the regulations." General Johnson was not put off so easily.

"Who writes the regulations?" he asked. After I responded, "We do," General Johnson said, "Change them." And we did. It is a phrase I have used many times since when told that something cannot be done because of the regulations.

Not long afterward President Johnson advised the secretary of defense that he wanted a black officer as one of his military assistants. I was nominated to be the Army's representative, and the nomination was approved by both the Army staff and the defense secretary's office. However, the White House further advised that the president wanted the Air Force Two pilot to be his senior military assistant. I was a serving lieutenant colonel and the Air Force officer was still a major. So Maj. Hugh Robinson, who was then on duty at West Point, was duly selected as the Army's representative. Louise could not have been happier. She would not have taken steps to stop me from accepting the position in Johnson's White House, but she was generally opposed to my doing so.

When my mother called in January 1966 and said that Dad was in the hospital, I was not terribly disturbed. I told Mom that Louise and I would be up to see him that weekend. Julius Wesley Becton III—Wes, as we call him—had been born only three months before, so he, of course, went with us to Philadelphia.

When Louise and I arrived at the hospital, we could hardly believe Dad was so sick. He had been working at his regular job just two weeks before, seeming to be his usual self. But still waters run deep. He probably had not been feeling well long before he was hospitalized.

I felt a tinge of guilt as I looked at Dad lying there in the hospital bed. I felt regret about not having spent more time with him and about not having told him I loved him and was proud of the kind of man he was. When I was growing up our household had never been free with hugs and kisses and expressions of affection. It was very unlike the home I had made with my wife and children. Make no mistake, however. There was plenty of love felt between my father and myself. We just never said much about it. I wished I had.

Perhaps I channeled the anger, disappointment, and frustration I felt at myself toward my brother Joe. He was a convenient target. We had never been close. There was always an underlying tension, based largely on Joe's perception that our parents favored me, the older child, and we were very different personalities. Some would say I was the studious one, and all Joe wanted was to do was have fun. In any case, he had joined the Navy at fifteen, then finished his education, and we had led very separate lives.

Joe had been to the hospital to see Dad, but when it looked like the end was near, Joe was nowhere to be found. I went out determined to find him. I did, and when we got back to the hospital, Joe and I had words. I said something to the effect that he was irresponsible for not being there with us at the hospital. Mom told me to knock it off.

Dad's condition worsened over the next hours. Mom, Joe, and I were at his bedside when he died on 21 January 1966. Louise, with infant Wes in her arms, had been run out of the room by the nurses. With a far-off look in his eyes, Dad said he was going home. We thought he meant that he was going to our home in Philadelphia, but that was not what he had in mind. A Code Blue was called, and the nurses and doctors came running with a crash cart. Dad was gone.

On his deathbed, Dad told Joe and me to act like brothers, to grow closer and look out for each other. We both failed him.

By tradition I could have dropped my "Junior" designation when Dad died, but I did not change my name. Retaining the Junior was my way of paying homage to my father's memory. Every time I write my name, I want to be reminded that there was one who came before me.

After I was turned down as President Johnson's military assistant, the Armor branch sent me to a new graduate program at the Institute for Defense Analyses (IDA). The program had been designed by the military services to produce officers trained in operations research and systems analysis— essentially, officers who could deal effectively with Secretary of Defense Robert McNamara's civilian whiz kids. Many of these youngsters were academicians with little or no military experience. They placed too much emphasis on econometrics and mathematical modeling, not recognizing that some things are just incapable of being modeled. For example, you simply cannot reduce human reactions under fire to a series of equations, factors, or other proxies.

My time at IDA turned out to be the toughest academic year of my life. The course was based in economics, but it covered four years of undergrad- uate mathematics and one year of graduate math in just two semesters of instruction. In our very first session Bob Kupperman, the instructor, asked the students, "What do you know about calculus?" After a long silence, someone in the rear of the room blurted out, "How do you spell it?" That was about where I was.

My graduate class spent half our time in the "paper-clip building" in Arlington, Virginia, where the IDA was housed, and half at the University of Maryland in the economics department. We received a master's degree in economics in January 1967. My thesis was titled "An Economic Analysis to Evaluate the Effectiveness and Efficiency of Proficiency Pay in the US Army."

Armed with my new degree, I reported to the Office of the Chief of Staff of the Army at the Pentagon. It was time to put into practice my expertise in systems analysis. I became a manpower analyst in the Office of Force Planning and Analysis (OFPA), a part of the newly established Office of the Assistant Vice Chief of Staff (OAVCSA) of the Army. The new office was not a very successful experiment in the judgment of many. For one thing its shared leadership structure that gave equal authority to a brigadier general and a senior civilian proved that two professionals cannot both have the same responsibility for running a bureaucratic office. One person must be in charge. For another, the OAVCSA became known as the "super rewrite staff." We rewrote almost everything the Army staff sent to the chief of staff. That was not a good way to establish rapport.

As the junior analyst in the office I became the recipient of a very "hot" piece of paper that everyone else had avoided. It was a handwritten note from General Johnson still serving as the Army chief of staff, expressing his desire that the Army develop measurements of effectiveness. He particularly wanted us to create a formula for determining how effective our forces were in Vietnam.

That piece of paper floated down the chain and landed on my desk, which gave me the opportunity to develop a new, improved way for figuring how successful the Army was. Being a young systems analyst, I thought, "Sure; no sweat. We can do this." How naive!

In every other war that this country fought, the Army's effectiveness could be determined by where it was on the land. Not so in Vietnam. Instead, there were pockets of North Vietnamese Army (NVA) and Viet Cong (VC) all over the place. As a result, miles of real estate controlled by U.S. forces were not useful markers of success.

For the Vietnam conflict we were using body count as a measure of effectiveness, which is a very poor metric because it so readily lends itself to inflation driven by the competition between units. Other measures that were bandied about during the course of my research included the miles of railroad we had recovered from the NVA, the number of hamlets we had secured, and the tons of rice we controlled. I never did derive a more effective measurement than body count, but I gave it the good old college try. And I was about to get a personal look at Vietnam.

In the summer of 1967, out of the clear blue sky, I received a call from the assignment guy in Armor branch. He asked, "Becton, how would you like to go to Vietnam?" A command was becoming available in the 101st Airborne Division that required an airborne-qualified armor lieutenant colonel who could be released from his current assignment. I fit the bill. The catch for me was to get released. My immediate boss, Col. Bill Manning, told me to go for it. My next stop was the executive officer. He said that the OFPA director would probably agree to my departure as long as the office received a qualified replacement. No problem!

For one more time in my life, the stars were aligned.

★　★　★

CHAPTER EIGHT

Command in Combat

I assumed command of the 2nd Squadron, 17th Cavalry, 101st Airborne Division, at Fort Campbell in Kentucky on 25 September 1967. I will never forget that day. The troop formation had passed in review, and the reviewing party was still on the reviewing stand when three UH-1 helicopters, flying rather low, came in for the final phase of the ceremony. Just as one of them reached the reviewing stand, one of its doors crashed to the ground. Fortunately, no one was hurt.

The assistant division commander, Brig. Gen. Frank Clay, looked at his watch, then at me. "Becton," he said, "this has been your command for thirty minutes. I want to know by tomorrow morning what happened."

Imagine my displeasure. Also imagine the displeasure of Maj. Jack Frost, my Air Cavalry Troop commander, who was in charge of the pilots.

As it turned out the helicopter crew had suspected that the door's retaining pin might be missing, but they confirmed their suspicions at an inopportune time. When they least expected it, the UH-1 door flew open and crashed to the ground.

My change of command took place on a Friday, and we had physical training the next morning. When I reported out with the unit, Capt. Jerry Walker, the assistant operations officer, asked me, "Sir, how far do you want to run?" I said, "Captain, do your normal thing. Run whatever you normally do." There was a formation of approximately three hundred soldiers, and I ran at the end. I had done a lot of physical conditioning before going to Fort Campbell, but I had not run more than two miles at a time.

The squadron ran, and they ran, and they ran. I was in great pain but determined not to stop running. If I did stop, I knew I might as well just walk out of the command and back to Washington. I made up my mind that if I passed out, they would have to carry me to the hospital, and I would come up with a good excuse about what had happened.

We finally stopped running, and I noticed that some of the soldiers looked as pained as I felt. Three months later in Vietnam, when we were sitting around the billets one evening, my men admitted they had run farther that morning than they had ever run before.

The squadron spent the two-plus months between my assumption of command and our deployment to Vietnam in intensive training, making sure we were qualified to do what had to be done. This posed a problem for me because the 2nd Squadron was the only cavalry squadron in the division. In exercises we often had to act the role of the aggressor so the other units could maneuver against us. We lost the opportunity to train the way we should be training. Cavalry is supposed to be the reconnaissance, the surveillance unit—or, as I translate it, "sneak, peak, and be damned cautious" group. You cannot learn how to do reconnaissance when you are constantly acting as the aggressor in training exercises.

In late October Division Commander Gen. O. M. Barsanti, with whom I had worked back in Korea, led a group of senior commanders to Vietnam for an orientation visit. While we were in country I had the opportunity to visit my counterparts, the squadron commanders for the division cavalry squadrons, and to see them operate firsthand.

Much to my chagrin I observed that virtually all these cavalry squadron commanders did was travel from one location to another carrying the mail and checking on the morale of their soldiers. They did very little that had to do with their squadron fighting as a unit.

Each brigade has three infantry battalions that have considerable firepower. The cavalry squadron provides not only additional firepower to the brigade commander, but also the wherewithal to do reconnaissance, conduct surveillance, and carry out cover and protection missions. These are realistic missions for a cavalry squadron. The division cavalry squadron normally has three cavalry units, but in at least two cases I observed in my first trip to Vietnam, the division commander had attached one Troop to each line brigade. This effectively meant that the cavalry squadron commander had no control over his line troops that were out in the field working with the line brigades. In effect, the brigade commanders led those cavalry troops.

I fully understood that the tactical scheme is the prerogative of the division commander. But when I returned to Fort Campbell, I felt I had to express my concerns to General Barsanti about how the cavalry squadrons were being used in Vietnam. I definitely did not want to find myself in the position of having no troops to command when my squadron was deployed.

I told General Barsanti, "If you want us to be a combat force, let us be a combat force and give us the same responsibility that you would give to an infantry battalion." I also explained that if he were to give me sufficient lift capabilities (i.e., helicopters) and give me a tank platoon or a tank company, my squadron would do what he wanted done and do it better than any other unit because we had more communications capabilities than they had.

General Barsanti thought long and hard about my proposal. He knew the kind of work I tried to do, and he eventually agreed. From the time we arrived in Vietnam, I always had my own separate area of operations, and we were able to do what we had to do.

When my squadron was deployed to Vietnam in December, we went in with fewer than three hundred soldiers. We should have had five hundred, but I was told I had to leave my C Troop—aviation—behind because there was not enough maintenance support in Vietnam. I thought then, and I continue to believe, that was hogwash. But I will say this: In country, I was never hurting for aviation assets. I was always given support from other units.

Before my squadron left, I reassigned C Troop's aerial rifle platoon, which was an airborne-qualified platoon of about thirty infantrymen who rode the helicopters, throughout my other units as mechanics, drivers, and clerks. Because they were not, strictly speaking, aviators, it was legal for me to take the infantrymen along. I reformed the aerial rifle platoon when we got to Vietnam, placing it under the leadership of Sgt. First Class Larry Joe Baker, who was a superb soldier. Also when we arrived, A Troop, which had preceded us to Vietnam under the control of the division's First Brigade, was reassigned to the squadron.

My squadron then picked up some replacements. I had first priority on any armor officer already within the division or just arriving, and one of the men available to me turned out to be Capt. Mike Shaler.

As Mike tells the story, he died a thousand deaths the first time we met. We were in our firebase, and I was in my "hooch" taking a shower. While showering, I noticed a captain walking down the road. After he got within hearing distance of my hooch, he asked, "Hey Buddy, where's the old man?" I said, "It depends on what old man you're talking about." Mike said, "The squadron commander," and I replied, "You're talking to him."

Mike was mortified. No one had told him that the squadron commander was black, and he just assumed that I was a sergeant major or something like that. His assumption that the divisional unit commanders were white was indicative of the times, and it was a reasonable assumption on his part.

Shortly after our arrival in country, one of our warrant officers, Loyal Nixon, came to me. "Sir, I think we can get some armored personnel carriers [APCs]," he said. "If I get them, would you approve it?"

I said, "Nick, as long as we are not breaking any laws, sure." Nick wound up getting six APCs from an American depot that was being used by the South Vietnamese. The five diesels and one gas-powered vehicles probably cost us a case of scotch.

An APC is like a moving fortress. As its name implies, it is armored-plated and designed to carry eight or nine soldiers comfortably. It will not stop rocket-propelled grenades or bullets from a .50-caliber machine gun, but it will stop AK-47 bullets.

We used our APCs more as fighting vehicles than as a means of transport, and we wanted every soldier in there except the driver to be able to fire a machine gun or some other weapon. Therefore, we built those carriers up, adding steel plates to the sides and positioning machine guns on top. We gave five of them to our B Troop, which ended up saving our lives more than any group in the squadron. We also painted the front of each APC with a large screaming eagle. We wanted the bad guys to know who we were.

When properly prepared, an APC is capable of "swimming." The splashboard in front must be brought down so water will not come in over the bow, and all the holes in the bottom of the APC must be plugged to prevent seepage. After these things are done, the APC can pretty much float like a boat. It cannot move very fast through a body of water, but it can cross it without a bridge.

On one occasion, Nixon's mechanics forgot to put in plugs and the driver managed to sink the gas carrier. They were determined to recover it before the division commander and I heard what happened. So one of the mechanics, who was a very strong swimmer from Hawaii, swam out with a rope and attached it to the sunken APC. The recovery team then got one ten-ton and two five-ton wreckers and winched the APC out of the water. They also managed to get it back in running condition before I even knew it had sunk.

I recount this incident to show the tremendous pride these men took in their work. In their eyes it was bad enough that the APC had sunk. They simply could not countenance the idea that they would be unable to recover it.

When I learned what had happened I had to focus on their extraordinary efforts to recover the APC. I felt good about the kind of men I had under my command, the kind of soldiers with whom any leader wants to go into battle.

Eventually, we were told by intelligence that the NVA or VC would just as soon go someplace else when they knew that we were in the area. This was fine with us. We wanted to put the fear of God in them.

Street Without Joy by Bernard Fall is about the Vietnamese struggle to end French domination in Vietnam.[1] Its title describes an area on the east coast in the vicinity of Hue from which the NVA and VC drove the French in the 1950s. Geographically, the area is almost a peninsula.

In April 1968, while my squadron was still fighting outside of Saigon, in the Ben Hua and central region, I made a reconnaissance to the Hue area because I knew my squadron would soon be taking over its defense. At the time it was controlled by the 1st Battalion, 7th Cavalry, 1st Cavalry Division. A very good friend, Lt. Col. Roscoe Robinson, was in command. Roscoe, a West Pointer, class of 1951, eventually became the Army's first black four-star general.

Roscoe and I sat outside his hooch in the base camp, drinking beer and discussing the area. He said he seldom had any contact with the enemy. "A piece of cake, Julius," Roscoe said. "No real problems."

The 2nd Squadron relieved the 7th Cavalry shortly thereafter. Within our first twenty-four hours in the area, we were in a firefight. The fighting continued to break out every couple of days for the next five or six weeks.

I have often thought about why Roscoe's unit had little or no action in the Street Without Joy and why my squadron had so much. I think he was absolutely correct about his assessment of the area. It was quiet when the 7th Cavalry was there because the NVA were in the area transiently. In addition, the 7th Cavalry was strictly ground walking. Our aerial capabilities gave us a better chance to detect the enemy. Finally, the NVA probably thought they could take advantage of the newly arrived division. If the latter was the case, the NVA quickly found out they were wrong. Our operations there turned out to be among our most successful, largely because of the way we maneuvered.

After we identified NVA or VC formations in the vicinity, we would establish a blocking position like an anvil to the south of the enemy, move forces north of where they were, and then drive down. We basically brought pressure down, leapfrogging our units into NVA or VC territory and blocking them in. This left them with only two directions to go—to the South China Sea or across the Pha Tam Giang River.

The 2nd Squadron was the only armored unit in that part of South Vietnam that was maneuvering this way, and our activities caught some very high level attention. Gen. Creighton Abrams, the deputy commander of U.S. Forces in Vietnam, became so interested in what we were doing that he came to our firebase about once a week to talk to us.

It is not every day that you get to shoot the breeze with someone in General Abrams' position, and he and I developed a very good relationship. He took a strong personal interest in my career, and I am proud to claim him as a mentor and a godfather.

I never underestimated the NVA forces. Any student of military science knows that underestimating your opponent is a foolish mistake that can have fatal consequences. In fighting the NVA I came to understand a good deal about their mind-set and ingenuity.

The NVA's professional soldiers could walk for many miles on minimum food and carrying unbelievable weight. They could also crawl through undergrowth that defied movement by us Americans, conceal large groups in underground holes, and make underwater river crossings using bamboo tubing as a breathing device.

As we were to learn, however, the U.S. Army had a major advantage over the NVA when it came to leadership philosophy. If we could knock out NVA leaders, we basically had them. If NVA units were told to march south, they would march south. But when they got south and there was no one to tell them what to do, there was a problem. The NVA troops did not know what to do next.

In the U.S. Army, by contrast, someone is always in charge, no matter how few are left. We make sure each soldier knows the mission so that if the leader is killed or critically injured, someone else can take over and the mission can be fulfilled.

Unlike the NVA, the VC forces were guerrilla units. In my estimation most guerrillas were true believers in their cause. One has to commend them for the guile, cunning, and control they displayed in fighting at night and their ability to mask their true feelings and conceal their identities during the day. The tenacious guerrilla you fought at night could be the person who cleaned your billet the next day or the barber in the compound or a cook. The VC guerrillas were almost like werewolves, except that werewolves have no control over their transformation.

My division commander's given name was Olinto Mark Barsanti. But he was always O. M.—"Old Man"—in the Army, and we used the name affectionately.

Barsanti had a Napoleon complex. He stood barely five feet, seven inches tall, and was a stickler about authority. He made sure everybody knew that he was in charge. Barsanti was also a very brave man. He had been awarded six Purple Hearts. And he cared about his people.

The Old Man would tell you in a heartbeat, "You're fired." Of course, he did not mean it. The old-timers who were with him his entire time in Vietnam—I was one of them—got fired as often as anyone else.

On one occasion, Barsanti had been visiting the units under his command, and he offered me a helicopter ride to division headquarters. There had been some incident that afternoon, and on our ride back, Lt. Col. Frank Garrison, the operations officer, briefed the general by radio. The Old Man got angry and yelled, "Garrison, you're fired." Frank answered, "Yes, sir." As we landed at headquarters, we saw Frank standing on the helipad with two bags. "Where are you going?" Barsanti asked. "You fired me, General," came the reply. Barsanti said, "Frank, get your ass back in there and go to work." Frank did. Later, I checked out his "luggage." It was two empty boxes.

I had my share of run-ins with the Old Man. One involved replacements. Units routinely receive soldiers to replace the ones who have been killed, hospitalized, or put out of commission for some other reason. One day my personnel officer told me we had gotten no replacements for some time. I asked if he had called the division personnel staff officer (G-1). He had. The G-1 had told him, "Your commander knows why."

I had no idea what that was supposed to mean, and I stormed up to see the chief of staff. I explained that my squadron had gotten no replacements, and he replied, "Well, don't you know why?" At this point, I was starting to

Change of command: reviewing the formation. Left to right: MSgt. Larry Baker, Maj. Dick Shimunek, Lt. Col. Bud Clark, and me. Commander of troops: Maj. Fred Crump. (Author collection)

get a little heated. No, I said, and asked what was going on. He said, "The Old Man said don't give you any."

It turned out that it was a mistake of the human ear. Barsanti had been visiting his units and had come across Lt. Col. Charlie Beckwith of the 1st Battalion, 327th Airborne Infantry, which had lost some soldiers. Barsanti was so angry about these deaths that he radioed division headquarters and said, "Don't give Beckwith any more people." The G-1 had heard, "Don't give Becton any more people."

I protested, "Hey, Chief; that wasn't me. That's not my unit. That's Charlie Beckwith." The chief went over to Barsanti's hooch. He told the Old Man that I was "really mad" about not getting any replacements. "We have not given him any replacements because you said not to," he said. "But, in fact, Sir, it may not have been Becton. It may have been Beckwith."

The Old Man's response was priceless. "Don't give *him* any, either," he replied. Needless to say, that was when I really hit the ceiling.

The next day my replacements started coming. The Old Man needed to save face. You could say whatever you wanted to say to him one-on-one, but you had better not publicly embarrass him, contradict him, or suggest that he was not in charge.

In 1970, when I was about to graduate from the National War College (NWC), Barsanti called me. He was the Third Army commander at Fort Sheridan in Illinois at the time. He wanted to know if I would come and work with him. I said, "Sir, if we were in combat, I would love to work with you. But in peacetime, there is no way that I could put up with your crap."

He growled and said a few profane words, but he understood.

I served with the squadron until June 1968, and it was one of the most rewarding assignments any soldier could ever expect. Our casualty rate was very low, our success rate was high, and we received the Presidential Unit Citation, which is the highest unit award.

I was also fortunate to serve with some of the finest soldiers I have ever met. The squadron had several recipients of the Distinguished Service Cross, the second highest individual award for valor, and Sgt. Bob Patterson received the Medal of Honor, the highest individual award. I was within a couple hundred yards of where the action for which Patterson was awarded took place that day in May 1968, but I did not observe it firsthand. The following excerpt from Patterson's citation tells the story:

> Sgt. Patterson . . . distinguished himself while serving as a fire team leader of the 3d Platoon, Troop B, during an assault against an North Vietnamese Army battalion which was entrenched in a heavily fortified position. When the leading squad of the 3d Platoon was pinned down by heavy inter-locking automatic weapon and rocket propelled grenade fire from 2 enemy bunkers, Sgt. Patterson and the 2 other members of his assault team moved forward under a hail of enemy fire to destroy the bunkers with grenade and machinegun fire. Observing that his comrades were being fired on from a third enemy bunker covered by enemy gunners in 1-man spider holes, Sgt. Patterson, with complete disregard for his safety and ignoring the warning of his comrades that he was moving into a bunker complex, assaulted and destroyed the position. Although exposed to intensive small arm and grenade fire from the bunkers and their mutually supporting emplacements, Sgt. Patterson continued his assault upon the bunkers . . . Sgt. Patterson single-handedly destroyed by rifle and grenade fire 5 enemy bunkers, killed 8 enemy soldiers and captured 7 weapons. His dauntless courage and heroism inspired his platoon to resume the attack and to penetrate the enemy defensive position.

The Army was reluctant to have an officer serve in combat as commander with the same unit for more than six months. One of the stated reasons is to prevent burnout. Another is to prevent people from becoming overly cautious because they have become too attached to the soldiers in their unit. So in July 1968, I was reassigned as the deputy commander of the 3rd Brigade, 101st Division, which was headquartered in Cu Chi. The brigade had three airborne battalions with a combined force of about three thousand, including headquarters and armor support personnel. My rank was still lieutenant colonel, but this assignment meant new responsibilities.

I was flown in a regular utility helicopter to a firebase outside Cu Chi. Four people rode in the helicopter—me, the pilot, the copilot, and Larry Joe Baker, my operations sergeant. Joe and I had developed a close relationship, and we were both fairly emotional about my leaving. The helicopter did not have any seats, so we sat on the floor, with Joe on one side and me on the other. Although it took nearly two hours to get to Cu Chi, I do not think Joe and I said five words.

The brigade commander was Col. Larry Mowery, who had been billeted adjacent to me at Fort Campbell. Naturally, I had heard a lot about him because there are not that many colonels in a division. And since I was the only black maneuver battalion commander in the division, Larry knew a lot about me. The morning after I arrived Larry left for rest and recuperation, or R&R, in Hawaii. His five-day R&R ended up lasting for ten, and during that period we got in to some very good firefights. It was comforting to know that Larry was not concerned about my coming in. He knew I was capable, and the division commander knew I was capable. My arrival was no big deal, no reason for Larry to delay his leave.

I was the number two person in the brigade. People of color were rare at my level. However, Lt. Col. George Peters, the commander of the 321st Artillery Battalion, which provided direct support to us, was black. George and I had met before and got along well. He was not going to let me fail, and I was not going to let him fail.

At Cu Chi we were under the operational control of the 25th Infantry Division. Cu Chi was our firebase, but our base camp was at Phouc Vinh. The normal operations that do not occur at the front lines took place at Phouc Vinh, including administrative activities such as maintenance of our logistics backup and the intake of replacements. Phouc Vinh was also the place where soldiers were brought to recuperate from injuries and to rest. Command and control headquarters was out in the field in Cu Chi.

When Larry returned to Cu Chi from his R&R, I flew back to Phouc Vinh, beginning a pattern of rotation that lasted for the duration of my assignment as deputy commander of the 3rd Brigade. When Larry was at one base, I was at the other. We always had senior leadership at both places.

While Larry and I were changing over, our executive officer, Lt. Col. Raymond Singer, remained at Cu Chi. Ray and I had known each other for quite some time, and we had been classmates in the IDA graduate school program.

Although the executive officer is an administrator, he is also a combat officer at the battalion and brigade level. There is a very good reason for this. The Army wants to ensure that every person in a combat position is capable of picking up a rifle, taking up a position on the perimeter, and firing, or, if necessary, becoming part of a patrol to go out and get the bad guys. The only true noncombatants in the Army are chaplains and medics. Even the members of the division bands—and each division had its own band—were capable of providing local security or going out on patrol. But when things really get tough and every red-blooded soldier is needed, even chaplains and medics have been known to pick up weapons.

The Geneva Convention protects noncombatants, but the Vietnamese we encountered did not care. The NVA did not respect the red crosses worn by the American and South Vietnamese medics; they would fire at them just as quickly as they would fire at anyone else. The NVA also routinely inter-mingled women and children among the soldiers as they marched toward our position, knowing full well that we would not fire. It is a part of our culture as Americans that we will run the risk of getting our own people hurt rather than retaliating or shooting back when women or children are in the vicinity. That is why the My Lai Massacre turns the stomach of every American soldier I know, particularly leaders.[2]

Just as the Vietnamese did not respect the Geneva Convention as its provisions applied to noncombatants, neither did they respect no fire zones that U.S. and South Vietnamese troops established. Although these areas were supposed to be safe havens for the civilian population, the NVA would fire into them.

As a battle tactic, we set up free fire zones in which anything is a target. We made every effort to ensure that the civilian population knew when an area was a free fire zone and advised them to vacate that area. Despite our efforts women and children remained in some zones. Some did so of their own volition, but others were forced to remain by the NVA. Of course, some of them were killed or injured when the firing started. Mortar and artillery shells cannot distinguish among targets; anything in the line of fire gets hit.

We had a change of command in July, when Col. Joe Conmy replaced Colonel Mowery. At about the same time the brigade moved north to join the rest of the 101st Airborne outside Hue in Firebase Eagle, the base camp for the division.

Conmy had been the commander of the 3rd Infantry Regiment, "The Old Guard," at Fort Myer. This is the regiment that is sent to protect the president and the one that is seen at the Tomb of the Unknown Soldier. It is also the one that, some twenty-one years later, my son Wes joined. Conmy was a West Pointer and had served in Korea, but he had not held a combat command in Vietnam prior to his assignment as commander of the 3rd Brigade.

He also was not airborne-qualified. Yet he was taking command of 3,000 soldiers who were all airborne-qualified and proud of it. There had been signs posted all over Phuoc Vinh that read "Repent legs; God is airborne." ("Leg" is a derogatory term for a nonjumper.) These signs were removed before Conmy assumed command, of course.

Removing the signs was easier than dealing with the underlying feelings in the brigade. Many found it untenable that a nonjumper should take command. I myself had only had six jumps, and the brigade knew that. But I had proven myself, and I was airborne-qualified. Conmy was not. The old-timers, the senior NCOs, resented this the most. I think this group is the worst kind when it comes to letting go of tradition, and I knew they were not above starting to quietly question Conmy's ability. So I took it upon myself to caution them. My message was very clear. I said, "This guy's a colonel. He's the commander. Don't you get caught doing anything or saying anything against him."

Following the chain of command is essential to the effective operation of the military. Someone is always in charge. It goes without saying, however, that this hierarchical structure allows subordinates to do what has to be done. Holding a certain rank means that you should know what you are doing. As the deputy brigade commander, I made the mistake of doing what needed to be done without letting Conmy know beforehand. This led to our first run-in.

After the brigade moved up north of Hue, our unit ran into some enemy troops one night, and we had a pretty good firefight. I was in my hooch when I got information about the action. I went to the operations center and took charge. I saw no need to wake the colonel up at 2:30 AM.

The action was mentioned at the morning briefing, and Conmy asked, "Who'd you tell?" The briefer said, "I told Colonel Becton." Conmy said, "You didn't tell me. Becton, you didn't tell me."

The other officers sitting around the map got very quiet. I said, "No, sir. I felt that I was qualified to do what had to be done. We did this, . . . this, . . . and this. . . ." Icily, Conmy said, "You didn't tell me. I think I'm the commander. You're not the commander." Then Conmy made it very clear to all of us how he would run things. Anytime anything happened, he would be told. Then, visibly angry, he stormed out of the briefing room. The staff looked at me, and I looked at the staff. Somebody said what I was thinking: "Well, Becton, I guess that takes care of you."

I was with the brigade for another six weeks. During that time, all the staff officers made sure that Conmy knew about everything that happened.

Fortunately, Conmy was the kind of person who did not hold grudges. He blew up, spoke his mind, and then it was over. And he turned out to be a really good guy. In fact, the Army thought so highly of him that the ceremony hall at Fort Myer is named Conmy Hall.

Comny, unfortunately, later got in trouble for the tremendous loss of life in a major battle along South Vietnam's border with Laos in May 1969. The 3rd Brigade assaulted Ap Bia Mountain, and our soldiers ran into a big firefight. American forces had control at the top and bottom of the hill, and the NVA controlled the area in between. The brigade tried rather unsuccessfully to link our forces from the ground up and kept going back into that meat grinder. Conmy's 3rd Brigade lost a large number of soldiers, which is why the operation became known as Hamburger Hill. Naturally, the operation caught the attention of Capitol Hill, and Democratic Sen. Ted Kennedy of Massachusetts led the list of politicians who set out to excoriate Conmy in the media.

The bottom line for a commander is this: You are held responsible for anything you do or fail to do. Under certain circumstances you may be able to demonstrate that all the actions you took were proper. At other times, you may not. The responsibility rests at your doorstep.

★ ★ ★

CHAPTER NINE

The Home Front

I returned to the United States in November 1968, and then two significant events occurred in short order. First, I was selected to attend the NWC. Not too long thereafter, I was promoted to colonel.

I also almost had a chance to work at the Joint Staff for Operations (J-3), the highest position in military service for controlling operations. But when my name and those of five others selected for the J-3 turned up on the NWC list, the J-3's administrative officer hit the roof. The war college classes started during the summer, which would have cut short our time at the J-3. The administrative officer turned us down, infuriating the three-star general who was his boss when he found out about it.

I was instead assigned to the Army's Special Review Board (SRB) in Bailey's Crossroads, Virginia. Most of us wore civilian clothing to work, and the SRB workday was entirely different from what I was used to. I had routinely worked twelve- and sixteen-hour days in Vietnam. At the SRB a typical workday was 0900 to 1700. In many ways, the environment was a shock to my system. I missed the adrenaline rush one gets from a combat environment, and I missed the contact with other combat soldiers.

Among the SRB's missions was to evaluate appeals by officers of their officer efficiency reports (OERs). While I was assigned to the board the Army ordered a complete evaluation of the OER system, and I was assigned to the study group. As the senior officer, I became chairman of the team, whose other members were Col. Jack Jorgensen and Lt. Col. Mike Malone. Mike was a behavioral scientist and a soldier's soldier who became a very close friend. Years later, when I was a division commander, I asked Mike to be my chief of staff, a position that almost surely would have meant a promotion to brigadier general. He declined, feeling he could be of greater service at the Army War College training young lieutenant colonels. He was that kind of guy.

From April to June 1969 my team evaluated the OER system. We studied how the performance of officers was evaluated from 1775 up to the present. We studied every OER form that had been used. Ultimately, we made major modifications to the officer evaluation system, and our version of the OER remained the standard for almost the next 20 years. In the early 1970s our work on the OER became known as "The Becton Study," simply because I was the senior officer on the team. To have your name attached to a successful program is not all bad.[1]

In early 1969 President Richard M. Nixon announced his desire to have a black military assistant. Bruce Palmer, who was the vice chief of staff of the Army and a four-star general, approached me. I did not feel the same excitement this time that I had at the prospect of becoming President Johnson's military assistant. The position did not have quite the same luster now. Plus, if I took the job, I would be locked in for two to four years, and would have to attend the NWC three years behind my contemporaries.

I knew General Palmer from Vietnam, and I think this positively influenced his reaction to my response. I said, "Sir, obviously, if you tell me I'm gonna go over there, I will do the best I can. But if you are asking me what my druthers are, I would much rather go to the war college and get on with the rest of my life." General Palmer said, "Colonel, you've got it."

I went to the NWC at Fort Lesley J. McNair in Washington, D.C., in the summer of 1969. There are five senior service schools: the Army War College in Carlisle, Pennsylvania; the Naval War College in Newport, Rhode Island; the Air War College at Maxwell Air Force Base in Montgomery, Alabama; the Industrial College of the Armed Forces at Fort Lesley J. McNair; and the NWC. These schools, as their names suggest, concentrate, respectively, on Army strategy, naval strategy, air strategy, the industrial base of the government, and national strategy.

When I attended the NWC was the smallest school, with a class of 145 students, including civilians from nonmilitary agencies such as the Atomic Energy Commission, the U.S. Information Agency, and the State Department.

Naturally, graduates of the NWC think we attended the best college. The statistics support our opinion. The NWC has had more graduates go on to the senior ranks of the military and the government than any other school.

The NWC program was incredible. We generally had a guest speaker every day, five days a week, and their caliber was unsurpassed. They included national and international experts on a variety of topics and chief executive officers of companies specializing in the subjects we studied. Secretary of Defense McNamara was among them, as was then–House minority leader and future president Gerald Ford, who delivered our commencement address.

Our class was divided into study groups of eight to twelve students. On a typical day we arrived at about 0800 and assembled into our study groups. At about 0900, we would gather to listen to the guest speaker, who talked for about forty-five minutes. After a break, there was a question and answer session for a select group of students and one or two faculty members. Then we returned to our study groups to discuss the speaker's presentation. We had a chance to ask questions during lunch. Afternoons were devoted to individual studies and preparation of research papers. There were no examinations when I attended the NWC.

All in all, it was truly a ten-month "gentlemen's course." We were exposed to the best the government had to offer. It was our individual responsibility to take maximum advantage of the opportunities presented.

Students at each service college take at least one trip overseas as part of their studies. The Middle East tour was my first choice, but because it was over-subscribed by Army officers, I was offered Africa. I said, "I don't want to go to Africa." So I went to Central and South America.

The trip lasted about three weeks. The group I was with visited Panama, Mexico City, Brazil, Peru, Chile, and Argentina. The purpose was to give us a strategic orientation to these countries. We were initially scheduled to stop in Columbia, but we did not because martial law had been declared there. Historic events help you remember where you were at a particular point in time. We were on the Panama Canal when *Apollo 13* had to abort, and the famous words, "Houston, we've had a problem," were heard around the globe. We were also on this tour when the killings at Kent State University took place.

In Peru, my group split into smaller ones to visit designated areas. On one of these sojourns, the entire group contracted a killer case of Montezuma's revenge. I have never felt so awful, and we had an audience in Lima with the president of Peru the next day. Our intestinal distress could not have hit at a worse time. During the audience every one in my entire group stood in the back of the room bent over in pain. Anyone could read the anguish on our faces. The other classmates reduced their questions to a bare minimum and our hosts took pity on us and cut the visit short.

I developed a standard for judging countries' wealth during that trip: You can tell the condition of a country's economy by its toilet tissue. If the paper is flimsy or coarse, the economy is poor. If the tissue is thick and soft, the economy is rich.

It was around this time that the Army implemented a new policy for aviation training that said you could become a pilot even if you wore glasses. The Army was getting more and more into airborne/air assault operations, but it did not have a sufficient cadre of senior officers who could fly. Rather than take aviators and make them into combat commanders, the Army did the reverse. It recruited proven senior officers who had demonstrated their combat skills and put them through an accelerated training program of six to ten months to become pilots.

I was very excited about the change in the Army's policy. I had been trying since 1943 to become a pilot. This time, when I applied for flight school, I was accepted.

But it is a truism that you can't have your cake and eat it too. In March 1970, just as I was accepted for flight school, I received orders assigning me to Fort Hood, Texas, as a brigade commander in the 2nd Armored Division. Combat arms soldiers live to demonstrate their professionalism with soldiers. I had been a company commander three times. I had commanded as a lieutenant colonel in combat. Now I had the opportunity to command three thousand soldiers at the brigade level. I was aware of the impact this would have on my potential to become a general officer. As much as I wanted to become a pilot, I turned down flight school and accepted the command at Fort Hood.

When I did, Joyce Wesley Becton became unglued. When the family moved, we would be taking her out of the school system she had been in since 1964, completing fifth through the eleventh grades, and taking her to Killeen, Texas, to become, in her words, a "kangaroo" (the name of the Killeen High School football team). Knowing full well that I could have gone to flight school instead, which would have allowed her to finish her senior year of high school in Washington, D.C., Joyce was beside herself. It took her a long time to forgive me.

The rest of the family did not put up as much resistance as Joyce, but I am sure they also regretted leaving Washington. They were pretty settled in D.C. Mom Thornton was happy there. Louise was working at Walter Reed Army Hospital, and it had been one of the few times in our marriage that she had been able to work uninterrupted for a fairly long period. Wes was five, Renee was ten. Shirley and Karen were now married, with households of their own.

Nevertheless, in the summer of 1970, the family packed up our 1959 Ford station wagon and headed west bound for Fort Hood.

Fort Hood is the largest Army Post in the United States. When I reported, it had two divisions and a corps headquarters, giving it a population of about forty-eight thousand people.

As my family and I were about to enter the post, a young black MP stopped us and asked to see my identification. This was very unusual. The registration was displayed on the car and so was the eagle insignia, signifying that the vehicle was registered to a colonel. I showed the MP my ID card, and with obvious surprise and pride he said, "Sir, you're the first black colonel I've ever seen." He saluted and we drove on.

Back then, black colonels were as rare as hen's teeth. When I assumed my command at Fort Hood, I was the senior black officer on post, and the only black colonel. Things have really changed. Today, the Army has hundreds of colonels who are black.

My family and I moved into temporary quarters because our house was not yet ready, and we were assigned a warrant officer from the brigade as our escort. He was probably in his mid-twenties, and Louise and I realized that he probably had not even been born when we were married. I quickly recognized that at Fort Hood I would be dealing with a whole new generation of soldiers. A significant difference between these soldiers and the combat-hardened group I had led from Fort Campbell to Vietnam was that the Fort Campbell troops were all volunteers, while most of the soldiers at Fort Hood were draftees.

The 2nd Brigade, 2nd Armored Division—the St. Lo—was the same brigade I had been assigned to in Germany from 1954 to 1957, but it had earlier been named Combat Command B. The brigade's nickname stems from its participation in the World War II battle for St. Lo in France. The outgoing colonel was Paul "Bo" Williams, who had replaced me when I left the Office of the Chief of Staff of the Army in 1967. We had become good friends by the time I arrived at Fort Hood. Bo's new job was to be the brigade operations officer (G-3) of the corps, which essentially made him the staff officer who controlled the operations at Fort Hood.

The three key positions in a division headquarters are the division commander, the assistant division commander, and the chief of staff. While the direct line of authority goes up from the brigade commander to the division commander, in reality the brigade commander, who is a colonel, also takes orders from the assistant division commander, who is a brigadier general.

Our division commander was Maj. Gen. Wendell Coats, a scholarly gentleman and a great guy. I liked his command philosophy. He let his subordinate commanders do their thing. He also had a unique way of speaking. He had not been around soldiers much, and he tended to speak in somewhat academic terms. After meetings with him, the three brigade commanders often met again to try and figure out what General Coats had said.

Brig. Gen. James "Alex" Grimsley was the assistant division commander. He hailed from South Carolina and was a graduate of The Citadel. Grimsley and I later had serious differences of opinion over how things should be done. The division chief of staff was Col. Jack Forrest.

Structurally, the division had five major commands: 1st, 2nd, and 3rd Brigades; Division Support Command; and Division Artillery. The 1st Brigade, which was also known as the Tiger Brigade, had three tank battalions. The 2nd Brigade had two armor battalions and one infantry battalion. The 3rd Brigade had two infantry battalions and one armor battalion.

Each command from the battalion on up has a senior enlisted person called a command sergeant major. Mine was Donald Horn, who was, despite being a year and two days younger than I was, a crusty but lovable senior NCO. If you did not mind hearing the truth, no matter how unappealing or unpalatable it was, you would ask Don Horn. He certainly never missed a chance to remind me I was his elder, and he quickly became my alter ego. The command learned that if Don Horn said something, it was just as if Julius Becton were speaking.

My brigade was assigned to be the unit that tested the M60 add-on stabilization system that was designed to permit the tank to fire on the move. That would be an entirely new capability. I can only speculate as to why we were selected to conduct the test. Perhaps this was a way to determine whether a black brigade commander could cut the mustard. It is also true that I had the necessary resources. I was the only brigade commander trained in operations research and systems analysis and that two of the three battalions under my command were armor. Whatever the reason was, we got the job.

Any job can be difficult if you have not done it before. I had never commanded a tank unit prior to coming to Fort Hood, and virtually every tanker under my command knew more about the M60 tank than I did. As a result, the stabilizer testing assignment posed quite a challenge for me.

I knew my own limitations, so I set out to learn as much about tanks as I could, pronto. I said, "Sergeant Major, you have a job to help me to understand about tanks. All of our free time is going to be spent in the motor pool where the tanks are." Don Horn and I spent a lot of intense quality time going over, around, and through tanks. This learning experience was very challenging and a lot of fun.

Despite this total immersion, I never commanded a tank down range. The reason is very simple: If I had had to shoot a tank in combat, we would have been in pretty bad shape.

One talent that has always served me well is my ability to select good people to do the job. I selected Lt. Col. Alfred Iller, the commander of one of my two armor battalions, as the point person developing the stabilizer test. Al was an aviator, which is a profession that requires a high awareness of systems. Additionally, he had a good battalion staff.

Those guys put together a plan that was beyond anyone's expectation. As a result, The 2nd Battalion, 67th Armor (2/67 Armor), Al Iller, and I earned quite a reputation throughout the armor community as the guys who tested the system and made it work.

Some of the new challenges I faced at Fort Hood had to do with the changing demographics of the Army during the early 1970s. One was a shortage of captains in Vietnam.

Due to the shortage the Army shortened the period of time that an officer had to remain in grade as a lieutenant. While I could understand the Army's rationale for making accelerated promotions, the policy had a negative impact on officers like me who had spent considerably longer periods of time as lieutenants. But it was not just a question of morale; the rapid-promotion policy also lowered the caliber of the captain corps. The new captains simply did not have the level of experience of their predecessors.

Additionally, many of the fast-tracked officers were aviators—former warrant officers who, after one or more tours in Vietnam, were given the opportunity to qualify for a commission as a first lieutenant and were then promoted to captain eighteen months later. They would attend a basic school in infantry, armor, or artillery and then be assigned as company commanders.

They had absolutely no basic troop experience, and they had never served with a peacetime unit in garrison.

There was nothing inherently wrong with the captains who had been aviators, but in the final analysis, they were competing with captains who had years of experience as ground commanders. Absorbing the captain aviators into the division posed a major challenge for the command.

Then there was the question of race. Every Army post had major race relations problems in the early 1970s, and Fort Hood was no exception. Almost every night, servicemen got into a fight over racial matters. The fight could be between two servicemen, or it could even be between units. The situation was ugly, and it spoke volumes about the soldiers' combat readiness. How could we fight the enemy when we were so busy fighting each other?

Many of the bad actors at Fort Hood were draftees who had come out of Vietnam and were killing time until their discharge. They were hardened by combat and felt that nothing worse could happen to them than what they had already experienced on the battlefields. Sure, they could be imprisoned, but by the time a soldier went through the military justice system, his discharge date would have come and gone. So these troublemakers were essentially ignored and left to run wild. In my opinion, this was a major mistake. They should have been taken to task for their actions.

I made it a point to visit my units at night and during the weekends. I spent a lot of time talking to my soldiers, trying to defuse the racial tensions, and I never personally witnessed any fights. I also started having meetings with all the officers, and on two occasions, I met with the entire brigade. Last, I made sure my battalion commanders maintained good order and discipline by meting out proper punishment.

The Army required monthly reports on each unit's operational readiness for combat. The reports were based in part on inspections by a team called Command Maintenance and Management Inspection (CMMI), which made unannounced visits to inspect a commander's maintenance program and the management of his unit. These inspections, which were run by Alex Grimsley, the assistant division commander, struck the fear of God into some commanders because they could be relieved of their command if their units failed to pass the inspection.

Many other officers, including me, however, felt that the CMMI visit was no more than a paper drill. Have you filed your paperwork? Do you have a receipt for that weapon? Is there a checklist that says you did such and such? Can everyone in the unit in the chain of command account for this piece of equipment? Few of those things spoke to our preparedness for war, and I definitely did not feel that my commanders' lives or their careers should hang on a paper drill.

I also had philosophical problems with the practical effects of having to pass the CMMI inspections. There was a strong incentive for units to take questionable shortcuts. The division's artillery unit was a case in point. If one of the five battalions in the unit got word that it was going to have an inspection, all five battalions would work together to make sure the paperwork was immaculate. While this practice certainly created teamwork, I did not think it was legitimate. I told my commanders to do the best they could, and to let me know if someone had not done what he was supposed to do. I did not want my junior officers to compromise their integrity. It was improper to utilize the assistance of people outside the unit because those people would not be with the unit in combat.

To give an example of how the CMMI system worked, we were notified in the fall of 1970 that two companies of the 2/67 Armor, commanded by Lieutenant Colonel Iller, were going to be inspected. This was the first battalion in the brigade to get a visit from the CMMI team, and it was a bit unusual for two companies from the same battalion to be selected. The next morning, the inspectors told us what they were going to do, then went about their inspection. At the end of the day, we gathered the entire battalion, along with all divisional battalion commanders and other key personnel, to hear the report. It was bad news. The two companies had narrowly failed the inspection, getting scores just short of the passing grade of 70.

Grimsley got up on the platform after the report had been given. This was a brigadier general talking to his colonel and all of his colonel's officers, NCOs, and soldiers, plus all the other battalion commanders in the division. He called us everything but a child of God. We had set out to embarrass him. We had set out to embarrass the division. We were a disgrace to the United States Army. It did not help matters that the inspection team was not a division team. Grimsley took it very personally that outsiders had seen how "bad" we were. When he had spent his fury, he pointed at me and Iller, and said, "I want to see you in my office tomorrow morning at 0700."

Iller and I knew Grimsley wanted us to fire the two commanders. I said, "Al, we're not going to fire anybody. If those captains failed, it is because we let them down. Somewhere there is something that we should have done that we did not do. Somewhere the division failed to do something that it should have done. You and I both know that these are good companies and the captains are good captains." Iller said, "Roger that."

The next morning Al and I walked into Grimsley's office and stood very rigidly at attention. The general was much calmer. He offered us coffee and donuts, which we declined. Then his first question was, "Who are the replacement company commanders?" Before Al could say anything, I said, "Sir, we're not going to replace them." As expected, Grimsley replied, "You know the rules. If you flunk, you're out." I said, "General, those may be the rules, but let's face it, I let them down, Iller let them down, you let them down, the division commander let them down. (And, oh, by the way, we don't have a system in the 2nd Brigade to do like some other units.")

Grimsley did not appreciate that comment. He said, "All right, Colonel. You flunk one more inspection and you'd better know who is going to get fired." I said, "Yes, sir. I can handle that."

Calm returned, and Grimsley asked Iller, "Well, what are you going to do?" Iller outlined his plan of attack, and Grimsley offered the use of the division CMMI team and whatever assets might be needed.

The word about what had happened spread in the brigade like wildfire. We never failed another inspection. The soldiers were not going to let their commander be embarrassed, and they were not going to let their brigade commander get fired. The soldiers would do anything we asked to prove that General Grimsley was wrong. Iller wrote me to say that my standing up for him and the company commanders was "the defining moment," and that it helped to restore the soldiers' confidence.

There is an interesting footnote to part of my career. General Grimsley made the following statement in my OER: "Col. Becton is an outstanding officer in every respect. Energetic, personable, and highly motivated, he continually examined all aspects of his brigade's activities. His leadership and professional ability were of major assistance to his subordinates throughout this period. Col. Becton possesses all the attributes required for a general officer and should be selected for promotion at the earliest opportunity. He and his wife are distinct assets to the division and to the post community. I would welcome having this officer in my command in any capacity."

During the early 1970s the nation was rife with civil disturbances. There were riots in the cities and huge demonstrations at colleges and universities.

The Department of Defense had the mission to be prepared to augment municipal or urban authorities.

Exercise Garden Plot was the code word for dealing with civil disturbances. Major urban areas were identified as part of the exercise, and each area was assigned a military unit to restore control if local authorities could not. The federal government made a strategic decision not to use local National Guard units in Exercise Garden Plot because local guardsmen could very well have ended up having to march against people they knew. Another concern was that local guardsmen might, in their private lives, be members of the group causing unrest. So the civic unrest plan called for federalizing National Guard units and moving them to other areas.

My brigade was assigned the Twin Cities of Minneapolis and St. Paul in Minnesota. The fact that we were stationed in Texas was of no moment. We had the wherewithal to get where we had to be when needed.

As part of the planning for unrest, I and other key people in my brigade made reconnaissance trips to the Twin Cities. We met with the chief of police, the local National Guard, the fire department, and other emergency response managers to determine how we would coordinate our efforts. We made sure our radios would work in the area and made note of any other special circumstances that would affect our response to a disturbance.

When we returned to Fort Hood, another challenge faced us. We had to make sure that our soldiers were prepared to deal with these situations. Nothing in the soldier's training taught him what to do when faced with a mob of civilians—American civilians—and he had to wear a facemask as he marched toward them in lockstep with his rifle at port arms, bayonet attached. Certainly, U.S. soldiers are not oriented to fighting their fellow Americans; the enemy is supposed to be foreign. We were never deployed for Exercise Garden Plot, but we were prepared.

The civil disturbances that were so prevalent in the early 1970s were symptomatic of much deeper changes affecting American society. For example, black people were feeling good about being black. Men, women, and children were growing Afros, dressing in African garb, and adorning their homes with African artwork. Signs of black pride were everywhere. James Brown's "Say it Loud, I'm Black and I'm Proud" had been a huge hit in 1968 and became an unofficial anthem when the Black Power movement was at its height.

The military was not immune to this growth of racial pride. There was a new awareness of and sensitivity to discrimination throughout the ranks.

Some black soldiers sought to use the heightened sensitivity to their personal advantage and alleged discriminatory treatment where there was none.

During my time at Fort Hood, Louis Stokes, a Democratic congressman from Ohio, received a letter from a black prisoner in the Fort Hood stockade. The prisoner invited Stokes, who also was black, to come see the "intolerable conditions" there. When III Corps headquarters received word that the congressman would be visiting, I was selected to be his escort.

The military judicial system is very fair. By the time a person ends up there, it is generally because he or she deserves to be there. Even though all the commanders at Fort Hood believed the facts would not lend credence to the prisoner's allegations, the matter was handled very delicately. The last thing the post needed was to be excoriated in the media about intolerable stockade conditions.

I met Congressman Stokes when he arrived at Fort Hood, explained what I knew about the situation, and escorted him to the stockade. I was not privy to his conversations with the prisoner. When Stokes had completed his interview with the prisoner, Louise and I took him to dinner at the Officer's Club. Apparently, he was satisfied that the prisoner was being treated fairly, for nothing further was heard about the matter.

My command tour was up eighteen months after I arrived at Fort Hood. This meant that I was supposed to come out of command in mid-January 1972. But Lt. Gen. G. P. Seneff, the corps commander, wanted me to remain at Fort Hood. He asked the Department of the Army to reassign me to corps headquarters as the staff officer in charge of community affairs (G-5).

Colonels are normally assigned to a major staff position such as division chief of staff or corps operations officer after they leave a brigade command. In the hierarchy of the army, the G-5 is not one of those career-enhancing jobs. However, Seneff was so concerned about doing the right thing, particularly with respect to minority soldiers, that he asked me if I would take the job for a year. I had been a colonel since 1969 and was eligible for consideration to be promoted to brigadier general. Seneff knew that. He gave me his word that if I took the job, he would do everything in his power to get me promoted. Because I knew the general, knew what he wanted to do, agreed with what he wanted to do, and knew the post and the community well, I decided to accept the G-5 assignment.

It was not to be, however. I was told in December 1971 that I was being reassigned to Washington, D.C., as the armor branch chief, a position that would put me in charge of all armor officer assignments below the grade of colonel for the entire Army. I was floored. All my formalized training had been infantry, and I had never been to an armor school. I had commanded armor units in combat, but I had never commanded just armor. Little by little, I began to grasp the significance of my new assignment. The Army had never had a black branch chief. I would be the first, and the armor branch had fewer black officers than any other.

I had been told to report to Washington in early January, so my new assignment created several challenges for my family. We had leased our previous house in Washington, and we no longer had a place to live there. Eventually, we rented a house on Upshur Street, NW, in the District. Our landlord was the estate of William Penn, who had been killed in a Ku Klux Klan–related incident in Georgia in the 1960s. His estate was renting the house for a ridiculously low price, and we were more than happy to sign the lease.

Fortunately for us, our eldest daughter Shirley, her husband, and their two daughters were living at Fort Myer in the Washington area. When we moved into the house, they brought mattresses, cots, and blankets for us to sleep on while we awaited the delivery of our household goods from Fort Hood.

I reported to work in a two-story building in an area adjacent to Fort Lesley J. McNair. The armor branch office had nine officers assigned at the time: five majors, three lieutenant colonels, and one colonel. Naturally, all the staff were the cream of the crop. Of the nine, all but three became general officers. I only knew two of the officers in the branch when I arrived. They were Maj. Richard "Dick" Behrenhausen and Maj. John Earl Toye, a black officer.

One of the first things I learned after reporting was what had happened to my predecessor, Col. Jimmy Leach. An armor officer assigned to the Army chief of staff's office was dissatisfied with his OER and took his complaint to Colonel Leach. Jimmy, who had a heart of gold, suggested to the officer that he file an appeal. Someone in the chief of staff's office took violent exception to the appeal, and Jimmy was relieved of his position as armor branch chief. Bill Coad, the senior lieutenant colonel, was the acting branch chief when I arrived. Boy, was he happy to see me!

But some thought I was unqualified to be armor branch chief. Perhaps the most vocal critic was then–Brig. Gen. George Patton, the son of the legendary World War II hero. The younger Patton was the assistant commandant of the armor school at Fort Knox, and he made it known to everyone who would listen that "it was a God-damned shame that the branch chief of armor has never been to the school and is not a graduate." I sent word back, "Sir, you can correct that. Give me an honorary diploma." I never received a reply.

My job as armor branch chief was to manage the career of all the officers, second lieutenant to lieutenant colonel, in the armor branch. My staff and I learned as much as possible about each officer. We encouraged them to visit the branch office when they were passing through Washington, to come in and sit down and talk—and to bring their wives and children.

We developed quite a dog and pony show to educate armor officers about the branch and their future, especially what the appropriate stepping-stones were to advancing in their careers. At least once a year staff members from the armor branch routinely visited every major Army post in the continental United States. We also made trips to Europe and Korea to meet with armor officers stationed out of the country. Of course, we routinely visited the branch school at Fort Knox, although I never was invited personally to give a presentation there. I did visit West Point to talk to the cadets, however.

My staff and I also developed what we called a "green tab file." The Army had started putting green tabs on the epaulets of all leaders back in the 1950s to identify them. We modified the concept to suit our purposes. We wanted to be able to identify captains and majors who could compete successfully against officers from any other branch or service for certain critical assignments. We culled through the entire population of captains and majors to identify officers with outstanding records and put a green flash at the top of the files of the most qualified officers.

Our strategy worked quite well for a time. If a request were made, say, for a major with X years of service, a certain kind of education, and so much experience, we could go right to a file of the officer who met the requirements and win the position for him. We won any job we wanted to win, whether it was at the Army, joint staff, or Defense Department level, the State Department, or the White House.

One day a senior officer in personnel started inquiring, "How is it that armor is cleaning up?" He eventually found out what we were doing, and our use of the green tab files came to a screeching halt. He said we were discriminating against the rest of our officers because we were identifying a certain select group from that population. Nothing we said could convince him otherwise. We had to go back to the old way of doing things.

Now the beauty of all this is that the officer who developed the concept of the green tab file was a major named Gordon Sullivan. In 1992, Sullivan became the 32nd chief of staff of the U.S. Army.

My assignment as armor branch chief turned out to be the shortest of my Army career. On 2 June 1972, the Army released the list of colonels selected for promotion to brigadier general. Five black colonels—the largest number in history—were on the list: me, Harry Brooks, Edward Greer, Arthur Gregg, and George Shuffer. Although I was not the most senior or the oldest, I was listed highest in the order of merit.

CHAPTER TEN

★ ★ ★

Life as a General Officer

T he day of 2 August 1972 was a memorable one for my family, for it was the day Karen, our second oldest daughter, delivered fraternal twins, Kimberly and Chris Brice. Also that very day, I became the sixth black American to be promoted to general officer status in the Army. Harry Brooks was promoted at the same ceremony.

Promotion: pinning on the brigadier general star—Gen. Bruce Palmer, acting CSA, and Mom. (U.S. Army)

Receiving line following promotion to brigadier general. Also, Wes at an early age enjoying a piece of cake. (Author collection)

While I was awaiting word of my next assignment, my boss, Brig. Gen. Gene Forrester, offered some advice. He said, "I know what kind of assignment you want, Becton. But keep in mind, no matter what they offer you, it is the best assignment that you could ever want and you have no choice but to like it." When Gene called with the news that I would become the deputy commander of the training center at Fort Dix, he re-emphasized the point. He said, "I know that you had wanted to become an assistant division commander, but you are going to become the deputy commander at Fort Dix, and you're going to like it, right?"

"Yes, sir," I replied. "Great assignment!"

I reported to Fort Dix in September 1972. In addition to the training center, the post was home to Walson Army Hospital, a reception center, a separation center, and a confinement facility. The confinement center was run by two men I knew. The commander, Lt. Col. Bob Harleston, had been in Verdun when I was there. Harleston's deputy was Maj. Joe Rozelle, who had served with me in Vietnam and was one of the men in my squadron who was awarded the Distinguished Service Cross.

Maj. Gen. Bert David, the post commander, was a West Pointer, infantry officer, and a great guy. He and his wife Shirley did all they could to make my family's move to Fort Dix as smooth as possible. As commander, he had responsibility for the entire post, but he put me in charge of the training center and left me alone to run it. Bert David worked very hard and expected his subordinates to do the same. He said, "You're here. You know what your job is. Do it. When you need some help, let me know." This was the way we began and continued working together.

The training center had four basic training brigades and one advanced individual training (AIT) brigade. Basic training in those days generally lasted from sixteen to seventeen weeks. It could be completed in just thirteen or fourteen weeks, however, depending upon the needs of the Army. AIT generally lasted from three to five weeks, depending upon the skill being taught. The AIT offered at Fort Dix was in technical skills for drivers, clerks, cooks, mechanics, and radio operators. Soldiers who were to receive combat arms training attended one of the dedicated schools at Fort Benning for infantry, Fort Knox for armor, Fort Sill for artillery, and Fort Bliss for air defense artillery.

I decided early on to participate in the orientation of every new group of basic trainees, which usually numbered about the equivalent of a battalion (i.e., 1,000–1,200 soldiers). Incoming personnel arrived weekly, and graduations were also held weekly.

Training center duty is generally not perceived as the best kind, particularly for combat arms colonels and lieutenant colonels. Such officers generally want to be with combat troops and feel that their careers are stalled during the eighteen to twenty-four months commanding training units. General David and I tried hard to change that perception.

Each brigade had a colonel and several lieutenant colonels, and I spent a lot of time trying to make these officers feel good about their work. My argument went as follows: This is an opportunity for you to try innovative ideas and to put your personal stamp of approval on your trainees. Granted, there is only so much innovation one can use in trying to teach a man how to stand at attention, shoot his rifle, use a compass, administer first aid, and feel good about himself. But here is a chance for you to try. If your initial approach does not work on one unit, you can try a different approach on the next. Over a year, you could have at least three training cycles. Over two years, you have a battalion commander impact on three battalions of soldiers. Think about it. You will have had an impact on five thousand soldiers.

In fact, I cannot think of any better human relations training than basic training because it deals with the individual. New recruits, as they say, "don't know their left foot from their right foot." Some know nothing about living adjacent to other people, and some do not know anything about "Army clean." Some may be used to taking showers once a week or so rather than every day. But recruits experience a miraculous transformation over their sixteen weeks in basic. When they reach graduation, they are standing tall and looking good. They have become a group of people any commander would feel confident taking into combat because they know they can do the job that needs to be done. I wanted to impress on my colonels how important and rewarding this was.

The drill sergeant is the backbone of a training center, the one who most directly makes a trainee into a soldier. He—and nowadays she—is with the trainees throughout the entire period of basic training. The schedule is grueling. For the first five weeks, drill sergeants work seven days a week, from 0400 or 0430 in the morning until 2000 or 2100 at night. It is humanly impossible to maintain this schedule for a prolonged period.

Early on the Army did not pay sufficient attention to what was happening among its drill sergeants: too much spousal abuse, too much child abuse, too many divorces, too much alcoholism. But when I arrived at Fort Dix, I began talking with my counterparts at other training centers—there were six of us nationwide—and we all agreed that something had to be done to protect our drill sergeants from burnout.

The first thing was to shorten the time for a person to serve as a drill sergeant. We finally settled on twenty-four months as the ideal term. We also recommended a change in the procedure for selecting drill sergeants. Heretofore, people had volunteered. We put an end to that by setting up a board to select drill sergeants competitively. Those selected were sent to drill sergeant school, and when they finished, they did their twenty-four-month tour and then went back into the forces with their new skills. Then another batch of drill sergeants was brought in, and the cycle repeated itself. Within a relatively short period, there was an Army-wide cadre of NCOs who were trained to be drill sergeants.

Of course, the new method for selecting drill sergeants meant that some people were chosen who did not want to become drill sergeants. If any of those people are reading, all I will say is "Sorry about that." You were a professional soldier, you were a noncommissioned officer, and you were selected to become a drill sergeant. The Army taught you how to be a drill sergeant, and it was your duty to do it well. We compensated you for that.

I do think, however, that the majority of drill sergeants loved their work and derived a tremendous sense of satisfaction from making soldiers out of the trainees under their control. And drill sergeants did not have to wait until graduation to find out how well they had done their jobs. They received earlier affirmation from visitors during the family orientation that was held at the end of the first five weeks. Parents were beaming. They were happy about what they saw. They were proud of the sons who stood before them, transformed from boys into men.

I did a fair amount of traveling while I was at Fort Dix, and one of my more delightful trips was in early spring 1973. Col. Paul O'Mary, an old friend, invited me to speak to the ROTC cadets at the University of Alabama at Tuscaloosa. I did not enjoy traveling to the South in the early 1970s, but I agreed to go because Paul had invited me.

Paul took me on a tour of the campus. As we approached the field house, he asked whether I would like to look in at spring practice and possibly meet the legendary Coach Bear Bryant. Naturally, I agreed. We went inside just in time to hear the coach blow one blast of his whistle, instantly assembling players who had been milling around—a response that would have pleased the drill sergeants back at Fort Dix.

After practice, Paul introduced me to Coach Bryant. I surprised everyone by blurting out, "Coach, I played center and linebacker in the mid-forties, and I want to commend you for having a Negro as your center." Back in those days, black Americans did not play center or quarterback, particularly in the South.

Bryant's response was typical of the man: "General, we use the best players in those key positions." The only thing left for me to say was, "Thanks, Coach!"

Three decades later that same center, Sylvester Croom, became the first black football coach in the Southeastern Conference, but at Mississippi State University rather than Alabama. The Bear must have flipped over in his tomb when Alabama's Board of Trustees refused to accept his All-American center as their school's new coach.

That brief meeting with Bear Bryant was not my only brush with legendary Americans during those years. When the *Pittsburgh Courier*, a major black newspaper, announced its annual Top Hat Awards in 1974, I was deeply honored to be a recipient. Fred Cherry, an Air Force colonel who spent seven-plus years as a POW in North Vietnam, was another.

The guest speaker at the awards dinner was U.S. Representative Barbara Jordan. The Texas Democrat was a powerful speaker, and she really bowled us over. After she had taken her seat, the master of ceremony, a Baptist minister, returned to the podium. "That was a great speech . . . tremendous speech," he said. "Spoken just like a man."

The air in the room became electric. Barbara Jordan came out of her chair, grabbed the microphone, and proceeded to browbeat that minister in front of the audience, showing no mercy. I am sure that tongue-lashing taught most of us men a lesson. Some members of the audience laughed and applauded, pleased to see Representative Jordan defend her dignity as a woman. Some, I am sure, felt a tinge of pity for the minister.

That same year, I even had a long-distance encounter with Colin Powell. Today, as a former chairman of the Joint Chiefs of Staff and U.S. Secretary of State, Powell is world-renowned. In 1974, I had never heard of him, but when I reviewed his file, I thought, "This young officer is going places."

In response to allegations of discrimination, the Army had established a policy that there must be at least one black American on every selection board, particularly on selection boards that require general officers. Given the fact that I was just the sixth black general in Army history, there really were not that many of us around in the middle 1970s. Add in the proximity of Fort Dix to Washington, D.C., and it is not surprising that I found myself sitting on every conceivable board in the nation's capital.

I was on the five-member board that would select lieutenant colonels to attend the senior service colleges in 1974. I was the senior officer on that board, so I served as its president. In those days the selection process was basically as follows: Each board member reviewed all eligible officers' records and then awarded a score of 1 to 6 points to each candidate. The scores were totaled and the candidates were ranked in order of highest to lowest score. If fifteen hundred officers were reviewed and there were a total of three hundred billets in the five senior service colleges, the next step was to identify which of the top three hundred officers would be assigned to which colleges.

On this board, the number one officer on the order of merit list (OML) was Lt. Col. Colin L. Powell. I perceived there was great potential for him to become a general officer, and I wanted to improve his chances by having him attend the best school—the one I had attended. So I announced to my fellow board members that he would be going to the National War College.

Three of the four members, all brigadier generals, were graduates of the Army War College.[1] They responded practically in unison, "No, Becton. He is the best Army guy on this OML. He goes to the Army War College." I said, "No, fellas. He's going to the National War College." One of the brigadier generals reminded me that I had only one vote. I agreed. "But let me tell you what is going to happen," I went on. "If Powell does not go to the National War College, I will make sure that every guy you have in mind for selection does not get it." How could I do that, I was asked?

I explained, "You've got a scale of one to six. If I find out that you have an officer who you really want to go to a school and everyone else is giving him or her a six, I will give him a one, and that is enough to knock him out." Of course, my fellow board members got very upset. But Colin went to the NWC. It is worth it to play hardball every once in a while.

The draft ended for all practical purposes in 1973, and volunteers were recruited to fill the ranks of the military. At the same time, the Army was downsizing, and Fort Dix was selected to be deactivated. Bert David and I felt it was inappropriate to close Fort Dix. It had been an entry point for recruits from the northeastern United States since 1917. Now that the country had gone to a volunteer Army, Bert and I believed parents from the Northeast would strongly resent having to travel halfway across the country to visit their sons and daughters at other training centers. Plus, the economic impact of a base closing on the area around Fort Dix would be staggering. We felt the decision was just plain wrong.

Because Bert and I disagreed so strongly with the decision to close Fort Dix, we visited the headquarters of the U.S. Army Training and Doctrine Command (TRADOC) at Fort Monroe, Virginia, to present our case. Our arguments fell on deaf ears. The policymakers knew better, they said, than a brigadier general and a major general.

But that was not the end of the story. Eventually, a lot of political clout came into play as the mayors of several eastern cities got involved in the effort to keep Fort Dix open.

Philadelphia is only forty-two miles from Fort Dix, so it would have been dramatically affected by the closing. I had an audience with Philadelphia Mayor Frank Rizzo at one point, and he asked my personal opinion about whether Fort Dix should be deactivated. I explained why I thought it was important that the post remain open. It was not difficult to prove my point. I said, "Mr. Mayor, how many folks from Philadelphia work at Fort Dix? How many youngsters come over to Fort Dix for training? How many soldiers from Fort Dix come to Philadelphia on pass for recreation?"

He was not a stupid man. After listening to what I had to say, Mayor Rizzo made some very profane comments, then summed it all up: "Nothing is going to happen to Fort Dix. It is going to stay open." And it did.

Back when I left the armor branch for Fort Dix, I had wielded some influence in favor of having Col. Paul "Bo" Williams assigned to be my replacement. Bo and I had already traded places a couple of times. He replaced me when I left the Office of the Chief of Staff of the Army, and I replaced him at Fort Hood. He later replaced me again as armor branch chief.

While I was at Fort Dix, our friendship led to a delightful chance to turn the tables on an old critic. Bo, by then a brigadier general, had replaced George Patton at the Army Armor School in Fort Knox. Patton had refused to invite me to address the students there, arguing that I was unqualified because I was not a graduate of the school. But Bo invited me, and I agreed, mentioning that I would really appreciate an honorary diploma. When I finished my speech, the faculty presented me with the diploma. Then Bo did something extra. He made me an honorary instructor, as well. I could not help myself. I sent copies of my diploma to George Patton with a note reading, "Now am I qualified to speak?"

At about that same time Bert David was reassigned to Okinawa, and Maj. General Thomas Upton "Tug" Greer became the new commander at Fort Dix. Whereas Bert David had let me have complete run of the post, Tug Greer wanted to do certain things differently. I said, "Fine." I had explained to all the people who worked on the post that a new guy was coming in, and I said, "He's the guy in charge, not me."

When Bert transferred in February 1974, he wrote on my second OER as a general officer:

Gen. Becton personifies what soldiers mean when they say a "soldier's general." He is without a doubt the most capable BG [brigadier general] I have ever served with. During this period I have observed him carefully and given him responsibilities, which allowed him to exercise his independent judgment as well as all aspects of his leadership ability. He never betrayed the trust and confidence that I placed in him. Mrs. Becton is a most valued member of the Fort Dix community and handled her responsibilities on the distaff side with dedication, sincerity and charm. Without any reservation I recommend Gen. Becton for immediate promotion to major general. I also recommend that the Army leadership provide this general officer a broader scope of responsibility. He has what it takes to lead men in the volunteer Army.

It was not too long before Bert's recommendation was acted upon. In the first week of June 1974 I was at Fort Benjamin Harrison in Indiana to address students. Just after I walked out on the stage, the secretary of the general staff of the post's commander rushed out and said, "You've got a telephone call." I asked, "Who is it?" He said, "The chief of staff."

Col. Jasper Johnson was the chief of staff at Fort Dix, and I said "Tell Jasper I'll get back to him." The reply was startling: "Sir, I'm talking about *the* chief of staff of the Army, not Colonel Johnson." I briskly went to the phone.

I couldn't think of any reason why Gen. Creighton "Abe" Abrams would be calling me. He was sick. He had cancer. The entire Army knew that.

When I got on the phone, I said, "Sir, this is General Becton." General Abrams said, "Julius, I want to tell you something. Congratulations. You're selected to be a major general." I said, "Sir, thank you, but you're supposed to be sick. You're supposed to be in a hospital someplace." He said, "Don't tell me what to do, Becton."

I have no idea what I told the students when I went back out to speak to them. I was on cloud nine.

I was promoted on 1 August 1974. Louise and Greer officiated in the pinning on of my second star. Abe died a month later.

There were then two major generals at Fort Dix when there should only be one. Greer was not very happy about that. He wanted to have a new brigadier general assigned so he could train a deputy the way he felt he should be trained.

Needless to say, Greer and I had a couple of interesting sessions. He was senior to me in rank, but I was older than he was, had been in the Army longer, and had no problem talking to him as a colleague. I was not insubordinate, but I was not intimidated. I wanted out as badly as Greer wanted me gone. In my heart of hearts, I wanted to command units.

Hoping for a quick departure, I called the assignment people in the general officer management office and said, "Okay, what am I going to do?" I was told, "Don't worry about it. It will be a good job. We're working on it." September, October, and November went by, and I still had no new assignment. Greer's patience was wearing thin, and so was mine.

I finally received word about my new assignment in December 1974. The call came from Maj. Gen. Bob Shoemaker, who was the commander of the 1st Cavalry Division. His unit was a test division called 1st Cav, TRICAP, which stood for "triple capability." Bob said, "Julius, guess what? You're going to be my replacement."

That was exactly what I wanted. And it got better: TRICAP would be phasing out, and the 1st Cav would become a true armored division at the same time as I assumed command. I would be a soldier/commander/manager, and I would be going back to Fort Hood to command. I could not have been happier.

I am sure that Tug Greer would have traded assignments with me in a heartbeat. He, too, had wanted in the worst way to command a division, but he was serving his two-star billet as a training center commander. He probably never would have another two-star troop assignment.

I think Greer gave vent to his frustration when he wrote the two-and-a-half-page narrative section of my OER, the longest I ever received. There were ten paragraphs. Nine were positive. The tenth, which follows, could have been the kiss of death for my career: "MG [Maj. Gen.] Becton's only weakness lies in his training supervision. Although knowledgeable in training matters, he failed to establish high enough standards of training, was not always discerning in detecting training deficiencies and was not demanding enough of subordinates in training matters. Although improvement was noted during the period of this report, he never reached expectations in these areas."

This could not have come at a more inopportune time. I had been selected to command a division. Certainly, Greer's assessment would give pause; perhaps a mistake had been made in my new assignment. I spoke with Greer about the efficiency report, but I was unable to persuade him to change it. He said, "Well Becton, that's the way I see it." I saluted and said, "'Bye."

★ ★ ★

CHAPTER ELEVEN

Change of Command

When Bob Shoemaker gave me the word about my assignment to the 1st Cavalry Division, he did not yet know what his own new assignment would be, but he wanted to discuss how we would handle the change of command. "What we're going to do, Julius, is ride," said Bob. The 1st Cav was one of the few divisions that still had horses—not many, but a platoon of ceremonial horses—and Bob was a serious horseman. I said, "Look, you had triple capability. You did those things. We're going to become an armored division now. I just think we ought to have a complete break. You go out there and ride, and I will stand still while you troop the line. Then we'll come back and change the flag, and I will be in charge. No riding." He said, "Okay. We'll talk about it later."

Not long afterward I heard from Bob again. He said, "Julius, I am going to become the corps commander at Fort Hood." He was going be promoted to lieutenant general and was going to be my boss. After I digested this fact he said, "Now, about this change of command. We are going to ride. You understand that?" I said, "Yes, sir."

I assumed command of the 1st Cavalry Division on 25 February 1975, and needless to say, we rode. I spent several hours with Bob's wife, Tukie Shoemaker, in the Horse Platoon riding area in the days leading up to the division change of command ceremony. Tukie was from the Old West, a real Annie Oakley type and *the* expert rider at Fort Hood. I felt fairly comfortable in the saddle after her tutelage, and the change of command went smoothly.

From my point of view, the 1st Cav had a somewhat questionable history. During World War II its troopers had treated black soldiers as second-class subordinates. As the white soldiers saw it then, they were the true fighters and those of us in the all-black 93rd Infantry Division were something else. I saw the same thing in Korea. But then things began to change.

The 1st Cav did have black soldiers and a few black commanders in Vietnam. When I assumed control over the Street Without Joy area, my unit took over from a 1st Cav battalion commanded by Roscoe Robinson, who was black. Still, for the brief period that we were under the 1st Cav's operational control in central Vietnam, my unit was assigned a "choice" piece of real estate between a sanitary fill and a dump for our bivouac.

All those bad things were completely forgotten on 25 February 1975, however.

There were two divisions at Fort Hood. The 1st Cav was nicknamed "First Team," and the 2nd Armored Division, commanded by Maj. Gen. Bob Fair, was known as "Hell on Wheels." As peers, Bob Shoemaker and Bob Fair had been fiercely competitive. Competition is healthy, but there are limits. Fair, who was very opinionated, wanted to be first in everything and was very demanding of his people. When Shoemaker became his boss, Fair seized every opportunity he could to slight him. For example, Fair seldom made it to corps commander meetings on time, while everyone else did.

But Shoemaker was not the sort of person to retaliate. He was judicious and evenhanded. He made a commitment early on that he would treat the two divisions under his command equally and that there would be no favorite. However, I thought he went overboard in trying to be to do this. If he found something wrong in the 2nd Armored area, he would end up in 1st Cav looking for something wrong. After about the third or fourth time, I said, "Hey, Sir, I really don't need this. Just because that other division has screwed up, don't pick on us."

I did not much like Bob Fair, and the feeling was mutual. In the spring of 1975 his senior assistant division commander Brig. Gen. Ollie Dillard was replaced by Brig. Gen. Richard Cavazos. Dick and I went back a long way. He and his wife Carol arrived at Fort Hood on a Saturday morning and spent the weekend with Louise and me. When Dick reported in on Monday morning, Fair asked where he had spent the weekend. Dick told Fair that he had gone to see his old friend Julius Becton. Fair said brusquely, "General, I don't think much of your judgment."

Just as Fair had bad-mouthed me, he had no compunction about disparaging other officers. When he spoke to his soldiers, he always seemed to be suggesting that no other officers knew what they were doing, particularly the lieutenant colonels and colonels. He was also small-minded about certain Army traditions. To note just one example our bands usually rotated in providing music during corps functions. On one occasion my division band was playing and struck up the cavalry song "Gary Owens." It is Army tradition to stand when a division song is being played. Of course, I jumped up. Bob Shoemaker, who was sitting next to me, jumped up. So did the other officers. Fair just sat there, but when he realized that no one else was still seated, he grudgingly rose to his feet, muttering under his breath.

Fair's philosophy of management ultimately caught up with him. He was promoted to three stars and left the division in the summer of 1975 to assume command of V Corps in Germany. He was fired a year or so later, however, earning the dubious distinction of being the only modern day corps commander to be relieved of duty during peacetime.

Fair's replacement was my old acquaintance Maj. Gen. George Patton. Despite our past differences, I was actually delighted that George would be taking over because I knew he would never abuse his soldiers. I immediately wrote to George, welcoming him to Fort Hood and offering any assistance I could provide. We ended up living two doors from each other, and our families became good friends.

While George and I competed in many activities, there was no longer any backstabbing. George and his wife Joanne also had a distinctly positive impact on the post, and relations between the two divisions improved greatly.

Normally, the Army chief of staff handpicks his own division commanders. It was a little different in my case. Before his death, General Abrams had made it known that he wanted me to take over the 1st Cav. Gen. Fred Weyand, who replaced Abrams as chief of staff in the summer of 1974, honored that wish. "If Abe said that Becton is going to command 1st Cavalry Division, Becton commands the 1st Cavalry Division," Weyand said.

Between the time I received word about my new assignment and the time I arrived at Fort Hood, the OER Tug Greer had prepared arrived in Washington. It included comments from Lt. Gen. Orwin C. Talbott, who nine months earlier had endorsed Bert David's generous appraisal of my performance by writing on David's report, "Gen Becton has fully evidenced the capacity for Division command."

Talbott expressed less confidence in me when he endorsed Greer's negative assessment of my command ability. He acknowledged that I was "liked

and admired, not by some, but all races and ranks." But he concluded with
the following: "Unfortunately, the comments in para 9 of rating officer's
narrative [Tug Greer's criticism of me] are correct. The quality of training at
Ft. Dix and especially the quality of the management of training left something to be desired. As training was the No. 1 mission of Ft. Dix, this weakness became very apparent."

My OER caused some consternation. It said I had failed in my primary
mission of ensuring the proper training of recruits. It said I was not the man
for the job, and it presented General Weyand with a dilemma.

Weyand visited Fort Hood post in March, just a month after I had
assumed command. I thought it was just a normal visit, but it was far from
that. I later learned that he wanted to see how I was doing for himself so he
could have some firsthand evidence to reconcile the extreme differences in
the opinions of Abrams and Greer.

Weyand talked to a lot of people during his visit to Fort Hood, including
Bob Shoemaker. He went away satisfied that what Abe had seen in me and
thought about me was true, that I was, after all, the man for the job.

By the end of 1975 I had put together an excellent team of officers. Col. Jack
Merritt, my chief of staff, was promoted to brigadier general and became
one of the two assistant division commanders. Brig. Gen. Jim Jaggers from
III Corps was the other. I brought in Col. Tim Bramlett from Fort Benning
as my new chief of staff. Col. Tom Spence replaced Col. John Crosby as
the division artillery commander. Col. Aaron Lilly replaced Col. Art Junot
as the division support commander. Walter Krueger was selected to be the
command sergeant major by Bob Shoemaker, with my concurrence.

Walter, who is now deceased, later wrote in a letter to Joe Galloway as Joe
and I were initially preparing this autobiography about something he never
told me about at the time:

> As an incoming ritual for new division commanders, the military affairs
> committees of the Chambers of Commerce of Killeen and Copperas Cove
> invited General Becton to lunch, the first being held at the Cactus Inn in
> Copperas Cove, Texas. As it was the general's custom, I was also invited.
> Upon arrival, we separated and went through handshaking rituals and
> during this activity a senior retired white officer, a longtime acquaintance,
> asked me how I "liked serving a nigger general." I was astonished . . . and
> didn't respond. A week or so later at a Killeen function, the same question
> was asked but this time, by a wealthy white businessman, also a longtime

acquaintance. Once again, my response was the same. This individual also asked me when and where I was going to retire—his assumption being that I would refuse to work for General Becton because of his color. . . . Subsequent to these two occasions I was asked the same question again and again, always by civilians or retired military and never once by a military contemporary.

My brigade commanders, all colonels, were Jerry Bartlett, Mike O'Connell, and Mickey Marshall. Marshall's arrival made ours the only division in the entire Army that had a black division commander and at least one black brigade commander. With two exceptions, every member of this team went on to become general officers.

The first exception was Tom Spence. Early on, wanting to make sure everyone was sensitive to racial issues, I established a policy that all incoming battalion and brigade commanders and command sergeants major would attend a brief orientation course arranged with the commandant of the Defense Race Relations Institute (now the Defense Equal Opportunity Management Institute). Tom Spence, the commandant reported, had a real problem.

The case of Mickey Marshall was more complicated. I was on temporary duty in New York City to give a speech when I got a call from Jack Merritt, who was in charge of the First Team whenever I left the post. "Sir, are you standing up or sitting down?" I asked, "Jack, what are you talking about?" Again he said, "Are you standing up or sitting down?" Even though I was not, I told him I was seated. Then he dropped the bomb: "Mickey just got charged with rape. He's in jail."

Mickey, too, had been on temporary duty for a speech at Fort McClellan in Anniston, Alabama. He had met a young woman who was in OCS there and who had previously been the driver for Command Sergeant Major Krueger. Mickey and the woman had gone out, and what probably began as consensual sex changed to rape.

I got back to Fort Hood as fast as I could and sat down with Bob Shoemaker. The first thing we had to do was get Mickey back under military control. Race relations were not great in 1975, and the civilian jail in Anniston, Alabama, was no place for a black man charged with raping of a Hispanic woman who looked white. It took some string-pulling, but we were able to get Mickey back under military authority at Fort McClellan. Then we whisked him to Fort Hood.

Now we had other concerns. Mickey's rape charge made the front page of the local newspaper in Killeen and was quickly picked up by *Army Times* and other international newspapers. I got calls from people from all over who wanted to commiserate and said things such as, "Oh, it is so bad that Mickey did that to you." I said, "What do you mean did that to me? He's a soldier, and he did something dumb."

We formed an Article 32 board to conduct a preliminary investigation into what the charges against Mickey should be, if any. Lt. Col. Cal Tichner, the division staff judge advocate, was on orders to Fort Leavenworth to attend the Command and General Staff College. Luckily for Mickey, however, Cal felt so strongly about the case that he gave up his leave time to make sure that we made no missteps. Cal's legal analysis was definitely on the money and confirmed why he was consistently promoted "below the zone" (i.e., ahead of his peers).

"Sir, we've got two charges," Cal initially told me. "We've got a charge of rape and a charge of adultery." I disagreed. "If you give a court two charges like that, guaranteed, they will find him guilty of adultery and, also guaranteed, they will acquit him of rape," I argued. "Also, I don't want to set a precedent of a general court-martial for people who commit adultery. We don't have enough jail space." Cal agreed with my thinking, and we prosecuted Mickey for one charge of rape.

Bob Shoemaker and I wanted to make sure that I retained jurisdiction over the case. If Bob had jurisdiction at corps level, the review would be conducted by someone off post at the next highest level. We did not want that to happen, so Bob appointed his deputy, Maj. Gen. John Hill, as president of the court. In a military trial, the jury is made up of the defendant's peers. In Mickey's case, this meant the jurors would all be colonels. So the division support commander, who was the only division colonel who was senior to Mickey, was made a member of the court. Bob Shoemaker also named three corps colonels as members.

As he was preparing his prosecution Cal told me he needed to ask a question of my senior officers. "Let's do it after church," he said. Some might find that odd, but I did not. Cal had once been a fun-loving soldier who partied as hard and drank as much as the rest of them, but he had undergone a religious experience and was now deeply pious. I suspect that he chose to see the officers after church because he would pray during the service that he would hear the right answers to his question.

Everyone met at my house for coffee after chapel. While our wives remained inside, the two brigadier generals, six colonels, one sergeant major, and I all went out onto the patio. Cal, who was junior to every officer present, was visibly uncomfortable. He turned to me first. "Sir," he said, "I have got to ask this question, and the answer will determine whether we go to court. I must ask you whether you have had any illicit relations with that woman." My answer was, "No. I did not." And around he went, polling every other man on the patio. Sergeant Major Walter Krueger was the last.

The woman had been Walter's driver, but we were not concerned about his answer. We all knew how devoted Walter was to his wife Betty and their four daughters. "No sir," Krueger said. Obviously relieved, Cal said, "We can go to court." I said, "Let's have a drink," and I did not mean coffee.

I had expected some fanfare surrounding the trial, but it was worse than I anticipated. The court-martial area was marked in tape, the media were present—TV vans, newspapers, and radio—and there were many spectators. It was a big show.

Louise and the wives of all the other senior division officers sat through the trial all day, every day, in a show of support for Mickey's wife, Toni, who also attended. Louise, in fact, had probably known about the rape charge against Mickey before I did. The evening Jack Merritt called me in New York, Toni went to our house to see Louise. As she entered, Toni said, "That fool has ruined his career." Her words were prophetic.

The court acquitted Mickey of rape. I do not think anyone doubted that he had intercourse with the young woman, but there was doubt about whether and when their relations ceased being consensual. In short, the jurors were not able to conclude that the woman's "no" was a clear "no."

Mickey came by my office the afternoon of his acquittal. He said, "Sir, can I have my brigade back?" While he was dealing with his legal difficulties, I had replaced him with another colonel. I said, "Mickey, you know better than that." Then I suggested that he call the colonels division, which was his assignment prior to joining the First Team and is responsible for the assignment of colonels worldwide.

He did. After about an hour, he came back to see me and said, "Sir, I am going to retire." I said, "Okay. What did they offer you?" They had offered him assignment as a National Guard adviser in South Dakota or as an Army attaché in Yemen.

In the Army's effort to attract volunteers, it had become quite permissive in certain matters relating to dress. Members of the 1st Cav wore berets, and when I first arrived, they wore berets of different colors: Infantry wore blue, artillery wore red, signal wore orange, and the support command wore green. The staff at division headquarters and the tankers wore black. It was a sight to see all those berets on display. One could not help but feel good looking at them.

Not everyone appreciated them, however. In the spring of 1975 the edict came down from Forces Command (FORSCOM) to get rid of those multi-colored berets. I read the order carefully. It said "get rid of the colored berets," not "get rid of berets." So in July 1975 I outfitted the entire division with black berets. As a result, out of the 16 divisions in the Army, 1st Cav and the 82nd Airborne, commanded by Maj. Gen. Roscoe Robinson, became the only two wearing berets. Ours were black, and the 82nd Airborne's were maroon.

I also had more significant problems to deal with, of course. Race relations was pretty high on the list. Before he died, Walter Krueger recalled an incident I had almost forgotten. Not long after I took command, he was following my vehicle on the way to a visit with the 13th Signal Battalion. As Walter told the story in a letter to me: "Approaching us on the sidewalk was a group of black soldiers. As we drew near them, instead of rendering the normal military hand salute to the general, they instead used the clenched fist, black power salute. General Becton virtually became unglued, stopped his vehicle and proceeded to reprimand these soldiers. I quickly intervened and took appropriate NCO action."

The Army set up all sorts of programs for enlisted personnel to deal with our race relations problem. I encouraged participation at every level.

The growing numbers of women who began joining the military in the mid-1970s posed problems as well. When I joined the 1st Cav, about six percent of the division's troops were women. Although they worked in different units, all the female soldiers in the division lived in one billet. Driving by the women's billet at night, I would see women in all manner of attire leaning out the windows and returning the abuse they were getting from the bunch of male idiots on the ground who were acting like dogs in heat. It was not long before I realized something had to change.

So we billeted the women with their units. This meant a female soldier became a member of the unit full time, not just during duty hours. It enhanced esprit de corps and made it more difficult for Sgt. Peggy Smith or

Cpl. Sally Jones to become a target for sexual harassment. Her male counterparts now treated her as a sister soldier deserving of respect.

It did not hurt that I had read the riot act to my commanders. I said, "I don't want to hear anything about how you can't control them. They are in your unit, and you hold everyone in the chain of command responsible." Eventually, the wild and outrageous behavior I had witnessed when the women were billeted separately stopped.

Although the 1st Cavalry Division was the first in the Army to billet women with the men in their units, the rest of the Army followed suit. The primary reason was economics: It was cheaper to billet them together. In addition, the change mirrored what was happening in society at large. Finally, billeting men and women together made good sense operationally because it helped maintain unit integrity.

The 1st Cav was out in the field for two or three days out of each month, running exercises, developing teamwork, and perfecting our ability to operate in a hostile environment. Infantry had to know how to charge up a hill, tankers had to know how to engage a target, and artillery had to know how to support the frontline units. But perfecting these techniques was not the main purpose of our field exercises. The main purpose was to exercise our command and control. I wanted to make sure that we could continue to operate no matter the circumstances.

While we were in the field the two assistant division commanders and I were routinely in different locations. We set up three command posts. The rationale for this was that if the commanders were separated and something happened to one, the others could continue operating.

Our command post had initially consisted of a formation of large stationary tents and the twenty or more trucks and vans used to transport the tents. I saw early on that we had to make changes. First, the command post was simply too large. It was big enough to be a target and an obvious priority for any enemy worth his salt. Second, it took forever to change locations.

So we dramatically reduced the size of our command posts to where they could be transported on just three or four vehicles. Unlike before, the enemy would have a very difficult time finding us and we could move around very fast.

After months of hard training, my unit commanders and I decided to set aside a day to celebrate. We just couldn't spend a lot of money. We scheduled

a dismounted division review for 17 October 1975. We even found two
retiring soldiers who had joined the First Team in the early 1940s when the
division was horse mounted, Col. Charles Wittlif and MSgt. James Holland,
to be reviewers. Since it had been some time since the two had been on the
back of a horse, the retirees would review the formation in a mule-pulled
wagon. Only Commander of Troops Brig. Gen. Jim Jaggers and I would
be mounted. I took the precaution to visit Tukie Shoemaker in the Horse
Platoon training area for a brief refresher course in riding the night before the
event. The Horse Platoon leader, Lt. Tom Hill, had selected a mild mount
named Old Bill for me.

October 17 was a beautiful day, with fluffy clouds and a mild breeze.
There were about 8,500 soldiers in the division formation, and several
thousands spectators in the stands. The band sounded off and resumed its
place on the extreme right of the formation, and it was time for us to troop
the line.

The two retirees were seated in the wagon, and Jaggers had moved
forward on his horse to meet me. Just as I was mounting Old Bill, the unexpected happened.

Several weeks earlier our division intelligence officer had had the notion
that it would be a great idea to get aerial photographs of the division on
review. So unbeknownst to me, he contacted his counterpart at Bersgtrom
Air Force Base near Austin and arranged for an RF-4 jet to take pictures
from the air.

The jet came in right about the time my right leg was going over Old
Bill. The deafening noise caused a chain reaction. The two matched mules
reared up on their hind legs, startling the wagon's passengers and spooking
Old Bill, who also reared up on his two hind legs. Old Bill and I crashed to
the ground, with me still in the saddle and my right leg under him.

Needless to say, cameras caught many action shots of this episode, from
the spooking of Old Bill to my remounting. Truth to tell, I remounted Old
Bill because my leg hurt too much to walk the entire division formation, and
I had too much pride to join the retirees in the wagon. The only other way
to troop the line was to get back on Old Bill. It had nothing to do with the
tradition of "Ride 'em Cav," even though Bob Shoemaker kindly wrote to
me later that "it was a classic demonstration of the spirit of the cavalry."

I was told later (I surely did not hear it at the time) that there was thun-
derous applause when I remounted Old Bill. I suspect that at least two people
did not applaud, however. Mom Thornton was there, making this one of

Spooked by those matched mules. (Author collection).

Still in the saddle. (Author collection)

You can see who they are worried about. (Author collection)

Back in the saddle. (Author collection)

the very few times she had attended a division formation. With horror, she turned to Louise and said, "He isn't going to get back on that crazy horse, is he?" And there were photos of Bob Shoemaker, his hands holding his head, which was bowed near his knees. I am sure he was thinking, "My God! I've got to train another division commander."

The next day the Austin newspaper had a front-page photo of me and Old Bill, reared up on his hind legs, with a caption suggesting that the division commander was hanging on. The *Army Times* carried a similar picture that gave the impression that Old Bill was about to throw me. No publication carried the photograph of Old Bill and me on the ground.

Obviously, I was very proud to be the commander of 1st Cav. I also think the same thing can be said for the men and women who served under me. Our esprit de corps was great, and it transcended the continental boundaries of the United States. Walter Krueger later ruminated in a letter to me on the great enthusiasm of the troopers, how "innovation was the name of the game," and the fact that "families were included in everything." As he wrote:

> I can not recall a plan, formal or informal, that took us from one point to another. It just sort of came together. . . . [M]any soldiers who served with the First Team during Gen. Becton's command have gone on to great personal successes and . . . they all attribute their success to participating in the First Team activities during the Becton Era. . . .

> [One incident] I recall vividly happened at 3 o'clock in the morning, standing on a ridge in northwest Fort Hood, overlooking the maneuver area and hearing General Becton say to me, "Sergeant Major, we've got it made. Many Americans pay good money to go camping and enjoy the outdoors and here we are, being paid to have so much fun"—it being about 17° F and raining at that time he is making this comment. And guess what? I agreed with him.

I reaped huge dividends at Fort Hood from the knowledge and understanding I had gained in other assignments. For example, while I had once had a pretty low opinion of my assignment at Verdun, at Fort Hood I was able to make significant use of the logistics I learned while I was there. And at Fort Dix I had learned a great deal about how to communicate, which ultimately enhanced my ability to command.

While I was at Fort Dix, Brig. Gen. Chappie James, a decorated combat fighter pilot who eventually became the first black four-star general in the U.S. Air Force, accepted my invitation to address the recruits. Chappie blew us away. He was the consummate public speaker, with an incredible ability to speak at the drop of a hat on just about any subject. I wished I could do the same. I later learned that Chappie used talking points for his speeches. With them as the basis of an outline, he could modify a speech to suit any audience and any occasion, and to fit the time allotted.

When I arrived at Fort Hood, I learned that Bob Shoemaker had formalized a list of thirteen principles that made up a First Team philosophy. I eventually adapted the First Team philosophy as the basis for my own talking points, and, over time, they became the outline of my own philosophy of command. Those principles, and how I have put them into practice, are as follows.

Be Professional

Under my definition there are three variables that are essential to being a professional: job knowledge, obedience, and initiative. First, know your job, and if you do not know it, learn it. Second, do what you are told to do. Third, in the absence of being told what to do, use that God-given gray matter to exercise some common sense and initiative.

The Boy Scout motto, "Be prepared," and the Army slogan, "Be all that you can be," capture the essence of what it means to be professional. Being professional has nothing to do with the type of job one is called to do, and everything to do with the manner in which the job is performed. My father was a janitor, but he was professional in every sense of the word. He did his job better than any other janitor I knew.

Integrity Is Nonnegotiable

If I had to choose the most important point, this would be it. As a commander I would not tolerate lies, and if I found out that someone had deliberately lied to me, he or she would be relieved of their duties. My team had no position for liars.

The battlefield will not accommodate lies. In a combat situation I had to be confident that if a subordinate told me he was at Position X, that is where he really was, and I could therefore shoot artillery at Position A. If he lied and was really at Position A, a lot of our own people could end up killed or injured.

I wanted the people who worked for me to understand that I would do everything in my power to conduct myself with the highest degree of integrity and to understand that I wanted them to conduct themselves in the same manner.

Loyalty Goes Down, as Well as Up

In my view it is absolutely essential that the people who work for you perceive your loyalty to them. It is important to demonstrate that you care about them. If you have not shown your loyalty to them, they will not trust you. And when things get down to where the rubber meets the road, you may or may not have people there when you need them. Loyalty is definitely a two-way street.

Chain of Command Works. Use It

From the time I was promoted to colonel, I followed an open-door policy. Anyone could come to see me if he or she felt that I was the only person left to deal with a complaint. All they had to do was call my office to make an appointment. After we met—generally after duty hours to ensure privacy—I would funnel the issue through the chain of command to someone who was responsible for following up and getting back to the complainant, again, through the chain of command.

My use of the chain of command to respond to open-door visitors and callers meant that I was committed to full disclosure. It also meant that I recognized that there are almost always two sides to every story. Later on, when I was a corps commander, I often met with all the battalion commanders—bypassing the brigade commanders, the division commanders, and the group commander who were all colonels and general officers—to talk directly to the lieutenant colonels. Some senior officers were extremely displeased and complained so much that I said, "Okay guys. I'll tell you what we're going to do. You can come to the meeting and you can sit in the back, but just don't say anything. I will not be telling them anything that you have not already heard."

My subordinate commanders eventually realized that I was not trying to circumvent the chain of command and that I was not trying to spy on them. They also came to understand that all they needed to do with respect to my open-door policy was to do the right thing and get their act together. I honestly believe that they realized I was merely trying to build a better unit, whether it was with respect to equipment, personnel, or morale, which are all essential for combat readiness.

Innovate: Seek a Better Way

When I ask, "Why are we doing it this way?" I do not want to be told, "We've always done it that way." No matter how well the job is being done, I maintain that there is a better way to do it.

A good example of what I mean was the way the 1st Cavalry field-tested different concepts for operational command posts. We tried new ideas, and some worked and some did not. Ultimately, we found a winner in the small operational command posts with low electronic signatures that could be rapidly moved about the battlefield.

Going to the moon is another example. On 25 May 1961, President John F. Kennedy announced the goal of landing a man on the moon before the decade was out.[1] The whole world was highly skeptical. But on 20 July 1969, Neil Armstrong became the first human being to set foot on the moon. That monumental step probably would not have been taken if President Kennedy had not challenged the scientific community to think outside the box. (By the way, in preparing to go the moon, the scientific community developed a whole array of new inventions, including watches that needed no winding, simply because people looked for a better way of doing things.)

Disagreement Is Not Disrespect

I have always believed that it is important for people to say what they really believe. I do not want parrots and I do not want people who tell me what they think I want to hear. I want to hear what people think, and it does not matter what the person's rank or grade may be. Everyone has different experiences, and everyone has something to offer.

I also maintain that how a person disagrees is just as important as what he or she has to say, maybe even more so. If someone approaches a subject in such a way that the other person just stops listening, then both people are just wasting time. And if someone is simply disagreeable, everyone has a problem. That is not demonstrating engagement or interest; it is showing disrespect—pure and unadulterated disrespect.

When properly done, disagreeing is both educational and good for morale. People like to have their day in court, and generally feel better after they have had their say.

Admit Mistakes

At some point during the many speeches I have given over the years using these talking points, I would ask the audience, "Is there anyone here who has not made a mistake in the last twenty-four hours?" Usually, there was no show of hands.

When I was a young lieutenant I witnessed an incident that underscored the point. A soldier who had been summoned by the first sergeant came into the orderly room. Before the first sergeant could say anything, the soldier said, "First Sergeant, I screwed up. I really screwed up. I did this wrong. I did that wrong. I'm an embarrassment to the unit, to you, to myself. I really apologize. I screwed up." What was left for the first sergeant to say? He had been completely disarmed by the soldier's admission.

But let me add a footnote: I can accept a person's explanation for making a mistake when life or death is not on the line because by that person's admission, he or she is promising not to do the same thing again. If that person comes back to me again with the same kind of mistake, I will remind him or her of that. But if the person does the same dumb thing over and over, we have a problem and I will help him or her correct it. The other side of admitting a mistake is having a boss who will help you to do better.

Be Sensitive to (and Intolerant of) Trooper Misuse or Abuse

To be sensitive, a commander must understand what his or her soldiers are feeling. And the only way to do that is to be out there with the soldiers, observing firsthand what they are going through. I am adamant about this. My subordinate commanders became quite accustomed to hearing me say, "If your soldiers are out there, I better see some leader out there too."

Fort Hood had a large number of vehicles, and there was routine daily vehicular maintenance known as "motor stables." It gets very hot deep in the heart of Texas, and in my estimation it is trooper abuse to call a motor stable when the sun is blazing down, the temperature is about 95° Fahrenheit, and the humidity is also about 95 percent. There is no good reason to put soldiers outside in that kind of weather when you do not have to unless the unit is undergoing training for deployment to an area of the world where such conditions are normal.

In protecting subordinates from misuse or abuse, a commander must be vigilant during off-duty hours, as well. I used to ride around Fort Hood during my off-duty hours to get a sense of what was happening. If I found something way out of line, I would have the battalion commander, the brigade commander, and—if it was really gross—a general officer summoned to meet me where the problem was.

Believe me, I only had to do this once or twice. Eventually, the commanders themselves started doing more of what I was doing—checking in during off-duty hours to learn what was happening in their commands. If the problem was there for me to see, it was there for them to see, as well.

Conserve Utilities, Money, and Property

This speaks to the wise use of resources, and its indictment against wastefulness is just as applicable to the private sector as it is to the military.

Back in the early 1970s Americans unwillingly grew accustomed to waiting in long lines to buy gasoline. Suddenly, the habits of the nation began to change. Many Americans modified their personal driving patterns and became members of car and vanpools. On a public level, highways were reengineered to feature special lanes for high-occupancy vehicles and mass transit systems were expanded. The automobile industry responded by manufacturing smaller vehicles with greater fuel economy. Conservation of motor fuel became everybody's business.

Challenge Assertions

Telling a young soldier that he or she should challenge assertions defies everything the soldier has been told about following orders. But the key to getting a soldier to understand how important this is lies in getting him or her to understand how an assertion differs from a matter of fact. I believe soldiers accept a commander's assertion because of the rapport already established.

Allow me to present an example: Soldiers in a unit are told there is no enemy over there. The logical question is, "How do you know?" If the commander replies, "I have been told there is no enemy over there," or "I believe there is no enemy over there," those responses are much different than him saying, "I know there's no enemy over there." There is a huge difference between when someone says, "I am asserting this," and when someone else says, "I know this as a fact."

Once a commander has established rapport with his or her soldiers and they understand where their commander is coming from, the statements the commander makes to them are facts, as far as they are concerned. There is no reason to challenge them as assertions. In essence, my advice to commanders is this: "Sergeant major, lieutenant, captain, lieutenant colonel, or colonel, make sure you have the kind of leadership in your unit that is the ideal leadership so that when you get to the ultimate place in combat, no one will be standing there and asking, 'Why are we doing this?' Instead, you have to have every confidence that they will salute and say, 'Let's go.'"

Maintain Your Sense of Humor

Taking yourself too seriously serves no useful purpose. Instead, it mires you in a negative or defeatist attitude. The ability to laugh at yourself helps you to bounce back and maintains a balance that other people want and expect to see. Humor is a great leveler and helps you to develop rapport. Even at some critical combat moment, if someone does or says something funny, the tension and stress in the situation are relieved.

Keep Things in Perspective

Certain things are expected of a leader. Falling apart is not one of them. Remembering that tomorrow is another day that will bring with it another chance to try and get things right will prevent breakdowns. A leader can only maintain the balance and ability to lead if he or she keeps things in perspective.

A story about a soldier in combat who had just gone through a horrendous firefight is on point. The soldier and many of his buddies had been injured. Others lost their lives. As the soldier was sitting in his foxhole, a chaplain came up to him and asked, "What do you want? What do you really want to do?" The chaplain did not anticipate the response. It was simply, "I wanna see tomorrow."

If You Charge Death Boldly, Death Will Move Out of the Way

Call it a handy cliché, a gimmick, a morale booster, or whatever you will, but this battle cry works. It is designed to make combatant soldiers believe that if they do what they have to do to the maximum of their ability and are determined to succeed, then they will overcome the enemy.

Does this mean no one will get killed? Of course not. But if there are one hundred soldiers who feel that they can overcome the enemy, the goal will be attained. Mission accomplished. A couple of soldiers may be lost, but if you are going to get done in, you might as well get done in doing the right thing.

During my days officiating high school basketball, there was a big, gangly kid named Zelmo Beatty on one of the teams.[2] Zelmo was a superb player, but if he ran into another player, he apologized. I saw him play for four years, in high school and at Prairie View, and I witnessed a complete about-face.

By the time Zelmo was a senior in college, he weighed about 265 pounds. And he had stopped apologizing. If he ran into you, he would put you on your backside. Reluctant to have this giant run over them, other players got out of his way.

The First Team Philosophy is a way of living and working that transcends the military. Its points can be applied to anyone in any phase of life, from the homeless man to the man sitting in 1600 Pennsylvania Avenue.

Perhaps the most important indicator of whether my philosophy of command worked is the evaluation of my superiors. In a General Officer Evaluation Report dated 26 January 1976, Lt. Gen. Bob Shoemaker wrote the following:

> Becton's great success as a commander stems from his ability to weld his officer and noncommissioned leadership into a large group pursuing the same goals with a common philosophy of leadership. I am not aware of any bickering or uncertainty among his subordinates as to the goal or the way to get there. There is no unhealthy, antagonistic competition between his brigade commanders—instead he has fostered a climate in which the development of battalion and brigade pride and esprit is encouraged but within the bounds of mutual support throughout the division. He has a special talent for getting the most out of his subordinates. This includes the perception to assign individuals to the right slot and then handling them in such a way as to bring forth their best effort. Although he is clearly in charge and a very visible front man, he does not permit his personality to dominate the organization. (My staff speaks of the "First Cav" not General Becton's outfit.)

One Sunday afternoon in early autumn 1976, after I had been in command for eighteen months, I received a call from Bob Shoemaker. "Come on over," he said. "I want to talk to you." Since I lived next door to him, I was there in a flash.

"I just got a call from the chief of staff," Bob said. "You are going to become the commander of OTEA." I responded, "Sir, I've got a command." Bob said, "I know that but you are going to command OTEA." The Operational Test and Evaluation Agency conducts troop tests for all Army equipment. Pausing briefly, I said, "Sir, I don't know a damned thing about OTEA or about testing equipment." "Oh yes you do," said Bob.

Why was I selected to become the commander of OTEA? There were several reasons. One, I was a proven troop commander. I had commanded at every level up to division. Two, I had experience in troop testing. I had supervised the add-on stabilization test for the M60 tank. A substantial amount of troop testing for other equipment had also been conducted with the 1st Cav. The third reason was unspoken. The Army had paid for my master's degree in operations research. This assignment was payback.

Louise and I thought 1st Cav was the finest command I ever had. Other folks apparently felt the same way. After I had turned over command to Maj. Gen. Russ Todd, Louise and I went back to our house one last time before our drive off post.

Unbeknownst to us, the commanders, the division staff, and the division band had assembled at our old house. There was a police escort there, and a horse and buggy to carry us off post. My driver was even there to bring our car.

As we rode by in the buggy behind the marching band, people stood and cheered.

★ ★ ★

CHAPTER TWELVE

The Honest Broker

My new command meant a move back to the Washington, D.C., area. As a general, I was provided a house at Fort Myer, Virginia. My family was not too keen on the location at first, which was not surprising seeing as how we were right next to Arlington National Cemetery. But living near Arlington was not all bad. Mom Thornton actually reached the point where she enjoyed the pomp and splendor of the almost daily funeral ceremonies at the post chapel.

When I assumed command of OTEA, the Army had three testing organizations.[1] The old Test and Evaluation Command (TECOM), located at Aberdeen Proving Ground in Maryland, was charged with engineer-testing equipment to see if it met specifications. When the engineers completed their testing, the equipment was put into the hands of operational testers (OTs) for the troop testing. First-level testing, or OT1, was done primarily by the branch boards, which served as the second testing organizations. OT2 and OT3 were mostly the province of OTEA.

Our mission was to make sure the equipment was soldier-proof, which is to say that we needed to ensure that equipment would perform under real-world conditions. Everyone knows all too well how things can work in a laboratory but not work outside of one. Soldiers can do things to equipment that no engineer ever thought of doing, and OTEA's job was to put new equipment into the hands of the soldiers who would use or operate it to see what would happen. We had no vested interest in whether the equipment did or did not do what its designers promised. We were the Army's honest broker.

Each of the services has its own testing organization, and we did a lot of information sharing with Navy, Air Force, and Marine Corps testers. As a matter of fact, all the groups eventually got to know each other quite well, which had an unexpected downside.

In 1978 a U.S. senator got it into his head that it was problematic for each service to do its own testing, suspecting that such a system fostered a vested interest in the equipment being studied. The senator wanted us to test each other's equipment instead—for the Army to try out Navy gear, for instance. The proposal made no sense at all. There was nothing in the history of our organizations to suggest that we were not being objective and an Army unit could not realistically or expertly put a Navy weapon through its paces. So all four commanders of the services' testing units found ourselves testifying at a hearing before a subcommittee of the Senate Armed Services Committee. This was a colossal waste of time, but we were able to prevent the proposal from going any further.

When I reported to OTEA's headquarters in Falls Church, Virginia, its staff numbered about four hundred, and the workforce was split nearly equally between civilians and soldiers. I had two deputies, one for testing and one for organizational structure, and I reported directly to the vice chief of staff of the Army, initially Gen. Walter "Dutch" Kerwin and then Gen. Frederick "Fritz" Kroesen.

Walter Hollis was my deputy for testing. He was my link to the scientific community—the way-out thinkers, the Ph.D.s, the university and academic community, and the various engineering laboratories. My first meeting with Walt was memorable. Walt asked to see me shortly after I reported, and when I saw him, he said, "I want to tell you that when I give you my best recommendation, it is my best recommendation. If you decide for whatever reason that you are not going to accept my recommendation, don't expect me to go before a congressional committee or anyone else to provide the support that I recommend against. When I think you are wrong I will tell you. And when you think I am wrong, I expect you to tell me." I looked at him and said, "Walt Hollis, you've got an agreement. You've got a deal!" Walt Hollis was a real pro.

Col. Thompson Rainey was the deputy for organizational structure. His duties included being the commander for the military folks. He was an armor officer, a good man with a very good professional reputation. In 1978 Colonel Rainey was replaced by Col. Raymond Singer, who had been a friend of mine since the mid-1960s.

One of OTEA's tasks during my tenure was to conduct the operational testing for a tank initially known as the XM1, and later as the M1 Abrams, tank. The armor community pushed hard to have the test conducted at Fort Knox. The Army Armor School and the armor boards were located there, and Fort Knox had the largest collection of armor officers, NCOs, staff, and civilian technicians.

On the recommendation of my staff, however, I decided not to conduct the test at Fort Knox. For one thing, we at OTEA wanted to avoid any suspicion that the folks at Fort Knox had been so anxious to get the tank that they had compromised the objectivity of the test. For another, because the range of the tank's guns was so great, safety would have required us to close down a large number of the ranges at Fort Knox. The third reason was tactical. We felt that we needed to conduct the test in terrain and climate conditions entirely different from those at Fort Knox. The fourth, and final, reason was that the real purpose of operational testing is to determine how a piece of equipment performs in the hands of a typical unit. The typical unit, unlike those at Fort Knox, would not have access to the best of everything in terms of armor, such as tank crews, supplies, and maintenance techniques.

In deciding against Fort Knox, I had the unqualified support of Dutch Kerwin, the Army chief of staff, and the secretary of the Army. But the decision infuriated some in the armor community. Matters were exacerbated because I had not attended the armor school and was relatively new to the business of armor. My detractors chose to ignore the fact that I had just finished serving as the commander of the newest armored division.

Never dreaming that the XM1 tank would become the M1 Abrams and be used to fight in the deserts of Iraq and Kuwait, we decided to conduct the OT2 at Fort Bliss in Texas and the nearby White Sands Missile Range in New Mexico. We chose Fort Bliss in part because the 3rd Armored Cavalry Regiment, an armor unit we could train to use the tank, was stationed at Fort Bliss. The missile range, whose desert sands and heat were a far cry from the environment at Fort Knox, provided an appropriately hostile environment.

So we moved the tank and the testing apparatus to Fort Bliss. I also moved Lt. Col. Steve Bettner, whom I viewed as a trusted officer and who had worked with me at Fort Campbell and in Vietnam. He was my point of contact with the program manager (PM), the tank developers, and the testing community.

The desert environment helped us detect and correct some deficiencies with the XM1 that we never would have discovered at Fort Knox. We found that the tank had a filtration system that handled dirt and dust poorly. We also found that the wrong sort of oil was being used in the tank.

The tank also created a need for another piece of new equipment, specially a replacement for the M113 APC. Because infantry and armor complement each other, it did not do the Army much good to have a tank that could go forty-five miles per hour and shoot on the move if the infantry vehicle could not keep up. What was needed was a vehicle that could keep up with the new tank, that could carry the requisite number of people, and that also had proper communications equipment and armor thick enough to withstand small arms fire.

The MICV—the Mechanized Infantry Combat Vehicle—was designed to replace the M113. The vehicle had been in the making many years and was at Fort Benning undergoing troop testing at the same time my group was testing the XMI. Walt Hollis had held serious reservations about the MICV for quite some time. He and I took a trip to Fort Benning in the spring of 1977 to observe the new APC's operational test.

After we saw it in action, Walt and I both realized that the MICV was not the vehicle the Army needed. It was not combat-reliable, its maintenance requirements were extraordinary, and its training requirements were onerous. I knew I could never recommend the Army's purchase of the MICV, so I ordered a halt to its testing.

This was a major decision, and I called Dutch Kerwin to discuss it. When I got him on the phone I said, "Sir, I'm down at Fort Benning, and I just stopped the MICV test because I don't think it is going to work." General Kerwin said, "Okay. What are some of the conditions?" After I explained, he said, "You are the commander of OTEA. Good." He accepted my word that the MICV was inadequate, and it went back to the drawing board, eventually to be replaced by the Bradley Fighting Vehicle that the Army still uses today. Kerwin's confidence in my decision set the tone for how I operated from then on.

Based on what I and my OTEA team saw in the filed, I blocked the fielding "as is" of a large truck called the 903 because it was road-bound; it had to be modified so that it was effective in areas that had no roads. We stopped testing of a replacement for the infantry M60 mortar because under certain circumstances it required the gunner to use both hands. During periods of reduced visibility, the gunner would presumably have had to hold a flashlight in his mouth. Our incredulous looks at the PM as we asked whether he really expected our soldiers to do this brought no response. He did not bother to say that these machinations could be done during the daytime. He knew better.

This brings up the subject of the PM, the Army officer who was responsible for shepherding a piece of equipment from the drawing board to the battlefield. The PM is normally assigned to the agency that develops, procures, maintains, and, finally, decertifies matériel. He or she has a vested interest in selling a widget to the Army. It was my experience that the vast majority of PMs were honorable, professional soldiers who were interested in producing the best possible equipment. But there were a rare few who considered OTEA to be the enemy, and who wanted so badly to have the Army choose the equipment that they were willing to compromise their principles.

Because we felt so strongly about the need to preserve objectivity, we started politicking for an operations and acquisition corps that was charged with acquisition from an operational testing standpoint. The Army established just such a corps in January 1990.

Another important change my OTEA team brought about was identifying and correcting problems well before things had progressed beyond the design and prototype phase. It seemed obvious to me that we might avoid significant costs and delays if the soldiers who would use the proposed equipment were consulted earlier in the development process. Eventually, then–TRADOC commander Gen. Donn Starry was able to convince equipment manufacturers to allow soldiers to work with the engineers when the equipment was being designed and assembled. This practice started with tanks, and it turned out to be very successful.

While I was commander of the 1st Cavalry Division at Fort Hood, the commander of the Israeli armor forces, Major General Musha Peled, had visited. Senior military officials from foreign countries routinely visit U.S. military installations for orientation purposes. Since Fort Hood is the largest Army base in the United States, with two of the four armored divisions, and Major General Musha Peled was a tanker, his visit made all the sense in the world.

We hit it off right off the bat, and he invited me to Tel Aviv. I appreciated his invitation, but as commander of the 1st Cav, there was no way that I could go, due to time constraints and my duties. I was not an ambassador.

I could seriously consider his invitation when I became commander of OTEA, however. My team was interested in how other countries conducted their testing, so I contacted Musha, thinking I might learn something on a trip to Israel. He said, "By all means. You come over here to Tel Aviv, and we

In the center, from left to right: Major General Peled and me. (Author collection)

Israeli soldiers and me. (Author collection)

General Gur and me. (Author collection)

will show you." (As an aside, we had a pretty good idea of how the Israelis tested their equipment. For example, if they wanted to test a gun system, they just pointed it at the "bad guys" and shot!)

I left for Israel in the early spring of 1977, accompanied by Walt Hollis, 1st Sgt. Harvey Gough, and Maj. Henry A. "Buzz" Kievenaar.

Harvey had been a very good friend of the 1st Cav at Fort Hood, and he had recently become a National Guard civilian. He asked if he could come along, and I said sure as long as he paid his own way. Harvey also had to abide by an additional stipulation. He is prone to be outspoken and to press an issue until it cannot be pressed any more. I had seen him in action many times by then, so I said, "When I say, 'Okay. That's it. Stop!' I mean it. I will lay the ground rules." He agreed.

Buzz had been Bob Shoemaker's aide-de-camp while Shoemaker had been the commander of the 1st Cavalry Division. Now, Buzz was a student at the CGSC at Leavenworth.

Musha had laid out the red carpet in Israel. We had complete freedom to travel as we saw fit. We were taken from the Golan Heights up in the northeast corner of Israel down to the Sinai Peninsula, and we were also privileged to have an audience with Mordecai Gur, the chief of staff of the Israeli Defense Forces. The Israelis were very open and forthcoming, and we learned a lot.

However, there was one question they would not answer. They would not tell us how many tank transporters they had. When they were fighting their many wars, the Israelis were always able to get tanks in front of their forces, whether it was in Egypt down in the south, Lebanon to the north, Syria off to the northeast, or Jordan in the east. We had always wondered how they moved their tanks so quickly. The tanks could not possibly be driven overland that fast.

We strongly suspected that when the need arose, the Israeli military tapped into every piece of equipment in Israel that could move a tank. An Army heavy equipment transporter today could very well have been a civilian truck last week. It could be painted purple, green, or any other color. All that mattered was whether it could carry a tank.

That same spring, I learned that my brother Joe was very sick.

He and I had not grown closer over the years since our father's death. The divide that existed when we were youths remained into adulthood despite Dad's deathbed wish that we take care of each other. Joe made it clear that he wanted me to leave him alone to live his life as he saw fit. I thought he partied too much, smoked too much, and was not the family man that I thought he should be. But who was I to judge?

Our lives had taken different paths. He had worked in the U.S. Post Office in Philadelphia and had taught for a while in the city's public school system. I had eventually redeemed myself with Dad, who was disappointed when I left Muhlenberg College and failed to fulfill his dream of having a son who was a doctor. Dad let go of his disappointment gradually as I rose through the ranks of the Army. He was proud of me in the end.

Joe did not resent my professional success, but he was not enthusiastic about it either. I wish things had been different.

I did not know that Joe was gravely ill until I got word that he had signed himself into Philadelphia's Veterans Administration hospital. He had been diagnosed with lung cancer, and the prospects of his beating it were not good.

I went to see Joe at the hospital, and it was clear that he was not going to make it. I was sad and worried about Mom, who faced the situation every parent dreads—the prospect of losing a child. In a perfect world, children would never predecease their parents. Ours is not a perfect world. Joe died on 14 March 1977.

Mom took his death hard. Even though she was a believer and had been a pillar in our church, she fell prey to a charlatan who capitalized on her grief and despair.

To my surprise, I learned that Mom had been paying money to a shady character in Philadelphia who had promised, for a fee, to help her communicate with Joe. I was finally able to talk some sense into her and make her stop that nonsense by telling her she was wasting the inheritance that she had planned for her grandchildren.

Rumors started flying in the summer of 1978 that I was going to be promoted to lieutenant general. I did not harbor any great expectations, but Arthur Gregg, another black Army officer, had been promoted to lieutenant general in July. Art and I had been on the same list for promotion to brigadier general in 1972.

In August Louise, Renee, Wes, and I took a rare family vacation. We went to a small National Guard camp post in West Virginia and stayed in its VIP quarters. We thoroughly enjoyed the time together. We had no television and no telephone, but we could fish in a nearby pond. It was very relaxing, and we relished our privacy.

We had planned on staying for five days. But on the second day, we had an unexpected visitor. A young white national guardsman came by our cabin. When I answered the door, he said, "I'm looking for General Becton." I thought his eyes were going to pop out of his head when I replied, "You're talking to him." Whoever had sent him to find me had obviously forgotten to tell him that the General Becton he was looking for was a black man.

After he collected himself the young man delivered the message: "You are to be at the chief of staff's office in the morning." Louise, Renee, and Wes drove me to the nearest airport, and I flew back to D.C.

Gen. Bernard Rogers, a Rhodes Scholar, was the Army chief of staff at that time. I was a bit apprehensive about being summoned to see him because I had crossed him a few times. The first was when he had ordered the elimination of the 1st Cav's colored berets. General Rogers was not for berets at all. I got rid of the colors but kept the berets.

The second was when my medical battalion commander was transferred and a Medical Service Corps officer was assigned as his replacement. I wrote a strongly worded note appealing the decision because I thought it was critical to have a medical doctor in command of my medics when we went to war, not someone who specialized in medical administration. Then I found out that General Rogers himself had made the decision. His office called and reminded me that I was a two-star division commander and had no right to challenge the four-star FORSCOM commander. I said, "Yes, Sir. Understood."

Then there was the time at Fort Hood when I was the director for a joint exercise involving the Army, Navy, Marine Corps, and Air Force. We had done an excellent job, and I felt really good about the day. I stopped by my garrison headquarters to check on something, and my staff officer told me General Rogers had called while we were out in the field and he wanted me to call back. I finally reached him at 0130. General Rogers made it clear that he had not called me, asked me if I knew what time it was, and hung up. I thought, "Well, there goes your career, Becton."

The next morning, General Rogers called me. When I picked up the phone, I could hear him but he could not hear me. Finally, I wrote him a letter explaining why I had called at 1:30 AM and how the telephone connection had failed. We eventually found out what had happened. On the day of the joint exercises, a call had come in from Alaska. Instead of two-way communication, they used back-and-forth, where people speak one at a time using terms like "Roger, over," which means "I have received the message and it's now your turn to talk," and "Wilco," which means "I will comply." The message was erroneously translated to mean that General Rogers had called and wanted to talk to me.

I recalled all these incidents as I entered General Rogers' office with some trepidation. The first thing he said was "I want to tell you that we have selected you to command VII Corps." I was elated. The assignment came with three stars and meant I would be the first black man in the history of the United States to command a corps!

I was admonished by General Rogers that I could not tell anyone outside of my immediate family about the promotion. Before it became official, my promotion would first have to be approved by Congress. Then the host country to VII Corps, West Germany, would have to be notified.

The promotion became effective on 31 October 1978.

Gen. George Blanchard, the commander of U.S. Army forces in Europe, happened to be visiting the United States when news that I would assume command of VII Corps became public. I had known Blanchard from our

days at the IOAC at Fort Benning when I was a young captain and he, a lieutenant colonel, was the second most senior student in our class. Blanchard
invited me to come to Germany with him to observe the ongoing Return of
U.S. Forces to Germany (REFORGER) exercise. REFORGERs were major
exercises that were conducted annually during which entire divisions were
moved to Germany. Blanchard wanted me to see the challenges of running
the exercise since my corps would be conducting a winter REFORGER in
February 1979.

When I returned from observing the exercise, Louise and I had three
weeks of language training in the U.S. Department of State language
program. One of the requirements for going to Europe as a commanding
officer is being able to speak the language of the host country at least halt-
ingly. Louise had taken German in high school, and I had completed three
semesters at Muhlenberg College. But my instructor had concentrated on
reading and writing, not speaking. We both had to work really hard to attain
some fluency.

When the movers came to our house at Fort Myer and started loading the
truck, we noticed that our cat Pisces was missing. We looked and looked, but
we could not find *her*. Renee was in tears. She was beginning her freshman
year at Lafayette University in Pennsylvania and had come home to see us
off to Germany. Now we could not find her cat. We had just about given
up when we got a telephone call from the warehouse where our household
items were being temporarily stored. The workers in the warehouse had
heard strange noises, investigated, and found Pisces under our sofa.

Our send-off from OTEA was memorable. We have come and gone
many times over the years, but this departure was particularly touching.
Louise and I had made quite a few friends while we were stationed at Fort
Myer, and a number of them assembled at Dulles Airport to extend their well
wishes. After we had bid farewell, we boarded a plane bound for Frankfurt,
Germany. The traveling Becton clan had shrunk considerably to Louise
and me, Wes, Mom Thornton, Pisces the cat, and Morton the dog. Shirley,
Karen, and Joyce were all married, and Renee was in college.

Maj. Bob Higgins, my appointed aide-de-camp, met us at Rhein-
Main Airport. Since Mom Thornton's mobility was impaired, Higgins
had arranged for a wheelchair to carry her from the plane to our ground
transportation. When we were about to get in the vehicles that would drive
us to our quarters in Stuttgart, we realized that we were one person short.
Mom Thornton was nowhere to be found. She turned up safe and sound

a bit later; her wheelchair had to take a different route than the one we had followed. But I am sure the intervening moments seemed like an eternity for Major Higgins.

Then we began the two-and-a-half-hour drive to Stuttgart. The countryside was as scenic as I had remembered it. I marveled once again at how clean the Germans kept their country. I think it is a matter of national pride.

We were all tired, and we arrived none too soon. Kelley Barracks, a quaint little Army post on the outskirts of Stuttgart, was the headquarters for VII Corps. The architecture was distinctively German. All the buildings were either brick or stucco and had steep colored roofs. The base was able to house about one-half of the 250 headquarters staff. There were approximately twenty-five single-family homes for the senior staff officers and senior enlisted, and apartment-type housing was available for junior officers and other enlisted. The rest of the headquarters staff lived on the economy. There was also an officers' club, an enlisted club, a bowling alley, and a gymnasium.

Our house was one of the nicest we had ever lived in. It was white stucco and had flower boxes that were filled with blooming perennials. On the ground floor it had a large foyer, a large kitchen and pantry, a small bedroom beyond the kitchen that Mom Thornton slept in, a dining room large enough to seat twenty-four people, a living room with a fireplace, a sunroom that led out to a small patio, one full bathroom, and a powder room. There were two full bathrooms on the second floor, one of which was located in the master bedroom. The house also had a full basement and a one-car garage.

I assumed command of VII Corps from the outgoing commander, Lt. Gen. Dave Ott, on 28 October 1978. General Blanchard had made it known that he expected all incoming commanders to give part of their speech in the language of the host country. I had practiced and practiced and finally had it down pat. I could switch with ease from English to German and back. The speech went beautifully that day. Too well, in fact. When the ceremony was over, and I was the commander of VII Corps, the German media descended upon me, asking questions in German. I had memorized my speech, but I did not have a clue what the reporters were saying.

This episode taught me a lesson I have never forgotten: Never try to be something that you are not.

CHAPTER THIRTEEN

★ ★ ★

Jayhawkland

About three weeks after I assumed command of VII Corps, which had been nicknamed "Jayhawk," I received a telephone call from Maj. Gen. Jim Hamlet, deputy inspector general (IG) for the Army. Jim, the third black general in the U.S. Army, was a very good friend. But he was not calling me just to say hello. Amidst the squeaks and cracks on his secure line, I distinctly heard, "Julius, I've got some bad news. I am sending over two colonels to investigate you." I did not have a clue what this was about.

It turned out that someone had complained about the fact that I had permitted someone who had no need to know to sit in on a classified briefing. My old friend Harvey Gough, who had accompanied me to Israel when I was at OTEA, had surprised me by coming from Texas to attend my assumption of command ceremony. After the ceremony, I was given a general defense plan briefing on where all the U.S. forces were located, what they were going to do, and so forth. I saw no problem in letting Harvey sit in. He was a national guardsman, after all, and he had the requisite security clearance.

The two colonels from the IG's office grilled me and everyone else associated with the briefing: Who was this Gough? Why did I do this? Why did I do that?

The investigation took place in December, but I did not get the results until June. I was at a quarterly commanders' meeting in Heidelberg, and when it was over, Gen. Fritz Kroesen, my new boss, said he wanted to see me. He was standing behind his desk when I entered his office. "I just got word from Washington that I am supposed to chew your ass," he said. I replied, "Yes, sir," and waited to be upbraided. He kept looking at me. I looked back at him. Finally, he asked, "What are you waiting for, Becton?" "Yes, sir," I said, and saluted and walked out. That was the end of the investigation.

I have often mused about what happened when the investigators from the IG's office interviewed Harvey Gough. I am sure they came away with the inescapable conclusion that legend had him pegged right. Harvey is an exceedingly generous and patriotic fellow who is part of the institution of the Army. He knows most of the former and current senior leadership on a personal basis, including the chiefs of staff. Everybody has heard about Harvey Gough. Everybody also knows that he is a certified nut.

Harvey is a native Texan, and, in typical Texas fashion, he does everything bigger and better than anyone else. He was long the proprietor of Goff Burgers, which served the best hamburgers in Dallas and had a ten-foot-tall statue of Vladimir Lenin in front. Harvey had liberated the statue from Odessa, Ukraine, and he mounted a plaque on it bearing the simple message "America won."

Harvey has nerves of steel. When armed robbers attempted to stick up Goff Burgers some years ago, Harvey dropped down behind the counter and let off a couple of rounds from his .357 Magnum. The robbers fled, much to the relief, I am sure, of then–Texas Gov. Bill Clements, who happened to be in Goff Burgers at the time.

After 11 September 2001, when the United States went to war to find Osama bin Laden, Harvey solicited donations from Dallas businesses and took one thousand full-course steak dinners to our troops in Afghanistan. He also cooked the steak dinners and served them to the troops.

Harvey also went to Baghdad not long ago. Gen. Tommy Franks, then overall commander of the forces in Iraq, is a good friend of Harvey's, but Franks had told Harvey not to come. Franks had been emphatic, saying, "Don't come here. I don't want you here. I don't want you in the way. I don't want you here at all." The general's words fell on deaf ears. As proof of that, there is a picture of Harvey, in the flesh, standing in front of Baghdad International Airport with a sign that says, "Hi, Tommy; I'm here."

Another interesting guest at my assumption of command ceremony was Manfred Rommel, who was then the mayor (*Oberburgermeister*) of Stuttgart and the son of Field Marshal Erwin Rommel, one of the greatest German generals of World War II. Field Marshal Rommel was not a Nazi. He was a professional soldier and a brilliant strategist. As commander of the Deutsches Afrikakorps (German Africa Corps), the field marshal constantly improvised to outsmart his enemies, a tactic that earned him his well-deserved nickname, the Desert Fox.[1]

Left to right: Gen. George Blanchard, *Oberburgermeister* Rommel, and me. (Author collection)

The field marshal's son and I became good friends, and I was privileged to hear from Manfred a personal account of his father's death. As is now widely known, Field Marshal Rommel was given the Hobson's choice of taking a cyanide capsule or standing trial for complicity in a plot to assassinate Hitler. Both choices meant certain death. Rommel chose the cyanide.

It was very moving to hear Manfred Rommel tell this story. At the time of his father's death, Manfred was fifteen years old and a soldier in north Germany. Hitler ordered Manfred home to be with his mother and to say farewell to his father. I do not think I would call this generosity. To me, it seems more like wanton cruelty. I cannot imagine how that young man must have felt, knowing his father was going to die and being powerless to prevent it.

As mayor of Stuttgart, Manfred Rommel was an outstanding supporter of U.S. forces. He hosted a meeting for all incoming American soldiers once a month, welcoming them to his city and briefing them about Stuttgart and Germany. His English was impeccable.

He was very sensitive to the needs of American soldiers, white and black, and he tolerated no foolishness from the citizens of Stuttgart. For example, if a taxicab refused to pick up a soldier and the soldier lodged a complaint, my staff got word back to the *Oberburgermeister*. Shortly thereafter, the discriminating cab company would be visited by safety inspectors, who would check its fleet to make sure all its vehicles were up to code. Similarly, if a restaurant refused to serve a soldier, the entrepreneur would find himself being greeted by a member of the sanitation department.

On 14 October 1979, Louise and I accompanied the Rommels to Ulm, where Field Marshal Rommel is buried. Once a year a few hundred people, mostly members of the Afrikakorps and local German military units, gathered at his gravesite in a solemn ceremony of remembrance. Louise and I were the only non-Germans present. The following year I presented a wreath on behalf of the American government.

I had initially encountered some opposition to making the presentation because Field Marshal Rommel had been an enemy of the United States. However, I was finally able to bring the opposition around to my point of view. I could see no harm in the gesture because it spoke to Rommel's expertise as a professional soldier.

Unlikely as it may seem, Manfred Rommel also befriended George S. Patton, son of the legendary American general who had been the senior Rommel's archenemy, when George was deputy commander of VII Corps. Both Manfred and he had been born on Christmas Eve, and the two took to celebrating their birthday together.

I think my coming to VII Corps caused George some consternation. He had every expectation that he would become the next commander, and when the assignment went to me, instead—an "old buddy" and competitor—it was a real shock. But when I reported in, he congratulated me and pledged his support.

I believe George aspired to the greatness of his father and mimicked his father's behavior in certain aspects. For example, during maneuvers or training exercises, he never had the top up on his jeep, no matter how miserable the weather. He would have the windshield up, but not the top. That is what his father did. But unbeknownst to most people, George had a heater under the dashboard so that he and the driver were pretty warm. His poor aide-de-camp, sitting in the back seat, did not fare as well.

Like the elder Patton, George was strong-willed and opinionated, which are not bad traits. I am strong-willed myself. However, George and I did not have time to butt heads. I had been at corps headquarters less than two months when he came to see me one day and said, "Sir, I'd like permission to go back to the States. I think it'd be probably best for you and me if I were to do that." I said, "General Patton, if that's your call, I will check."

So I went to see my boss, Gen. George Blanchard. Blanchard agreed to George's departure. Word came back from Washington in fairly short order that George's request to be reassigned had been approved.

Shortly after Christmas of 1978, George sent his wife Joanne and son Ben back to the United States. He remained in Germany to participate in the February REFORGER exercises. After the REFORGER was over, George came back to see me, and took me by surprise. "Sir, I like the way you operate," he said. "I'd like to change my mind. I'd like to stay here." Once again I called General Blanchard. I will never forget Blanchard's response: "Hell no. He's gotta go."

George Patton was the kind of soldier with whom I would want to serve in combat. So was Maj. Gen. Will Latham, who replaced George, and so was Maj. Gen. Dick Boyle, who replaced Will. I had a truly extraordinary staff during my command of VII Corps, many of whom were later promoted beyond the grade they held while in my command.

There are far too many to mention, but they included Maj. Gen. Fred Mahaffey, commander of the 3rd Infantry Division, and Maj. Gen. Glenn Otis, commander of the 1st Armored Division, both of whom later were promoted to four stars. So was John Shalikashvili, the commander in charge of the artillery in the 1st Armored Division, who years later succeeded Colin Powell as chairman of the Joint Chiefs of Staff.

When I had to replace my outgoing G-3, I chose Gordon Sullivan, who was then a lieutenant colonel recently selected for promotion to colonel. It was an unusual choice since the G-3 should normally be a serving colonel. But I had worked with Gordon before, and I had no doubt about his ability to do the job. My staff and commanders tried to change my mind almost en masse. I finally had to remind them that I was the commander and would do what I damn well pleased. And within one month all the naysayers were singing Gordon's praises. He later retired as Chief of Staff of the Army.

There were many other exceedingly talented officers who worked with me in VII Corps. I have often joked that when the powers that be saw that I was going to be the commander, they knew I needed help and gave me the best they had to make it work.

For the first five or six months that I was at VII Corps, I spent a lot of time visiting my subordinate commanders. I wanted to see them firsthand on their turf and give them an opportunity to hear a bit about my philosophy of command.

VII Corps, located in the German states of Baden-Württemburg and Bavaria, covered an area twice the size of South Carolina. Fortunately, General Blanchard, the Europe commander in chief, had a train that was available to the two corps commanders. It was a single-engine train that had rather plush self-contained living and dining quarters that were comparable to those in first class of any train in the United States today. And it had once belonged to Adolf Hitler. When Louise and I first boarded, I knew Hitler just had to be rolling over in his Aryan grave at the thought that such "inferior" human beings were occupying his quarters.

During the first tour I made of VII Corps forces, I traveled by train from Stuttgart to the northernmost unit in my command, which was the 3rd Infantry Division. I then swung south, eventually reaching the 1st Armored Division, and returned home by way of Augsburg, which was the site of the corps artillery headquarters commanded by Brig. Gen. Harvey Williams. All in all, it took us five or six days to cover the command.

I believe the trip was productive. I had accomplished what I had set out to do, and I believe my subordinate commanders felt pretty good about my going out to see them. My talking points, which I described in chapter 11, came in handy in helping me to explain my philosophy of command. I also had some help from a management tool known as the Transition Model. Maj. Sam Morton, one of the VII Corps organization effectiveness officers, acted as my consultant.

The Transition Model is designed to reduce an incoming boss's downtime by improving communications with staff, enabling the boss and staff to get to know each other better personally, giving the boss the big picture (e.g., identifying issues, educating the boss on how the team operates, spelling out expectations of how time can be spent most productively), and giving staff the new boss' philosophy, vision, and priorities.

Under the model, the first step in the transition process is having a consultant conduct a series of forty-five-minute interviews with all the participants. The purpose is to gather information for the new boss, as well as for team members. That information should include everyone's hopes, fears, concerns, and priorities and what the organization should continue to do, start to do, or stop doing. It should also include the boss's leadership

Secretary of the Army Clifford Alexander and me on one of my visits to Washington while commanding VII Corps. (U.S. Army)

style, methods, expectations, and aspirations, and it should pass on the team's "street wisdom" about the organization. The information-gathering interviews are designed to help shape the agenda for the first forty-five to ninety days under the new leader.

The Transitional Model had been developed at the Army's Organization Effectiveness School. The information gathered was given to the commander who requested the assessment and was used as the commander deemed appropriate for his or her introduction to the command.

Simply stated, the Transition Model works. I have continued to use it—and to employ Sam Morton as a consultant—in all the posts I have held since I commanded VII Corps.

VII Corps was very different from my previous commands because of the sheer number of people under my command. The corps consisted of about eighty-eight thousand soldiers. The 1st Cav at Fort Hood, with some twelve thousand troops, was a far distant second.

Both VII Corps and V Corps, which was headquartered in Frankfurt, were NATO forces, with signal brigades, air defense, and other support units. To my south was the II German Korps. To the north of V Corps was the III German Korps, and the British were to the north of the III German Korps. I reported to an American general who wore two hats, commanding both the U.S. and NATO forces. My boss reported to a German general in charge of Allied Forces Central Europe, and the German, in turn, was under the Supreme Allied Commander in Europe, headquartered in Belgium.

The sole purpose of the REFORGER exercise was to give U.S. forces an opportunity to train with the people with whom they would go to war. Pretty much all eighty-eight thousand people in VII Corps participated. Because we did not have enough units of our own in Germany, the rest of the 1st Infantry Division were brought from the United States to join the 1st Infantry Division Forward, which was already in country and under my command permanently. At a certain time in our emergency alert escalation, we were to receive the German 12th Panzer Division, which, assigned to VII Corps, would fill the gap between V and VII Corps.

The REFORGER exercise I directed began in February 1979 and lasted several weeks. The first major effort was to make sure the forces could draw their equipment from in-country, prepositioned storage sites. The real exercise began once the equipment had been drawn and the forces had moved to their assembly areas. As exercise director, I controlled both the good guys and the bad guys. The aggressor force was the 2nd Armored Cavalry Regiment, and the friendly force was the rest of VII Corps.

Bob Wagner, commander of the 2nd Armored Cavalry Regiment, was the sort of commander I would have liked to have been out front leading the way if we were on the road to Moscow. As the aggressor, Bob would move his forces at night so the friendly forces could not detect them, even though night movement was prohibited during the exercise. Bob is fiercely competitive, and he played to win.

But we were not on the road to Moscow, and the commanders of the friendly forces also wanted to win. They thought Bob's night movement was not playing fair, and they were really peeved when they could not detect his forces at the beginning of each day. One evening near midnight, I called a halt to the exercise. All of the commanders were assembled, and I made myself very clear: "One more violation, and somebody's gonna get fired." Needless to say, the night movements ceased.

Louise and General Haig at his departure ceremony. (U.S. Army)

When we started the REFORGER, the ground was frozen. Then, halfway through the exercise, the weather turned warm, the ground thawed, and we started tearing up German crops. Several thousand vehicles and more than three hundred tanks weighing seventy tons each can do a lot of damage to the countryside. The result is called maneuver damage, and it is very costly because the U.S. government had to pay the Germans for the crops that were torn up during the REFORGER exercise. We had to terminate the exercise early, at great expense. Continuing was economically infeasible.

There was some pulling of rank over who would actually terminate the exercise. As corps commander and exercise director, I thought I should terminate the REFORGER. General Blanchard said he should do it. Ultimately, neither one of us put an end to the exercise. In the midst of the discussion, Gen. Alexander Haig, the Supreme Allied Commander in Europe, came to visit VII Corps. Because Haig, a fellow graduate of Lower Merion High School and someone I had known for years, was the top dog, it was he who finally terminated the REFORGER.

There was a change of command at Heidelberg during the summer of 1979. Gen. Fritz Kroesen replaced Gen. George Blanchard as the commander in chief. Haig left at about the same time, and Bernie Rogers replaced him as the Supreme Allied Commander in Europe.

Helmut Schmidt, the chancellor of West Germany, invited me and other major commanders to the farewell reception for General Haig. It was a major ceremony and protocol was supposed to reign. As we were seated at the large dining table, Louise and I were assigned to a protocol position higher than General and Mrs. Kroesen. There was nothing I could do about it. We sat where they told us to sit.

General Haig glanced over and smiled at me. He knew exactly what was happening. I was not amused, and although he did not make any comment about it—he was a soldier—I do not believe General Kroesen was either.

I had gotten to know quite a few people by this time. Being a black American and a three-star general, I was an oddity. When I first arrived in Stuttgart, the German press repeatedly referred to me as "the black corps commander." However, I had traveled so extensively throughout West Germany and Louise and I had benefited so much from Manfred Rommel's policy toward American servicemen that we became accepted anywhere we went. And after we had been in Germany for about thirteen months, the public affairs folks informed us that the German press now referred to me simply as "the corps commander."

Among the many people who made Louise and me feel welcome was Franz Josef Strauss, who had been the West German minister of defense and was then president of Bavaria. All German states consider themselves to be equal, but Bavaria considers itself more equal than the others. It is the only state with its own president and, for all practical purposes, its own language. A person from northern Germany would have a difficult time understanding a Bavarian, and a Bavarian could not care less. Bavarians are very independent people, kind of like Texans in the United States.

Strauss was a big, roly-poly fellow, a very hail-fellow-well-met gentleman. At any social gathering he attended, Strauss was in charge, and he always welcomed Louise and me with some fanfare. As we walked in Strauss would stop the music, have the trumpets play—"Da, Da, Da, Da"—and then say, to applause, "Ladies and gentlemen, we now have the U.S. VII Corps commander and his lovely wife." This was quite an ego boost, and we enjoyed it.

I still made an occasional misstep. On one occasion after an exercise involving different countries, there was a press conference, and General

Kroesen asked me to represent him. It was a fairly large press conference. I came into the room dressed in my battle attire, walked up to the podium, and introduced myself. "I'm Julius Becton, commander of VII Corps," I said. Then someone asked, "How do you spell that?" I said, "Julius, just like in Caesar. Becton, B as in boy, *E-C-T-O-N*."

The next morning at least one French newspaper reported that I thought I was Caesar.

While I was at VII Corps, we undertook a number of new initiatives. One of them involved computers. The machines were gargantuan and unwieldy in 1980, and also nowhere nearly as powerful as they are today. But there were some visionary people who were beginning to see how useful computers could be.

One of them was Gordon Sullivan, who definitely had a talent for thinking outside the box. Working with a computer wizard named Maj. A. J. Foyt, Sullivan came up with an exercise simulation for VII Corps using computers. While computer simulations are now routine, they were a real innovation in 1980. The exercise, called Cold Reason, was a computer-generated war game of our general defense plan.

We assembled all our major commanders in the gymnasium at Kelley Barracks and laid out on the floor a map of the area in which we would fight. The enemy forces—East Germans, Poles, Hungarians, and Russians—were depicted in front of the commanders' units. The commanders were then asked to plot their positions on the map. We then input the information about the initial lineup of forces, our weapons and ammunition, and every-thing else that could be germane to the action into the computer.

Our intelligence folks had fed additional information into the computer before we even started the exercise with the commanders. This allowed us to play possible scenarios, to see "If they do that, this is going to happen." "If they do this, that is going to happen." We tried to examine every conceivable response we might make to the enemy's actions.

At the end of every hour or so, we stopped the action and got a computer printout of what had happened. Then I went to each commander, from the front to the rear, asking, "Okay, what are your actions and orders based upon what you know?" Then we cranked our next move into the computer, and the process was repeated, with me continually querying each commander about his actions and orders.

We conducted this simulation for a day and a half, and it was an over-whelming success. Face-to-face communication is invaluable. We had the benefit of being able to really pick the unit commanders' brains because they were all in the same building under one roof.

A commander also learns a lot from visiting the troops on their own turf. Something I learned from the VII Corps armor garrison in the town of Bölingen led to some rather dramatic reforms in the way VII Corps did business.

The first time I visited the compound at Bölingen, I beheld a very odd sight. The trees were full of boots, like Christmas ornaments. Hanging up the boots, I learned, was the soldiers' way of saying, "I've got my orders, and I am going home." Aside from the time and effort to clean them up, the treed boots did not cause any harm. But another Bölingen custom was consider-ably more disturbing. If a woman showed up anywhere on the compound, the male soldiers would hoot and holler, catcalling her wherever she went. It did not matter if she was a soldier, family member, or visitor. This was pure and unadulterated sexual harassment.

Part of the problem was a pervasive culture of machismo. But there was also the fact that our female service members were then segregated from the male troops. Women were housed in special barracks called "WAC shacks" in the vernacular. When a unit was out in the field, women were lodged in a special section cordoned off with barbed wire. In the eyes of too many male soldiers, the special treatment demonstrated that the female soldiers could not cut it and should not be around them.

The situation at Bölingen reminded me of what I had seen happening at the women's quarters at Fort Hood. Integrating women into their units had helped put an end to sexist behavior in Texas. I saw no reason why it would not work in Bölingen.

So I ordered that the barracks be integrated. Room assignments alter-nated by sex, so that in any given row, the first room would be for a male, the next for a female, the next for a male, and so on. There were separate bathrooms for men and women. To no one's surprise, the hoots and hollers stopped, and sexual harassment was significantly reduced. The men and women were comrades who just happened to be of different genders.

Still, integrating U.S. Army barracks was virtually unheard of in 1980, so naturally some eyebrows were raised. Despite suggestions in some quarters that I was compromising the morals of our young men and women, I was eventually vindicated. By 1984, Army barracks were completely integrated.

In the spring of that same year, my staff and I decided to tackle some broader questions involving all women in the military, not just the ones in uniform, but also the Army Department civilians such as teachers, nurses, and family members. I had been concerned about how the Army was using them and how they were treated ever since I was a brigade commander—and for good reason.

To get to the root of some of the issues facing women, we conducted a symposium on women's issues. We started by soliciting input from the sergeants major. They all had units that included women or dealt with women in their area, and having them on our side was half the battle; they could ensure the support of their commanders and help enlist the coop- eration of community organizations. We also solicited input from major organizations such as the U.S. dependents' schools, the Red Cross, and the NCOs' and officers' clubs.

As a framework for our information gathering we posed three questions: 1) What are we doing that we should not be doing? 2) What are we doing that we should continue to do? 3) What should we be doing to improve the lot of women? The whole purpose of this effort was to sensitize people to women's issues, with the ultimate goal of improving the fighting effective- ness of each unit.

After we had collected and sifted the input from the sergeants major and the various organizations, we identified four key issues: violence against women, images and perceptions, sexual harassment, and upward mobility.

That fall more than two hundred representatives from the various orga- nizations attended a four-day seminar at Nuremburg. Because I had been pulled back to Washington to sit on a general officer selection board, Louise and Will Latham, my deputy commander, ran the seminar. More than one hundred specific issue items requiring action were identified during the seminar. Some were big deals, and some were not so big, depending upon your perspective, but each needed to be addressed. For example, a source of irritation to many people, including my spouse, was the use of the term "dependent" to describe the spouses and children of servicemen and servicewomen; Louise, as she often said, was not dependent on me. We finally convinced the folks in VII Corps to substitute "family member" for "dependent."

We also eliminated some rules that did not make sense. For instance, until we changed the rule, a woman soldier, private or sergeant, who wanted to see an obstetrician-gynecologist first had to go to her first sergeant and announce, "I want to go on sick call." Her sergeant would, of course, want to know why. After she explained and was released to go the dispensary, she had to report in to a medical corpsman, who was usually a man. Again, she would have to ask to see an ob-gyn and tell the medic why. Then she would see a physician's assistant or maybe another corpsperson and go through the same ritual. If she was lucky, the physician's assistant would make an appointment for her with the ob-gyn at the local hospital. We eliminated this nonsense and allowed female soldiers, like family members, to simply pick up a phone and make an appointment.

The treatment of women in matters of employment was another irritant. Because of the existing policies, not too many women had to worry about hitting the glass ceiling. For example, a female family member coming to Europe who had civil service status in the United States lost it when she arrived in Europe and had to start accumulating seniority all over again. And when female family members left Europe and returned to the United States, they could not take their "employment status" with them. They were penalized for coming to Europe, and they were penalized for returning. Either way, they could not win.

Long term, the Army developed a Family Action Plan modeled on the VII Corps women's symposium. Louise was a principal speaker at those gatherings from 1981 to 1984. As she worked on the women's symposium, she had realized that there was a need for standards of living to which family and community members should aspire.

She wanted to emphasize that nonmilitary family members owe a responsibility to their community and to drive home the point that they were not mere appendages of the family member who was on active duty in the military. Ultimately, we developed a philosophy for family members that embraced the following standards:

- I am the community and will become involved.
- I will speak up and speak out.
- Disagreement is not disrespect.
- I will stay informed.
- My spouse's career is not on the line.
- I will contribute my talents to a volunteer group or individual act.

- I will become a better citizen by voting and participating in the political process. (I am still a citizen and I should be voting.)
- I will respect the rights, privileges, and property of others.
- I will conserve energy.

By the time the women's symposium was organized Louise had already learned a great deal about life in the military. She had ample opportunities to see how the wives of some senior officers threw their weight around, lording their husband's position over the wives of junior officers as I was working my way up through the ranks. Louise recoiled against this type of treatment. Why should she—or any other wife, for that matter—have to grovel or be submissive to the wife of a senior officer? Similarly, why should a husband's career depend upon his wife's interactions with the wives of his superiors? His OER should reflect his own performance, not that of his wife.

Louise wanted to clear the air so the wives knew what the ground rules were. She wanted a wife to know that her husband's career should not be affected if she did not join ladies' clubs or participate in coffees and teas. Louise also wanted to give family members the incentive to become full members of the military community and to help foster pride in it. She understood that just as our neighborhoods are only as clean as we keep them, our community is only as good as we make it.

Early on my German counterpart to the south and I discussed ways the allied commanders could get to know each other better. We came up with what we called a senior commander retreat.

The German general sponsored the first retreat, which was held in 1979 in the Alps. We invited all the generals in his command, and I invited all the senior generals in my corps and V Corps. Even though France was not a member of the NATO military alliance, we invited the French commander. We also invited the commander of the Canadian brigade, General John de Chastelain, who later became the chief of staff of all Canadian forces, as well as the Italian northern corps commander, and the Swiss and Austrian senior officers. Although Switzerland and Austria were neutral, their officers agreed to come.

Our spouses accompanied us, and we all wore civilian clothing and drove our own cars. The idea was to avoid attracting attention. I think the French, Swiss, and Austrian officers might have had some difficulty explaining why they were in the Alps with members of the NATO military alliance.

There were no speeches, lectures, or formal programs. We did not talk tactics or strategy. We went for walking tours into the mountains, and had good food and drink. We had a great time, and we really got to know each other. This is really important in the time of war when you are going to put your life on the line. When de Chastelain or anyone else said, "I'm over here. I'm with you," it was important to know he damned well was there.

I hosted the second retreat in 1980 in the Black Forest. The reason I picked the Black Forest—nothing racial—is because the German wife of one of my sergeants major suggested that we use her family's chateau there.

The Black Forest is a wooded mountain region in the southwestern part of Germany. Its name refers to the heavy stands of fir on the upper slopes whose foliage is so thick it actually looks black. The area is filled with upscale villas, specialty shops, and restaurants. Mineral springs are abundant, and the forest boasts such well-known health resorts as Baden-Baden and Bad Wildbad. The villa where the retreat was held even had an indoor firing range in the basement. There were also walking trails and streams where we could fish.

Once again, the retreat, which lasted for two and one-half days, was a smashing success. Including the spouses, about thirty people attended. We all abided by the previous ground rules that there would be no military talk and that we would use the occasion to get to know one another better. The scenery, the facilities, the food, and the amenities were absolutely superb. Everything was free-flowing, and we had a great time.

I suspect that the commanders from the other governments did what I did. I did not tell my higher-ups about the retreat until after it was over because I did not want to run the risk of having someone say that I could not do it. It is often easier to obtain forgiveness than permission.

In December of 1979 Louise and I took a trip to Berlin with our daughter Renee, who was visiting from college. Because Berlin was behind the Iron Curtain in East Germany, our trip ranked as more than a typical tourist outing. And because I was the third most senior American military officer in Germany, our trip was regarded as sensitive. We had to follow protocol, which meant obtaining clearances and giving proper notification to the Russian forces that a senior American officer would be visiting Berlin.

There were eight people in our touring party: Louise, myself, Mom Thornton, Renee, Wes, my pilot, my aide-de-camp, and my driver.

We took the "duty train," a military train that ran between Frankfurt and West Berlin transporting equipment, supplies, and people. The duty train was operated by the Germans but was restricted to U.S. military personnel. It ran overnight, and once en route, it did not stop until it arrived in Frankfurt or Berlin. Because of my senior position and the size of our party, we were assigned to a separate car on the train.

Once we crossed the border between East and West Germany, we were in Russian-controlled territory. However, because we were on the duty train we were treated as if we were on U.S. embassy grounds. After we arrived in Berlin, we had a car that had been set aside for the corps commander's use. We stayed in a very plush villa that had been taken over by U.S. forces after World War II and was being used as VIP quarters.

We had decided to visit a museum in East Berlin that was the site of the World War II surrender signed by the German government and the Allies. I had been advised that no one would object to our outing because of my senior status. However, I was also warned by USAEUR security personnel that when we arrived at the museum, I would immediately recognize a very tall, stern-looking woman in her early forties who was an agent of the KGB, the Russian secret police. I was told that the agent would not say anything to us, but she would follow us everywhere. Sure enough, it all came true. I found it amusing that the Communists did not even try to conceal the fact that they were monitoring all our actions.

We also visited the Soviet War Memorial, where German and Russian soldiers were buried. Contemplating the huge number of war dead buried in the cemetery was sobering, even though they were from armies that had been and were enemies.

And then there was the Berlin Wall, which was truly a sight to behold. I had seen pictures of it in books and magazines and on television, of course, and I knew its infamous history, knew how in 1961, to stem the tide of East Germans escaping through West Berlin, East German police built a barrier between the city's two halves.

But there was nothing like seeing the Berlin Wall up close and personal. Better than any words, the three-foot-thick brick wall with its control towers manned by East German soldiers with machine guns and heavy barbed wire depicted the ideological division between East and West.

Spotlights shone continually to discourage escape under the cover of darkness. There were land mines, too, although we could not see them.

Seeing and sensing all this made me appreciate more than ever the desperation of East Berliners who attempted to escape to a better life.

The Wall finally came down in 1989, and that was cause for jubilation. I have two pieces of the Wall, one of which was presented to me by Gen. Mike Speigelmeir, who served as the last commander of VII Corps. Every time I look at them, I am reminded that brick walls cannot block out ideas or extinguish humans' desire for the individual liberties that we take for granted in the United States.

My mother came for a visit the year after the trip to Berlin, and my best man, Dr. Bob Williams, his wife, Betty, and their youngest son, Bruce, came along. For this visit, Louise and I planned a trip of a different sort.

VII Corps was responsible for the front between West Germany and East Germany and the border between West Germany and Czechoslovakia. That front was comparable to the Berlin Wall in that it was demarcated with a barbed wire fence, land mines, dogs, and, of course, guards armed with machine guns. VII Corps had forces stationed on one side, and the East Germans and Russians were on the other.

Louise and I decided that we would tour the front lines with Bob and his family and my mother. Taking two cars, we started at the northernmost point of the area controlled by VII Corps and wound our way south, stopping to spend the night wherever we happened to be at the time.

In effect, I was visiting my soldiers and the others were just observing. I later learned that we drove the East German and Russian intelligence folks crazy. They detected us early on because we were not hiding, and they carefully tracked our movements. They knew who I was, but they did not know what we were doing, which caused them much heartburn. Our intelligence folks monitoring their communications heard them passing the word, "This general is out here. He's inspecting, and something is going to happen, but we don't know what it is."

This episode made me think of my own distress some time before when my intelligence staff officer informed me that we no longer had spies in East Germany. Our human intelligence capabilities had been cut by Central Intelligence Agency Director Stansfield Turner with the concurrence of the president because he believed electronic intelligence could do the job adequately by itself. Although there was nothing I could do about it, I hit the roof. The truth is that nothing can take the place of human intelligence, which is something the U.S. military has learned again most recently in Afghanistan and Iraq.

Lee Ewing, the publisher of *Army Times*, arranged an interview with me in the spring of 1981. We spent the better part of three hours talking about every conceivable aspect of VII Corps, which was then the largest combat corps in the Army. Eventually, we came to the subject of female soldiers, who were generally in key positions such as MP, signal, military intelligence, and maintenance—positions that would require them to fight if necessary.

I was convinced that pregnancy of single soldiers presented a major problem. About 10 percent of my 80,000-plus-member command was female, so I had the potential to have a large number of pregnant soldiers in my corps. A pregnant female soldier is not, per se, a problem. However, a pregnant female soldier who is not married and is about to become a single parent is definitely a problem because the soldier will not be combat ready. There are no day care centers on a battlefield.

During the interview, I flippantly said that if a single soldier on her first enlistment got pregnant, she had a decision to make. She could abort and remain in the military; carry to term and put her child up for adoption; or leave the military. I said this without any consideration of the moral aspects of abortion. I was speaking solely as a commander of soldiers who must be prepared to fight.

Army Times published the interview on the front page with the headline: "Corps Commander Says Abort or Get Out."[2] Not surprisingly, the article created a furor. The Roman Catholic Church let its displeasure be known all the way up the line, and the Army was forced to distance itself from my statement.

If I had it to do over again I would choose my words more carefully, but I stand by my reasons for making the statement. The pregnancy of unmarried female soldiers was a problem in 1981, and it remains a problem today.

By the time I left Germany, the *Army Times* article had been published. I hoped that the storm it created would blow over, but I confess I did have some doubts about my professional future.

On 29 June 1981, the day of my fifty-fifth birthday, I turned over command of VII Corps to Lt. Gen. Bill Livesey. The farewell celebration consisted of several events throughout the corps area. As Louise and I traveled from one event to another, I felt good about my command and looked back with satisfaction on what I, Louise, and my staff had accomplished militarily and for Army families. Today, with the benefit of 20/20 hindsight, I can see that VII Corps made a significant contribution to winning the Cold War, and I am even prouder of playing a part in that.

CHAPTER FOURTEEN

★ ★ ★

The Final Salute

My new assignment was as deputy commander for training at TRADOC at Fort Monroe. Donn Starry, whom I had known for at least twenty years, was the commander of TRADOC. Starry had convinced the Army chief of staff, Gen. Edward C. "Shy" Meyer, that he needed a second deputy commander for training and that this person should also be the Army inspector of training. I would be the second person in the U.S. Army to hold that position. The first, Baron Friedrich Wilhelm Ludolf Gerhard Augustin von Steuben, had reported to George Washington and is credited with organizing the Continental Army during the American Revolution. I was getting ready to fill some mighty big shoes.

Of course, Baron von Steuben's responsibilities were dramatically different from mine. Much had changed over the intervening two hundred years.

My job was based more on personality than anything else. I had to be able to deal with my own boss, all the other major commanders, and the Army chief of staff. As the Army inspector of training, I met with the chief of staff one-on-one every month. It might have been an awkward situation because I was reporting on my boss's performance, but things worked out fine. I was perceived as objective and fair, and the command climate was such that everyone felt comfortable.

Major TRADOC responsibilities included developing training doctrine for the Army, coordinating combat development efforts, and publishing "How to Fight Manuals" dealing with the requirements and operational capabilities of new equipment. While the Army Materiel Command is charged with developing a piece of equipment, it is TRADOC's job to supply the language to teach soldiers how to use the new equipment.

Training is something that must be constantly improved. This is true of every aspect of training, and it is perhaps particularly true of simulated weapons training. Over time, equipment is enhanced and ammunition becomes more lethal and more costly. Knowing this, TRADOC never looks at simulator training in isolation. TRADOC teams look at a training package in its totality to determine what will be required to fully train soldiers efficiently and at minimum cost. They try to determine which aspects of training could (or should) be done with simulated weapons, how the simulation should be done, the amount of training a soldier needs to become proficient, and where simulators should be located. A routine initial question is whether a soldier should begin training with a simulator or whether experiencing the actual sound and feel and recoil of the real weapon will be more helpful.

One task I took on as deputy commander for training at TRADOC was establishing a general method for determining how many rounds of live ammunition a soldier needed to fire to become proficient in the use of a given weapon. Training can be very expensive and wasteful if too many rounds are fired, and it can be very ineffective if too few are fired. Given the high price of shells for tanks and artillery, especially, TRADOC has tried to simulate the actual operational environments under which a weapon would be used in as many instances as possible. Instead of firing a $10,000 round down range, then, soldiers can operate a simulation that achieves the intended result at a fraction of the cost. The U.S. Treasury will also be better off for such efforts.

I also asked whether the Army could afford to have a simulator for every unit, and if not, where they should be located. For example, Fort Knox and Fort Hood each had a huge training facility for tanks and APCs. Because the Pentagon could not afford to put similar facilities at every post, crews from other parts of the country were scheduled for training at Knox and Hood.

There were also more mundane matters on my plate. In those days, for example, the Army required soldiers in physical fitness training to run in combat boots. Most of the running was on asphalt and concrete, which is entirely different from running over ground and grass. My staff and I concluded that having soldiers run in boots, beating up their ankles and legs, made no sense. On my watch, soldiers began to do their physical training in running shoes.

There was vehement opposition at first. One of the most resistant units was the 82nd Airborne Division, traditionally great runners who believed in running in combat boots. Even so, we went ahead with our decision and then set out to determine the best type of running shoes. Because of the potential contract opportunity, a host of shoe companies were more than happy to give us the shoes we needed to conduct our tests.

I am happy to say that the opposition has acknowledged that I was right, though it took nearly twenty years for all the holdouts to come around. Surprisingly, the last group to stop running in combat boots was the U.S. Military Academy Corps of Cadets. Because it was not part of the Army, per se, I could not impose my will on the Corps. Some traditions have a viselike grip and die a very slow death.

During my tenure as army inspector of training, TRADOC set up two new schools: the U.S. Army Physical Fitness School (USAPFS) at Fort Benjamin Harrison in Indianapolis and the Army Physical Fitness Research Institute (APFRI) at the Army War College at Carlisle Barracks in Carlisle, Pennsylvania. The first was established to turn out experts in physical fitness, drill sergeants, and other NCOs, and was subsequently moved to Fort Benning.

While the USAPFS looks at how physical training should be done, the APFRI evaluates the components of the physical training program to determine what specific exercises and methodologies should be used. The APFRI started analyzing the physical requirements of soldiering in a very sophisticated way using a process called anthropometric analysis. Additionally soldiers no longer simply stepped on scales to be weighed; they were also dipped in pools to have their body fat calculated.

As a result of the work done at the APFRI, the Army implemented a three-event Army Physical Fitness Test (APFT) consisting of a timed two-mile run, push-ups for reps, and sit-ups for reps that is still employed today. This test clearly evaluates stamina and upper body strength, and it requires a soldier to train in order to pass it.

The new focus on physical fitness testing in the early 1980s also directed attention to whether the same standards should be applied to women and men. The cards were stacked against women, and it sometimes seemed as if the Army was oblivious to the fact that women are different from men. For example one of the exercise devices commonly used for physical training had ladder rungs that were too far apart for many women to reach. So female soldiers faced an unfair challenge in taking this test. In discussions with the organization responsible for designing the test, members of my TRADOC team asked, "Why don't you put the rungs closer together so women can reach them?" Aha! They agreed that was the thing to do.

One argument used to justify identical standards for women and men was that soldiers have to be able to pick up and carry heavy things such as toolboxes or aircraft mechanic kits. Granted, a female soldier needs to transport such equipment, but why must she have to carry it herself? We suggested the development of a dolly so women could pull the equipment instead of carrying it. There was, of course, a good reason for why such changes had not been made earlier. The Army did know all along that women and men have different physical capacities, but the placement of women in combat support positions was relatively new, and the number of women in the military had been low up to that time.

Overall, the research school at Carlisle was a real boon to the Army's physical fitness program. It did not hurt that the researchers had a ready-made, constantly replenished population of study participants made up of incoming officers. Each new student was required to take a complete physical upon entering the program and again before graduating because we wanted a benchmark for each individual. Spouses were also invited to take the APFT, and the AFPRI is credited with having saved lives because its tests detected heart conditions that would not have been picked up during routine checkups.

But in its enthusiasm for anthropometric analysis, the Army went overboard in the importance it attributed to body fat. If a soldier's body fat exceeded a certain percentage of his or her weight, that soldier would be discharged. I had misgivings about the wisdom of that regulation, and since I traveled more than most people at my level, I decided to have my body fat checked at every place I visited. Lo and behold, none of my body fat measurements were the same. In less than a twelve-month period, the measurements fluctuated from a low of 17 percent to a high of 25 percent.

I was troubled by the variation and concerned that the Army was likely discharging soldiers based upon inaccurate body fat measurements. Citing the evidence I had gathered, I recommended that the Army reassess the body fat regulation. Body composition was subsequently eliminated as a reason for discharge.

When TRADOC was setting up the two new schools, the secretary of the Army was Jack Marsh, a former Democratic congressman from Virginia. Jack was something of a physical fitness buff, and he suggested during one of our meetings that he and I each do an APFT. Jack suggested that we go to Fort Benning. I suggested Fort Benjamin Harrison instead, explaining that TRADOC was setting up the USAFS there. Jack agreed, so we flew to Indiana.

It was a miserable day. Jack was a month and a half younger than I, and he beat me. I did thirty-eight push-ups, and he did fifty. We matched each other in sit-ups. I thought I was the leader of the pack in running, but I did not lead anything that day. In effect, as I said to some people, "He clobbered me."

As I was flying back to Fort Monroe and he was heading back to Washington, D.C., I called Jack on the radiophone. I said, "Look, I certainly can't take anything away from what you did. But I know your people are going to try and publicize this, and I suggest you give some thought to it. Do you want the message to get out that the physical fitness test is so 'easy' that even an old man like the secretary of the Army can do it?" I saw one press release and nothing more after that.

I have seen Jack many times since that day at Fort Benjamin Harrison. Every chance I get I tell him, "Mr. Secretary, do you remember when you embarrassed me? Let's go out and test now. I'll beat your butt. I could have, but I didn't do it then."

All of the training centers for incoming soldiers were under my direct control. I also had responsibility for the trainers at officer training schools. The Army had OCSs at Fort Benning for infantry, at Fort Knox for armor, at Fort Sill for field artillery, and at Fort Bliss for air defense artillery. There was also the Sergeants Major Academy at Fort Bliss.

The Sergeants Major Academy was relatively new at that time, having been founded in the 1970s. During my tenure as Army inspector of training, I made it a point to address each incoming class at the academy, and I had a lot of fun doing so. The academy trained soldiers in the top two senior enlisted grades (E8 and E9) about across-the-board Army matters. Because sergeants are specialists of sorts, the academy courses are designed to broaden sergeants' horizons and expose them to areas with which they may have little, if any, familiarity.

This gave rise to some interesting situations, as I was in someone else's backyard evaluating enlisted trainers who were subject to the control of their immediate commander. My visits were ripe for conflict and demanded careful choreography. While I did not want to infringe on someone else's authority, I also had to do my job. Being able to deal with people was critical to the success of my efforts.

And I was good at dealing with people. At one point, although it was not specified in either of my job descriptions as TRADOC deputy commander of training or Army inspector of training, I assumed responsibility for mending some fences. There was bad blood between TRADOC and FORSCOM, which was located at Fort McPherson in Georgia. The tension arose from turf battles dating back to the creation of the two commands in 1973, when the Continental Army Command (CONARC) had been split in two. FORSCOM had taken active command of the combat forces, and TRADOC took command of training and doctrine.

About a month after I first became deputy commander of TRADOC, FORSCOM got a new commander in the personage of Gen. Dick Cavazos, who was a very good friend of mine. In an attempt to break down the historical barriers to cooperation between the two commands and to demonstrate to our people that FORSCOM and TRADOC were working together, Dick and I agreed that whenever he visited posts under his command, I would accompany him if there were a TRADOC activity at the post. This worked out very well. We demonstrated a cohesiveness and rapport that put an end to the infighting. Attitudes flow downhill.

During one of our visits to the 4th Infantry Division at Fort Carson, Colorado, Dick and I learned that the division commander, Maj. Gen. John Hudachek, and the assistant division commander, Brig. Gen. Colin Powell, were having problems. Colin was so distressed by the situation that he was talking about retiring from the Army. We said, "Don't do anything dumb." Fortunately, Colin hung in there, and when we returned to our home stations, Dick and I got the problem corrected. As they say, the rest is history.[1]

Not all of my efforts were so successful. Back at Fort Dix I had to deal firsthand with the perception that officers in combat commands are better than those in training commands, and that perception lingered. In fact, when the time came to make selections for the advanced schools and other choice assignments, there was a tendency to favor officers in combat assignments over those in training jobs.

Almost single-handedly, I took on the challenge of balancing the books and giving officers in training assignments a fighting chance. I first had to convince the officers in training jobs that they could advance in the Army if they did their jobs well. Then I had to convince the boards and the Army chief of staff that penalizing people in training assignments was bad business because it hurt the Army's combat readiness and negatively affected the morale of its soldiers. Unfortunately, in the final analysis, I never could change the unfavorable attitudes toward training assignments.

Louise and I knew Wes had the smarts. He had the ability to do as well as he wanted to, but he had never shown much desire to excel in school. He had fallen into the habit of getting by. I am sure a reason for his lackluster academic performance was that he wanted to fit in with the other kids. Fat chance. Just as there were privileges, being the general's kid came with burdens. It was difficult being regular and just one of the kids when on base, where we lived, other people would not treat you that way because of your father's position.

I had received a brochure from Valley Forge Military Academy (VFMA) in Pennsylvania and had left it on the desk in my office in the house. At the time, Valley Forge was an all-male college preparatory boarding school and a two-year college on Philadelphia's Main Line whose campus was not far from where I grew up. VFMA did not accept black students when I was in high school, but times had changed.

Wes saw the brochure and was intrigued. He had been in JROTC since he was a freshman in high school, and he had done pretty well. Academically, it was his best class. I had never tried to influence him to pursue a career in the military. Perhaps it was a case of reverse psychology, but I was still somewhat surprised when Wes said he would like to visit VFMA and possibly enroll.

This was another time when past relationships proved beneficial. I knew the VFMA admissions officer Dick Schoendorfer very well. Dick had worked for me at Fort Dix as both a battalion commander and a staff officer. He was very receptive to my call, and he was delighted that Wes had expressed an interest in attending VFMA. When we drove up to visit, Dick laid out the red carpet. Wes was sold on the school.

When Louise and I dropped Wes off at Valley Forge to start his senior year of high school in the fall, any intention he had of blending in was completely shot. The school just about had a parade in my honor. Wes later learned that the cadet officers had been warned not to haze him for fear of the general's kid telling on them.

In late August 1982 Glen Otis, who had replaced Donn Starry as TRADOC commander, advised me that I was not going to be promoted beyond the grade of lieutenant general. I was disappointed, of course, but not really surprised. In the final analysis, I think I was a casualty of "abort or get out."

I had a mandatory retirement date coming up in 1983, and I had originally thought that I would retire in May of that year. But Louise had a request. She said, "You know, I've done everything you've asked me to do. Can you see if we can stay here through the summer? I'd really like to do that." We had been at Fort Monroe since July 1981, and we had a beautiful home overlooking the Chesapeake Bay. I could not blame Louise for wanting to stay there just a little while longer.

During one of my monthly sessions with the chief of staff, I broached the subject of remaining at Fort Monroe through the summer. He said, "Becton, I don't give a damn when you retire." I replied, "Thank you, sir. But I really . . ." Interrupting me, he said, "Did you hear what I said? You retire whenever you want to retire." End of conversation!

So I retired in August and Louise got her chance to enjoy living in our waterfront house for one more summer.

I really had not planned on having a retirement ceremony. I had been to so many of them over my nearly forty years in the Army, and I just did not feel up to the emotional drain of attending my own. But when I told my boss that I was going to just sign my discharge papers and disappear, he gave me a hard look. "I don't think you want to do that," he said. "You owe it to the soldiers and to a lot of people to have a ceremony."

After much relentless prodding and pleading from my staff, I relented. TRADOC headquarters had a regular retirement ceremony for all those retiring in a given month, and I said I would participate in that. Two other officers were retiring at the same time as me, U.S. Air Force Col. Tom Barnes and Army Col. Fred Kaiser, both of whom I knew. The date was set for 23 August.

The weather was unremarkable that day—hot but breezy. The ceremony, however, was nothing like what I had expected. Every one of the eighteen black flag officers then serving in the Army was in the audience, including Maj. Gen. Colin Powell. There were other luminaries, too, both civilian and military representatives of the Defense Department and the Army.

Most of my family members were present, as well. Karen and her twins, Kim and Chris, Joyce, USAF Lieutenant Renee, VFMA Cadet Wes, Al and Dot Horton, and another first cousin, Lonnie George attended. My mother, who had cancer by then, wanted to be there, but I felt that the heat would be too much for her and convinced her to remain in Philadelphia.

After the U.S. Continental Army Band played a musical salute to my family, a seventeen-gun salute was given as Gen. William R. Richardson,

TRADOC commander and host for the ceremony, was escorted to the podium. General Richardson spoke after the presentation of medals and commendations to the retirees. Here are some excerpts from his kind remarks:

> General Becton reached the highest ranks by what those of us who know him believe is just steady hard work on the part of a great soldier, constantly proving himself, to himself and to the Army, that here was one who could stand apart in terms of his great abilities. We call him a soldier, not necessarily because of the uniform, but because of what he represents inside that uniform, and we mean that in its ultimate terms. He experienced as a soldier the moral and physical challenge of battle and he never faltered through three wars. We call him a leader because he spent a lifetime preparing himself to train the people under his charge—the men and women in peacetime and those in wartime that he led in combat.

> But he was more than a trainer. Julius Becton was a teacher in the best sense of that word because he guided and shaped people in the image that we like to see happen from our leaders. Julius Becton probably knows more about the workings of the Army than most generals. I say that because he concerned himself with people who make up the Army probably more so than anybody I know in all of my service. . . .

> Here . . . we know him as the deputy commander for training and the Army inspector of training, the first of that position to bring focus and shape to the training effort for the whole U.S. Army. His knowledge of that system helped all of us, especially those of us in the Training and Doctrine Command who believed that what he said was important to the institution of change and the enhancement of training throughout our system as well as throughout the rest of the Army. He could find the soft spots and work them. He could find the needs of our noncommissioned officer corps and those of initial entry training and cause us to work those. He not only made training better in the Army; he made the Army better. . . .

> But I suppose that we would remember Julius Becton for his strength of character and the cherished professional attributes that all of us aspire to have. He is a man, I think with a deep sense of loyalty up and down, great responsibility to those who he serves above him and especially those who he serves below him. . . . He is a man concerned with other human beings, one concerned with fair play, concerned with great self-respect, with the dignity

of the individual. He set the hallmark of all those attributes for so many . . . and we are the better for it.

Finally he was a man possessed with great integrity, a man of principle that truly is a leader in the classic sense in our profession. . . .

So ladies and gentlemen we honor today three of the finest in our profession. They gave much to the military profession. Their exemplary performance is a guidepost to old and young alike. They patterned their lives on the best traditions of the military. They exemplified the meaning of service to country. They are two soldiers and one airman we will not soon forget. They are retiring officially but we will count them as here with us always. General Becton, Colonel Barnes, Colonel Kaiser, with great pride and deep respect, I salute you.

I thanked General Richardson on behalf of myself and the others, and than spoke a bit about the Army. "The leadership that we have today has the potential to be just as good as any I have seen in almost forty years of service, provided they do certain things," I said. I then went on to talk about those things:

I suspect I am one of the few soldiers still in uniform who heard a shot fired in anger in the Big One, World War II. The patch I wear on my right shoulder represents one of those World War II divisions, the 93rd Infantry Division, an all-black division. . . . You see, when I joined the Army, it was a segregated Army. In that division, we had all black enlisted soldiers, many black junior officers, and few, very few, black field-grade officers. The rest of the leadership was white.

There is no need for me to relate to this group the progress made since those days. The fact that we have black men and black women of all ranks, be they commissioned or noncommissioned, attests to the principle that we are truly an organization that not only talks about, but demonstrates daily the subject of equal opportunity and equal treatment. In 1948 the Army had one black colonel. In the audience this morning there are at least fifteen general officers who happen to be black. Today Command Sergeant Major Bill Peters is the command sergeant major for this great command, and throughout the Armed Forces there are similar examples. I am very proud to have been a part of that success story.

But on a higher plane we must all keep in mind that we are not made up of, or fight because of, our blackness, our whiteness, our being Hispanic, or

Native American born or whatever. We fight because of our leadership, our training, our cohesion, that thing called esprit. So it is on that note that I intend to close. The spirit of the Army today is as good as the leadership it has. My concern now, and has been for some time, is the need for a leadership that is willing to take risks, not do dumb things, and certainly not gambling, but a leadership that recognizes that the essence of the Army lies in its people. As General Abrams so aptly said, "The Army is people and people is the Army." We need leaders who dare to be different and to make a difference, to act rather than react. Our young soldiers or young officers will do exactly what they see their leaders doing. If in that risk-taking, that is so important to winning on the battlefield, we forget about our history—the fact that battles were won by men and women who refused to accept the status quo and did something about it—if we forget, we fail our great Nation. We will win on future battlefields as long as we have those troopers, regardless of grade, who take that calculated risk based upon their best professional judgment.

However, that calculated risk and the ability to make those judgments must be refined and honed in training before we can expect to do them in conflict. Back in 1981 the secretary of the Army, Jack Marsh said, and I quote, "Many potential creative leaders in military and civilian life do not make it through the middle level. They become casualties on the battlefields of their career. They are the walking wounded about whom others speculate as to their great potential which was never realized."

We must have leaders who really know their job and can teach others. We must have leaders who are willing to stand up and be counted. . . . We must have leaders who are sensitive to the needs of their soldiers, airmen, sailors, and marines, and demand that they sweat in training rather than bleed in battle. We must have leaders who are intolerant of abuse of our troopers, regardless of the source of that abuse. And lastly, we must have leaders who know how to have fun and can maintain their sense of humor.

There is one last segment of our community that is key to our success. . . . We have been tremendously fortunate to have had the support of our family members. I know I wouldn't be here today if it were not for Louise's support, and I am sure that Tom and Fred feel the same way about Ellen and Selby. . . . I would like to say publicly and officially: Thanks to these grand ladies, Louise, Ellen, and Selby, who have been with us through thick and thin. And to thank all the other family members, those who are here and those whose paths we have shared, thanks for caring, thanks for your concern, thanks for your loving.

Now we are not about to say goodbye because as we take off our uniforms and transit into some other field of endeavor, we will always remember, we will always reflect on what you have meant to us. So rather than say goodbye, let me try this: Adios. Auf Weidersehen. Farewell. Our paths will cross again. On behalf of the Barnes and the Kaisers and the Bectons, we say thanks again for sharing this moment with us. Good luck and God bless.

After the band had finished playing each of our favorite songs—Louise had requested "Stars and Stripes Forever" for me—Colonel Barnes, Colonel Kaiser, and I stood with our wives for the final salute. Then the announcer directed the audience's attention to the vicinity of the gazebo. From behind it, flag bearers in the uniform of each unit that I had commanded during my Army career emerged, complete with color guards, then marched toward me one at a time to each unit's song. They marched until they were directly in front of me, carrying the colors of the 2/17 Cavalry, the St. Lo Brigade, the 1st Cavalry Division, and VII Corps.

Then they saluted. I had maintained my composure rather well up until then, but that did it. Both Louise and I had water on our faces. In that very short time, a capsule of my life as a commander flashed before me. That truly was the Final Salute.

CHAPTER FIFTEEN

★ ★ ★

The Politics of Disaster

I was still unemployed five months after I left the Army. I had gone on plenty of interviews, but the outcome was the same each time. A potential employer would ask what I had done. I would reply truthfully: "Well, during my last command, I commanded and managed about eighty-eight thousand soldiers, seventy-six thousand civilian family members, and twenty-three thousand employees and supervised a payroll totaling about $1.2 billion dollars." That was not what they wanted to hear. More than once, I was told I was overqualified. I even tried playing down my résumé, but to no avail. I think the biggest strike against me was that my credentials made me a threat to existing personnel, maybe even to the boss.

My luck changed when I spoke with an old classmate from Leavenworth, Dr. William "Bud" Mayer, who was the assistant secretary of defense for health affairs, and Bud's wife, Heidi, who was working for the U.S. Agency for International Development (USAID). Heidi suggested that I might be interested in working for USAID. The incumbent director of the agency's Office of Foreign Disaster Assistance (OFDA) was about to get fired, and his job would be open. At first, I had little interest. One sticking point for me was that under the rules prohibiting dual compensation of federal employees, I would not be able to draw retired military pay along with my regular compensation if I took the OFDA post.

Meanwhile, Louise had gone to work as a staff nurse at the Hospice of Northern Virginia. She was thoroughly enjoying working the facility, which is known as Capital Hospice. Nursing was Louise's first love; hopefully, I was a close second. Sometime in early December 1983, while Louise was at work and I was unemployed at home, I got it into my head to help her out by "organizing" the kitchen. As I have told all my friends since then, "Do not do that!" I rearranged the cans and bottles by size and put them in alphabetical order. I even made sure that all of the labels were facing out. Then I proudly waited for Louise to return home to admire my handiwork.

Louise was not pleased. She promptly reminded me that 1) it was her kitchen, 2) she did not use condiments based upon the alphabet or the size of the container, and 3) unless I was prepared to take over the cooking responsibility, it would be best if I stayed out of the kitchen. Two things came of this. First, I faced the realization that I had to get out of the house. Second, I began rethinking my concerns about my pay.

I advised Bud that I might be interested in working for OFDA. He recommended me to the right people. Since I was a registered Republican, I was accepted to start the interview process, beginning with White House personnel folks and Robert C. McFarlane, who was then President Ronald Reagan's national security adviser.

I became OFDA director on 4 January 1984, and shortly after I reported to work, I got word of one of the greatest losses of my life. My niece, Crystal Becton, called to tell me that my mother had died.

Mom had been battling what turned out to be pancreatic cancer for some time, and she had undergone extensive surgery at the Philadelphia Naval Hospital in November 1982. It was determined at that time that nothing else could be done. I was with my mother's physician when he arrived at that prognosis. The doctor told me what his team had determined and asked whether he or I should break the news to Mom. I opted to do it.

When I returned to her room, I told Mom the doctors had done all they could. "How long do I have?" she asked. I told her they had said three to six months. She lay there for a few minutes in complete silence. Then the doctor came in. Mom asked whether she could go home. He said yes, and gave her a list of dos and don'ts. Mom then said that she had a few things to do in her remaining time, including telling off a few folks.

With that, I took her back to her house. Her granddaughter Crystal became my mother's primary caregiver, and she had a regular visiting nurse. Either Louise or I went up to Philadelphia every week for a visit.

Although the cancer was ravaging Mom's body, it never touched her spirit. She owned a rental property in Caroline County, Virginia, and the tenants had gotten behind in their rent. Woe unto them! Louise drove Mom down so she could have a word with the renters. Mom was never one to let people take advantage of her.

I was with Mom the Sunday before she passed. We watched TV—her favorite sport, football. Before leaving, I administered her shot of morphine, kissed her, and said I would be back next weekend.

Someone observed that Mom waited until I had a job before she went home.

OFDA was celebrating its twentieth anniversary in 1984. It had been created to coordinate U.S. government aid to nations struck by natural or man-made disasters. The international counterpart of the Federal Emergency Management Agency (FEMA), OFDA mobilizes U.S. government resources and coordinates with voluntary agencies, international organizations, and other donors when disaster strikes outside the United States. OFDA also maintained five regional stockpiles of supplies that could be delivered to a disaster site in as little as twenty-four hours. On average, OFDA responded to thirty-seven disasters per year and monitored forty situations that had the potential to become disasters.[1]

The U.S. government's history of foreign disaster assistance goes back to 1812, when Congress made its first foreign aid appropriation of $50,000 for the victims of a powerful earthquake in Venezuela. The Marshall Plan in 1947 formalized foreign disaster relief. When an earthquake devastated the city of Skopje, Yugoslavia, in 1963 the uncoordinated stream of contributions from numerous U.S. agencies highlighted the need for a central office to supervise international aid efforts. The U.S. Foreign Disaster Assistance Program was established as part of the USAID a year later.

By 1984, OFDA had become an independent office within USAID and had a staff of thirty. Thirteen or fourteen of the staff members were disaster specialists. The OFDA and its staff were structured into three geographic divisions, one each for Latin America and the Caribbean, Africa and Europe, and Asia and the Pacific. These divisions provided regional and country-specific expertise on relief needs and disaster preparedness.

When disaster strikes, the U.S. ambassador to the afflicted country first ascertains whether the country is capable of handling the response on its own. If not, the ambassador issues a disaster declaration. The role of OFDA when I became director was to authorize the immediate expenditure of up to $25,000 and then coordinate the disbursement of any additional relief money. I managed this effort and reported directly to USAID Administrator Peter McPherson, whom the president had designated as special coordinator for international disaster assistance.

I could call upon experts to assess the damage and determine the best response and either bring those experts to the OFDA office or send them to the disaster area. In 1984, I had at my disposal a budget of approximately

$96 million, but the amount appropriated for OFDA activities was often unrealistic from year to year because it was impossible to predict what disasters would occur and how much the office would need to spend. I could request additional funds if necessary, and OFDA was never without the money it needed.

The very first disaster I handled as director took me to Costa Rica. On 29 February 1984, the Costa Rican government reported a fire at a warehouse in the capital city of San José. The warehouse stored medical supplies for distribution to regional centers that served all the hospitals and medical posts in the nation. Losses were estimated to be more than $2.5 million and the potential for a national health crisis was discussed. Facing a two-month wait for newly ordered supplies, Costa Rica requested assistance from the United States in obtaining a two-month supply of critical stocks. The U.S. chief of mission in San José issued a disaster declaration, which my office supported, and OFDA coordinated the shipment of $25,000 of critical drugs and supplies.

It turned out that we had been had. Our regional consultant, Paul Bell, arrived in country shortly ahead of my team. Bell's contacts quickly alerted us to the fact that the warehouse actually contained considerable amounts of alcohol and that most of the "lost medical supplies" had been either nonexistent or very much outdated.

It was not long before I was learning quite a lot about disaster politics. My first good lesson resulted from a drought that struck the Caribbean islands of Antigua and Barbuda in 1984. The islands generally experience a drought every decade, but few measures for conserving water in an emergency were in place, and lower-than-expected rainfall had left supplies far short of what was needed. By April 1984, Antigua's main source of water, the reservoir formed by the Potsworks Dam, had dried up. A disaster was declared on April 13.[2]

I flew to Antigua. On the way from the airport to consult government officials, my car passed three or four large estates and lavish hotels where the grass was being watered. But downtown, I saw a line of people waiting to get water from a single spigot. It turned out that the government was reluctant to publicize the water shortage for fear of hurting tourism. There was little I could do except threaten to cut off deliveries of emergency barged water to the island.

Our own countrymen also played political games with OFDA. A year after the Antigua drought, on 11 May 1985, a fire swept through a wooden stadium in Bradford, England, engulfing a grandstand that seated about three thousand. Within seconds, spectators found themselves in a furnace of intense heat and fallen debris. Serious casualties were few, however.

Although it was certainly one big fire, I highly doubt the United Kingdom could not handle its effects. There was no need for OFDA to provide $10,000 in assistance to one of the wealthiest and most industrialized nations in the world. That my office did provide the money came down to a political nicety: The U.S. ambassador to the U.K. wanted to offer visible assistance to the British.

Then there was my encounter with Oliver North. At that time, the U.S. government was allegedly supporting and supplying the Contra rebels in Nicaragua. North was the action guy in the White House. He contacted OFDA, asking to use our aircraft to fly "humanitarian supplies" into Central America.

We wanted to know what kind of assistance they wanted to fly in. North would not tell us, so I refused the use of our aircraft. He then enlisted some of my former colleagues in uniform to badger me. "Why can't you help this guy?" they asked. "Because, God damn it, my job is to move humanitarian assistance," I replied. "You tell me what the cargo is, and if it falls within my charter, I'll move it. But I'll be damned if I'm going to use our aircraft not knowing what it's going to be used for."

That was a good decision on my part.

During my twenty-two months as director OFDA experienced one of the worst years in its entire history. A total of 22,703 people had died as a result of declared disasters during fiscal years 1980 through 1984. In grim contrast, during the single fiscal year 1985, 427,073 lost their lives to disaster.[3] It was the year of the worst industrial accident in history—the release of toxic gas from a Union Carbide pesticide manufacturing plant in Bhopal, India. There were powerful earthquakes in Mexico that brought enormous devastation. And drought and famine killed hundreds of thousands in Africa and harmed millions more.

The nations afflicted by the drought had experienced several years of insufficient rainfall and reduced harvests. In addition, environmental degradation and deforestation in many countries had reduced domestic food production, making those nations increasingly reliant on imported supplies.

Compounding such problems were seemingly endless wars, the crimes of warlords, and epidemics of communicable diseases. Oftentimes, government programs simply made bad situations worse.

By 1985, much of Africa was in the midst of a full-blown humanitarian crisis. In Ethiopia, an estimated 7.75 million people were at risk of dying from starvation. Drought conditions reached their peak in Niger and reduced nationwide cereal production by almost 40 percent. Millions of refugees were on the move, trying to get away from the drought-stricken areas.

To counteract the worsening situation, the U.S. government created the Task Force on the African Famine (TFAF) in October 1984. The TFAF was an interagency organization, with representatives from the Departments of State, Defense, Agriculture, Health and Human Services, and Transportation; the National Oceanic and Atmospheric Administration; the White House's Office of Management and Budget; and the National Security Council. I was asked to lead the task force.

When it was created, I was in Africa with a party of four OFDA staffers assessing the impact of our relief efforts. We had visited food distribution centers in Mauritania, and then headed north to what had to be one of the most desolate parts of the country. There we witnessed unimaginable horror. People were waiting to be fed or to die. The villagers' emaciated bodies were little more than skeletons covered with skin. As one of my colleagues later described the scene, "It was pitiful. Picture an area the size of a football field with several tin-roofed sheds to offer shelter from the sun. Children with swollen bellies and orange hair, symptoms of starvation. Children crawling because their joints were too swollen to support their weight. Food contributed by us and other donor nations was the only reason these people still survived. From the looks of it, many would soon be dead."[4]

The African drought precipitated a massive worldwide outpouring of sympathy. The hit single "We Are the World" came out of the relief effort and was immensely successful, raising an additional $60 million for the Ethiopian relief effort.[5] Even so, food shortages persisted and even worsened.

Particularly in Ethiopia, relief efforts were stymied by politics. Ships laden with food often sat idle for more than a week before being unloaded. Then their cargoes sometimes sat on the docks for weeks longer as the food rotted. Ethiopian officials used any missing paper or signature as grounds to prevent aid from getting through.

My first trip to Ethiopia was a real lesson. I had expected to see the president in the capital, or at least a senior representative from his office, but I ended up meeting with an official from the transportation department who was quite rude. At one point as I and my contingent of three or four plus several of his colleagues sat in his small office, the transportation official made a statement I did not hear. I just stared at him, waiting for him to say something more. When he did not, I eventually said, "Well, I guess it's time to leave." I just walked out. When my team and I left Addis Ababa, our embassy folk said that Ethiopian government officials had a complete change of heart all of a sudden. Anyhow, after that, we got along much better.

Having been in combat situations, I had seen human beings maimed, mutilated, scarred, and killed. Despite this, what I saw during my time in Ethiopia was so ghastly and horrific that it will remain with me until I die.

The primary government response was to uproot large numbers of peasants from the drought-affected areas in the north and resettle them in the southern part of the country. The Soviet Union provided military aircraft to assist in this relocation. The Soviet flight crews carried out their mission by herding people into inhumanely crowded planes. Some of the evacuees would defecate or vomit all over the place during the flight. When the Soviets reached the drop-off location, they unloaded their cargo, removing the corpses of those who had not survived the trip. They then used a fire hose to clean out their aircraft before they returned for more human cargo.

The Soviet plane crews knew as well as we did that this did not have to happen. One million people did not have to die.

I made other unforgettable trips to Africa during my tenure at OFDA. At one point, I was invited to Ghana to inspect that nation's disaster response system. But for me, that trip meant far more.

During the heyday of the slave trade, millions of Africans were shipped to North America alone, and many of the slaves passed through the region of Africa that is now Ghana. While I was visiting that nation, I had the opportunity to stand before "the Door of No Return" on the Gold Coast.

It is difficult to describe the emotions I felt as I stood in that place where my ancestors may well have stood as slaves in chains. I was aggrieved. I felt a tremendous sadness as I contemplated the terror, anguish, and despair most certainly felt by the slaves who passed through that door at Elmina Castle. Part of an enormous vaulted dungeon has also been restored at the castle to show the "condemned cells" where troublesome slaves were kept. The room is dark, with hardly any ventilation. One small window lets in air and light.

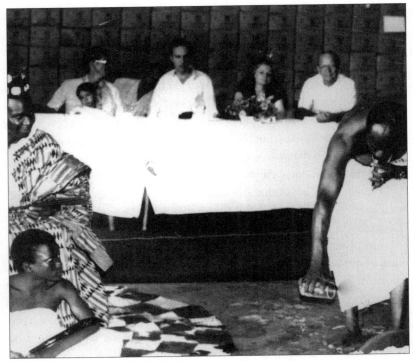

My enstoolment. (Author collection)

And yet that trip to Ghana also produced one of my more pleasurable experiences in Africa. During a visit to Ashanti, a former kingdom and British protectorate located in central Ghana, I was "enstooled." This meant I was attired from head to toe in African garb and escorted by a court of young boys. Members of my traveling party tried to convince me that this ceremony was designed to claim me as a descendant of the area.

Apartheid was alive and well in South Africa during this period. One day when I was back in Washington, D.C., my agency received a call from the government of South Africa, which wanted our assistance. The number two guy from the South African embassy came over to the agency and was told to see the OFDA director, who could help his country get aid. No one bothered to tell the guy what the director looked like. He came into my office and damn near died. His face turned beet red, then pale white. I listened to what he had to say. When he left, I told my secretary Frances Vanech, "We'll never see that guy again." We did not.

On the morning of 19 September 1985, an earthquake measuring 8.1 on the Richter scale struck the southwestern coast of Mexico. The next day, a second quake registering 7.5 on the Richter scale struck southeast of the first earthquake's epicenter. Even though both quakes occurred hundreds of miles away, they caused massive damage in Mexico City due to a phenomenon appropriately named the Mexico City effect.[6] The soil under the city consists primarily of soft sediments that tend to amplify seismic energy and magnify the ensuing devastation.

Never wanting to rely on its powerful neighbor to the north, Mexican officials were at first reluctant to request aid from the U.S. government. It quickly became obvious, however, that Mexico could not handle this disaster by itself. Working through the American Red Cross and the International Committee of the Red Cross, OFDA finally convinced the Mexicans to request aid. Once the request came through, I went to Mexico City with an eight-member multidisciplinary team.

Riding in from the airport, I saw complete and total destruction. There was rubble everywhere. Many of the structures were not up to earthquake code, and the majority of those destroyed were residential buildings. Between four million and six million residents of Mexico City were without water, and there were major breaks in the city's sewage pipe system.[7]

Shortly after the Mexican earthquakes, and despite my objection, First Lady Nancy Reagan, USAID Administrator Peter McPherson, and Assistant Secretary of State for Inter-American Affairs Elliott Abrams visited the disaster site. Rescuers were still trying to free people who by that time had been buried beneath rubble for six days. But all work stopped while Mrs. Reagan was there.

Did people who might have been saved die because of that work stoppage? I would wager that some did. The other result of that trip was that the U.S. government gave $1 million to the Mexican government that came out of OFDA's budget. No one told me about that until after the fact.

Wes had done very well at VFMA, and he attended the ROTC Basic Camp at Fort Knox in 1983, finishing the six-week program as a cadet company commander. I was asked to be the graduation speaker at the end of the camp, and I gladly accepted the invitation. Louise warned me not to get too emotional, but I could not help it. After nearly forty years of soldiering, it was really something to see my only son as a cadet commander.

At the end of the graduation ceremony we received word that Wes had won a two-year ROTC scholarship to attend Valley Forge Military Junior College. We were bowled over. It helped ease our financial burden. But even more important, Wes felt great about being able to pay his own way at school.

With the ROTC scholarship came increased responsibility, and Wes excelled in both his academic classes and military science. Ultimately, he became the top cadet and just the second black regimental commander. After his second year, he was commissioned a second lieutenant in the U.S. Army at the age of nineteen, which was the same age I had been when I was commissioned in 1945. Wes then went to George Washington University (GWU) to finish his college education.

At GWU, he met Ingrid Ahlman, his future wife, and it was not long before things between Wes and Ingrid got pretty serious. Louise and I got to know Ingrid pretty well, and we did not care at all that she was not black. As long as the person Wes brought home was a decent human being and cared about our child, it was all right with us.

We did not meet Ingrid's parents until graduation. The Ahlmans had accepted our invitation to brunch at our home after the commencement, and I thought I should introduce myself, so I scoured the crowd looking for them. I eventually spotted Ingrid, and it was fairly easy to identify the rest of her family because they all have carrot-red hair.

Robert and Tobie Ahlman and Louise and I hit it off. After we had settled in at our house after the drive from Washington, we talked about everything under the sun. Wes and Ingrid were hilarious. They kept running in to see how we were getting along, conducting surveillance for tension or strain. There was no hostile activity to be reported.

★   ★   ★

CHAPTER SIXTEEN

Taking Charge of FEMA

FEMA Director Louis Giuffrida officially resigned on 1 September 1985. His professional relationships with other Reagan administration officials had been deteriorating for some time, and the resignation came as no surprise.

Frankly, I do not remember who first asked me whether I would be interested in running FEMA. But I was interested. It meant higher pay and a new challenge, and I was flattered to be asked.

There were other candidates for the job. In fact, when I asked Virginia Rep. Frank Wolf if he would sponsor me, the Republican apologetically declined, explaining that he was backing someone else. But I got the support of both of Virginia's Republican senators, John Warner and Paul Trible. And it did not hurt a bit that I had the backing of Vice President George H. W. Bush and of Colin Powell, who was then a major general and the military executive to Defense Secretary Caspar Weinberger.

I was given a stack of briefing books by FEMA staffers and set about preparing myself for a nomination and Senate confirmation hearing. I knew that I brought much to the table, but preparing to answer the list of prehearing questions still required a lot of hard work. The questions covered a range of issues about the agency and the issues it faced, from rebuilding morale (I knew that had to be my first priority) to FEMA's seven-year plan to relocate the civilian population from cities to the countryside in the event of nuclear attack. (I certainly was not about to commit to making changes to that plan until I had a chance to give it more careful study). There was also the National Flood Insurance Program. (I did not think that the program, whose rates were heavily subsidized by the government, was as sound actuarially as it should be, and it made no sense to me that the government was, in effect, subsidizing construction in areas that were highly susceptible to flooding). And the National Earthquake Hazards Reduction Program had just been created by Congress after considerable review. (I allowed as how revisions might be necessary based upon subsequent analysis, but for the moment, the program represented what was believed to be necessary to reduce U.S. vulnerability to earthquakes.)

In response to one of the prehearing questions, I made it clear that I had made no commitments with respect to FEMA policies and programs other than to be completely objective in my assessments of them after confirmation.

The hearing took place before the Senate Committee on Governmental Affairs, which was chaired by Delaware Republican William Roth. Tennessee's Democratic senator Al Gore asked me how members of the committee should address me. "Call me General, Director, Doctor, Mister, or anything," I replied, "but just don't call me, 'Hey you' or 'boy.'" There was considerable laughter when Gore said, "Yes Sir, General."

Senators Warner and Trible talked about me as if I were the greatest thing since night baseball, even though I had only spent thirty minutes at most with each of them and neither really knew me. But I appreciated their glowing words very much.

Overall, the hearing was friendly. And shortly I received the committee's unanimous support, and my nomination went to the floor of the Senate, where I was confirmed.

I reported to work as director of FEMA on 7 November 1985, and Vice President Bush officiated at my swearing in. I had my work cut out for me.

Within my first ten days on the job, I had to cut FEMA's budget by $13.8 million. Two grand juries were looking into alleged questionable practices in the agency, and more than thirty investigations by the FEMA Inspector General were under way.[1] Add to this the unflattering press the agency regularly received in local newspapers and the fact that no funds had been available for travel, recruitment, or training for the prior ten months, and it was little wonder that employee morale was low.

One of my first personnel actions was to find a chief of staff who could help change the climate at headquarters and establish greater staff accountability. One of the senior staffers recommended Bill Tidball for the job. Bill was a deputy regional director from Texas, and he was participating in a training program at a FEMA facility less than ninety minutes from headquarters when he was recommended, so I had a chance to meet him in

My swearing-in as the director by Dr. William (Bud) Mayer, ASD (HA), with Louise and Vice President Bush observing. (Courtesy of the White House)

person. He was everything people said he was—the ideal civil servant and an honest-to-goodness business manager with broad experience in emergency management. Bill had worked in just about all of the areas with which FEMA deals at one time or another.

Our chemistry was good, and I had no doubt that Bill and I could work well together. I had no idea about the heartburn the move would cause his wife Ann. She was a doctoral student in sociology at the University of North Texas when Bill accepted the position as chief of staff, so there went her program. It took a long time for her to forgive me for disrupting her life and the lives of their two daughters.

About twenty-four hundred people were employed by FEMA, and half of the staff was at agency headquarters in Washington, D.C. The other half was dispersed throughout ten federal regions,[2] each of which was headed by a regional director who was a political appointee. As a result, the regional directors varied in expertise. They owed their positions not so much to what they knew about disaster response or FEMA, but to their political connections.

It has always been a priority for me to get to know the people with whom I work and to give them an opportunity to get to know me. So I visited each of the ten FEMA regions at least once during my first three months, and I also held an orientation for all the regional directors at the FEMA's training site in Emmitsburg, Maryland. I expected that some would depart after I became director, some at my urging and others of their own volition. I was right. The first director replaced was the one in Denton, Texas. In the vernacular, he had "wandered off the reservation." He had made commitments over and above his authority, and he only complied with FEMA policies when it suited his desires. Further, I wanted to send a message to all of the political appointees. Bill Tidball and Spence Perry, the FEMA general counsel, paid the Texas regional director a personal visit to collect his credentials.

The second regional director to be replaced was headquartered in Kansas City, Kansas. My first clue that he might not make it came at the meeting in Emmitsburg. Everyone else wore a coat and tie, but he appeared unkempt, and I noted his disdain for me. In preparation for my initial visit to the Kansas City Region, there was a discussion about what meal they should serve the director. "Fried chicken," the regional director said. "That's what folks like him like."

The regional staff, put off by the director's remarks, got word back to my staff. Tidball said, "I can handle it." I said, "Do it."

When we removed a regional director, we had to explain the move to the member of Congress who had sponsored the director for the position. Only once did I run into any opposition. The director of the region that includes New York and New Jersey was a good guy, but it was against his philosophy to participate in nuclear preparedness exercises. A nuclear power plant was being built on Long Island, and he could not do what had to be done, so he was relieved of duty. Republican Sen. Alfonse D'Amato of New York went ballistic. He said, "You can't do that." I said, "Oh yes I can, Senator. If he can't do what I am telling him to do, he has to go."

Mine was not the last word on that matter, however. Some time later when I was testifying before a House subcommittee, Senator D'Amato, who was sitting in on the panel, really blasted me. Before I had a chance to respond, he excused himself, and went to the floor of the Senate, where he demanded that I be fired. New York's senior senator, Democrat Daniel Patrick Moynihan, and Republican Alan Simpson of Wyoming told me not to worry about it. I did not.

At the time I came on board, FEMA had been in existence for just over six years. President Jimmy Carter had created it, effective 1 April 1979, from four separate federal agencies that were previously run by the General Services Administration and the Departments of Defense, Commerce, and Housing and Urban Development.

It was clear to me early on that FEMA's original mission statement was no longer adequate by the time I became director. The agency was required to do far more than had been envisioned for it at its birth. An updated mission statement was definitely in order. After a detailed review of the agency's current functions, the senior agency staff produced the following:

> Under the direction of the President, the mission of the Federal Emergency Management Agency is to plan for and coordinate the protection of the civilian population and resources of the Nation, to include planning for the continuity of constitutional government in time of emergency.

> To accomplish its mission, FEMA acts as the focal point for all levels of government in developing a national emergency management capability that can deal effectively with any major emergency. Toward the creation of this capability, FEMA:

> - develops and coordinates programs and activities to prepare for, mitigate, respond to, and recover from natural, technological, and attack-caused civil emergencies.
> - develops program guidance and plans to assist government at all levels in planning to cope with and recover from emergencies.
> - supports state and local governments in disaster and emergency planning, preparedness, mitigation, response, and recovery efforts.
> - coordinates federal assistance from Presidentially declared disasters and emergencies.
> - develops programs for population protection, including warning, shelter, and evacuation planning, and emergency public information.
> - administers the United States Fire Administration program, aimed at reducing the nation's loss of life and property from fire through better fire prevention and control.
> - administers the National Flood Insurance and Federal Crime Insurance Program and directs floodplain management activities.
> - develops programs to lessen the effect of natural and technological hazards.

- develops and provides training and education for federal, state, and local fire
  service personnel and emergency managers to enhance the preparedness and
  professional development of all levels of government.

I had often said that when I retired from the Army, I would like to become
a vice president of a college or university. After November 1985, I jokingly
said, "Now I own one."

FEMA's National Emergency Training Center in Emmitsburg consisted
of the Emergency Management Institute (EMI) and the National Fire
Academy. The center has a 107-acre campus and offers the finest in educational resources. It has fully equipped air-conditioned classrooms, lodging
for students, a learning resource center, and dining and recreational facilities.
There also are several specialized facilities, such as the simulation and exercise
lab, a television studio, and two computer laboratories that are integral to
instruction for many courses.

FEMA personnel were eligible for training at EMI, as were others
involved in emergency preparedness activities at the federal, state, and local
levels. The institute offers training in a broad array of topics, including
natural hazards, radiological hazards, hazardous materials, and community preparedness. It also offers programs in professional development. The
National Fire Academy is open to the fire community throughout the nation
and also offers a wide range of first-rate instruction.

The National Fire Academy was of particular interest to the U.S. Fire
Administration, which is the only department within FEMA that has its
own, quite powerful, constituents. When I became director of FEMA, there
was a rift between the parent agency and the fire administration, which
basically wanted to secede and become an independent agency. The fire
administrator was an old professional firefighter and also a politician. He
was good at both roles. Every member of Congress has firefighters in his or
her community, which means the fire community finds many sympathetic
ears on Capitol Hill.

I did not particularly endear myself to the fire administration. For
one thing, I refused to sit by and let it secede from FEMA. Perhaps more
importantly, I also made a serious blunder. I said paid firefighters are professionals and volunteer firefighters are not. It was as if I had blasphemed
against what everyone in the fire community held sacred, and they let me
know, quickly, how very wrong I was. I apologized, swearing never to make
that mistake again.

Marilyn Quayle and me at the National Fallen Firefighters Memorial. (Courtesy of FEMA)

Then, when time came to draw up FEMA's 1987 budget, I proposed eliminating the U.S. Fire Administration. All federal agencies were subject to the congressional budget-cutting and -balancing mandate known as the Gramm–Rudman–Hollings Act.[3] So in my testimony before a subcommittee of the Senate Committee on Appropriations, I explained: "The 1987 request proposes the elimination of the U.S. Fire Administration for a savings of $7,364,000 and twenty-two work years, made necessary to reach Gramm–Rudman–Hollings targets. . . . In calling for elimination of the U.S. Fire Administration in 1987, we are asking state and local governments, the private sector, and volunteer organizations to share in supporting and maintaining of the fire safety programs."[4]

This was sheer gamesmanship. I had no honest desire to eliminate the U.S. Fire Administration. I was simply recommending a cut that I knew was not going to happen. I knew, with almost absolute certainty, that if the funding for the U.S. Fire Administration were cut, it would be restored. I was just as sure of that as I am sure that my name is Julius Becton Jr. Such games are played every day in Washington.

I was not against Gramm–Rudman–Hollings in theory because the law was merely a requirement to reduce expenditures by the federal government as a whole. But I was opposed to across-the-board budget cuts. Such a blanket approach renders all programs less efficient. My preferred approach would have been to take any program that could be easily done without and to offer that up for elimination. If no one screamed about it, fine. We would come in under budget, and the most valued programs would remain intact. If opposition arose to putting a program on the chopping block, then I would have gained an ally to help me save it if that is what I really want to do.

Need I state the obvious? The U.S. Fire Administration was not eliminated. But having to dodge the budget axe left members of the fire service with a bitter taste in their mouths, and it left me with a soured relationship with that community.

That was not my last mistake. The EMI and the U.S. Fire Academy were both at the National Emergency Training Center, but the two institutions coexisted with little coordination. It did not take a rocket scientist to see that FEMA could easily save some money if the institute and the academy consolidated some of their activities. Why couldn't the same employees handle the registration of students at both institutions, for instance? And why couldn't students attending the schools be housed in the same buildings?

The fire community went berserk when I suggested these changes. I even incurred the wrath of Maryland's Democratic senator Barbara Mikulski because she thought my proposal would mean lost jobs for her constituents. This whole fiasco was my own fault for refusing to recognize those things that I could not change.

For obvious reasons FEMA worked closely with a number of other U.S. government agencies. It was a member of the National Disaster Medical Service, working closely with the Departments of Defense, Health and Human Services, and Veterans Affairs to plan a coordinated medical response to disasters. FEMA also had a cell of eight employees in Colorado Springs, home of the North American Air (now Aerospace) Defense Command, or NORAD. FEMA's role in missile defense was to represent the emergency management aspect of the command and to coordinate state emergency management services if an attack occurred.

FEMA also had a limited but important international dimension. NATO has a Senior Civil Emergency Preparedness Committee (SCEPC), and, as FEMA director, I was the U.S. representative to the committee. The agency had an office in Brussels staffed by five employees, and the SCEPC held semiannual meetings in Brussels that I was required to attend.

The SCEPC coordinated information sharing on civil emergency preparedness among the member nations. As an example of this, during my tenure as FEMA director, the agency participated with the Canadian government in joint exercises that explored what would happen if nuclear weapons were suspected of being on a ship in the Great Lakes. The idea was to play the "what if" game about everything that could happen, from the intelligence suggesting the possibility of a disaster to the military tracking the suspected weapon and to FEMA and its Canadian counterpart preparing for the worst.

More often, however, the disasters faced were real. On 26 April 1986, the world learned that something had gone terribly wrong at the Chernobyl nuclear power plant in the Soviet Union.[5] The Federal Emergency Response Committee, headed by National Security Advisor Colin Powell and under the leadership of Vice President Bush, assembled immediately in the Old Executive Office Building. The committee, made up of representatives from a range of government agencies, discussed what little was known about the accident and what, if anything, should be done. FEMA's responsibility was not to test the atmosphere to determine the level of radiation. That was the responsibility of the National Oceanic and Atmospheric Administration. FEMA's job was to receive the information and ensure that it was disseminated to every state.

FEMA conducted continuity of government exercises every six months. The idea was to practice the procedures that would have to be followed in a crisis situation.

In the United States, the chain of succession runs from the president to the vice president and then, in order, to the Speaker of the House, the Senate majority leader, and the cabinet members, starting with the first cabinet position activated and moving in order to the last. Since the secretary of state was the first cabinet-level position activated in our government, the secretary of state would follow the majority leader in assuming power. Continuity of government plans are designed to make sure that an attack on the United States does not completely decimate the nation's leadership. As a precaution dictated in those plans, the president, the vice president, and all the cabinet members will never all be present at a single public event. A highly visible example of this is during the State of the Union Address when at least one cabinet member is always absent.

FEMA's role in ensuring continuity of government was obviously not to select the person who would become president. The chain of succession answers that question. Rather, FEMA's responsibility was to know who was next in the chain and where that person was so he or she could be kept up to date on emergency situations and transported to where he or she was most needed or could be kept safe. As part of the exercises, we even used helicopters, picking up key governmental officials in Washington and flying them out to a safety. Some people scoffed at the idea of having hideouts for senior leadership, but I think the terror attacks of 11 September 2001 invalidated that school of thought.

During my four years as FEMA director, my senior staff and I briefed every cabinet member on the chain of succession, except for one who just never had time for "such foolishness." As part of the briefing, we gave each cabinet member an ID card with information on the steps they should take if there were an emergency, where they should go, and what they should bring with them. We always explained that we would be conducting exercises and encouraged them to appoint stand-ins to participate in the exercise. All did, again, except for one. She said, "General, I will not have anyone act in my behalf. I will be there." And she did participate. As I have often joked, she was not about to give up her chance to become president for a day.

The U.S. Supreme Court preferred to make its own plans for continuity of operations in an emergency, but FEMA did make preparations for Congress. A lot of money was spent building an underground facility in West Virginia whose secret location at the Greenbrier resort outside of the town of White Sulphur Springs later became public. Since the facility was for members of Congress only, I always wondered whether we could really expect them to go to the site, leaving their families behind. It is very doubtful, but that was the plan.

The West Virginia facility was not the first whose location was inadvertently disclosed. In December 1974 a Trans World Airlines plane crashed into a fog-shrouded mountain in northern Virginia and burned, killing all ninety-two persons aboard.[6] People who went to the rescue noticed much more than the federal government would have preferred. The rescue crews found it mighty strange that cars were parked in the middle of nowhere near the mountaintop, and that was how the cover was blown for Mount Weather, which is a classified, underground shelter for a sizeable number of people near the Pennsylvania border.

Years later I was contacted by CBS's TV newsmagazine *60 Minutes* because Mike Wallace's office wanted me to authorize a visit to Mount Weather. Of course, I refused. "Why not?" the caller asked, adding, "The Russians know about it." I still refused.

I would argue that there is a continuing need for such secret sites despite the fact that the Cold War is over and the possibility of a full nuclear attack against the United States has become pretty remote. The Mount Weather site is still in use today.

Mom Thornton was not just my mother-in-law. She had been a member of our household almost since Louise and I were married, and as an adult, I had spent more time with her than with my own mother. I called her "Mom" because she treated me like her son, and that was how close I felt to her. I must admit that I had grown to rely on her support when Louise and I had a difference of opinion because Mom Thornton usually sided with me. I doubt many sons-in-law can say that.

Sadly, Mom Thornton was growing increasingly frail by 1987. She was ninety-two when she started failing, so I should not have been surprised by that. But I do not think anyone is ever totally prepared to accept the imminent death of a loved one. Mom Thornton had a bout with ovarian cancer in the late 1940s, and she beat it. Four decades later, it was not cancer that threatened her life. It was just old age.

Mom Thornton's decline began gradually. She started staying in her bedroom for longer and longer periods. Eventually, she stopped joining the family for meals. She got progressively weaker. For about a year, she was unable to come downstairs at all and remained in her room. Then the dementia set in. Although she had lucid intervals, they became infrequent. It was hard to watch. Even so, Mom Thorton almost always had a smile on her face.

Louise was working at the Hospice of Northern Virginia during this period, and she loved her work there. A psychiatric nurse by training, Louise felt strongly about allowing people to have a peaceful death and derived tremendous satisfaction from being able to assist terminally ill cancer patients in transitioning to their deaths.

But it is different when you are watching your mother slowly decline. Louise was the primary caregiver, and it was terribly hard on her, bringing all the attendant feelings of frustration, anger, and just plain fatigue. Sometimes, it was a thankless task. Mom Thornton would occasionally become angry, unreasonable, impatient, and irritable. Perhaps she was actually paying her daughter a backhanded compliment when she did that. It may have been that taking the liberty to let it all hang out—to reveal her vulnerabilities and fears—to Louise was a sign that she felt safe with Louise.

We hired a nursing assistant to stay with Mom Thornton on the days that Louise was scheduled to work at the hospice. Louise needed a break just like the family members she interacted with at the hospice.

All the kids were saddened by Mom Thornton's illness. Joyce lived in the area, and Wes was a student at GWU. Since the university campus was just a hop, skip, and a jump from our house, he was able to come home fairly frequently. Hearing about Louise's experiences at the hospice helped all of our children handle the experience with their grandmother.

Wes and Mommom, as the children called her, had a history of arguing. Wes would say something, and Mom Thornton would disagree. And vice versa. On one of the occasions when Wes was home from school, he was sitting with Mom Thornton in her room. She opened up to him and shared her fears about dying and how she was afraid to let go. He told her it was okay, that she could let go.

Mom Thornton must have taken him at his word. The ordeal ended on 18 April 1987, a short time after their conversation. The morning before she died, it became crystal clear to us that Mom Thornton was in extremis and probably would not make it through the night, so we took her to Walter Reed Army Hospital. She died the next morning. She was buried in Arlington National Cemetery in the same plot where Louise and I will be buried.

During my tenure as FEMA director, the Seabrook Station nuclear power plant in New Hampshire was being brought online. The Nuclear Regulatory Commission is responsible for testing each reactor facility's emergency preparedness plan for inside its perimeter. FEMA is responsible for testing emergency preparedness outside the perimeter.

I had no concern about the manner in which FEMA was completing its responsibilities. But New Hampshire's Republican governor, John Sununu, did not share my view. He did not think FEMA was completing its testing fast enough.

Sununu called me in the spring of 1988 to complain that FEMA was dragging its feet and to say that he expected us to speed up the process. The second phone call from him ended with a dial tone. He hung up on me before I had a chance to say good-bye. Then he showed up unexpectedly in my office. After I told him I was satisfied with FEMA's pace, he stormed out, threatening to go straight to the White House.

I never received a call from the White House instructing me to do what Governor Sununu wanted done. Although I knew our encounters had not been pleasant, I did not think there was any bad blood between Sununu and me. As far as I was concerned, he was simply trying to get what he wanted, and I was doing my job by refusing to cave in.

My encounters with Sununu all took place before the 1988 presidential election. The governor was very active in George Bush's campaign, and after Bush won, he appointed Sununu his chief of staff.

I received a call from Bush's transition team asking if I would be interested in becoming secretary of the Department of Veterans Affairs, which would be elevated to cabinet status in March 1989. Louise did not want me to take the job, but I jumped at the opportunity. I would have loved to become the department's first secretary.

But it was not to be. I was edged out of the position, I believe, by a political debt that had to be paid. Edward J. Derwinski, a former Democratic congressman from Illinois who had held various positions in the Reagan administration, needed a home, and the job went to him.

John Sununu, the chief of staff designate, did not offer any objections to my becoming secretary of Veterans Affairs. But a bit to my surprise, in the course of his short-lived tenure in that job, he did follow up on his frustrations with FEMA. He announced in early 1989 that I would not continue as the agency's director.

It was quite obvious that he would have his way. Even my personal contacts with the influential members of the FEMA Advisory Board* were not sufficient for President Bush to overrule his chief of staff. I was facing a somewhat uncertain future.

That spring, I was contacted by several friends who asked whether I would be interested in becoming the president of Prairie View A&M University. I

---

*Membership: Dr. Wesley Posvar — Chairman, Dr. Harold Agnew, Dr. William O. Baker, Robert H. Flax, Dr. Jacques S. Gansler, W. H. Krome George, Gen. Andrew Goodpaster, Dr. Samuel P. Huntington, Gen. Glenn A. Kent, Dr. Lawrence J. Korb, Dr. Robert H. Kupperman, Dr. William E. Mayer, Gen. Paul Nitze, Honorable Stewart L. Pittman, Robert L. Ratchford Jr., Gen. Roscoe Robinson Jr., Gen. Brent Scowcroft, Francis M. Staszesky, Dr. Albert M. Stone, Dr. Edward Teller, and Dr. Eugene P. Wigner.

did not have an earned doctorate, and I was considered a military man rather than an educator, but I jokingly said, "Sure, put my name in the hat."

Since there was no real pressure from the White House for my immediate departure, I had time to consider other options, most of which were not particularly appealing. In mid-June Connie Newman called to say she had mentioned me to Tony Welters, the CEO and owner of American Coastal Industries (ACI). The company was involved in the production of steel sheds for transporting armor vehicles overseas on commercial ships and supplying computers to the federal government. I met Tony, and we hit it off immediately. My last day at FEMA was my birthday, 29 June. I became chief operating officer at ACI on July 1.

My final days at FEMA were rather emotionally charged. My immediate staff and I had weathered many storms and developed friendships that last to this day. And during the countdown to my departure, someone sent me a copy of the 13 June 1989 *Congressional Record*. I was pleasantly surprised to find that Rep. Norman D. Shumway, a Republican from California, had paid me a tribute. An excerpt from Shumway's statement follows:

> While none of us enjoys dealing with severe disasters, I am sure we can all agree that General Becton has made such emergencies more manageable. His leadership, experience, and combat-proven abilities under pressure made his stewardship at FEMA impressive. . . . Under his command, FEMA's 2,400 employees provided rapid, effective response and relief to disasters, be they natural or man-made. During his tenure, FEMA has mitigated 73 disasters and emergencies of sufficient severity to be declared eligible by the president for federal assistance. His prioritizing has seen some $1.5 billion well applied.
>
> General Becton has dedicated 44 years of his life to federal service, 39 of them in the U.S. Army. His military career reflects his determination, drive and excellence: he rose through the ranks from private to lieutenant general. His meritorious service, courage, and valor have been recognized repeatedly: he won 13 awards for meritorious service and 7 decorations for valor in combat during World War II, and the conflicts in both Korea and Vietnam. . . .
>
> I am pleased to have this opportunity to express my appreciation and commendation to Gen. Julius Becton for a job well done. Additionally, I know that my colleagues will join me in wishing the very best to him, his wife, Louise, and their family as they enter another challenging chapter of their lives.[7]

In 1989 Louise and I gained both a daughter and a son. Wes and Ingrid were married on 16 September at the chapel at Fort Belvoir, Virginia. It was a military wedding with all the pomp, including dress blue uniforms and saber arches. Wes had two best men, and I was honored to be one of them.

Approximately 175 people from all over the world attended their wedding. As it happened, 16 September was the day Hurricane Hugo hit the Mid-Atlantic states. A few wedding guests were involved in automobile accidents because the rain was so torrential. The basement of the church flooded, and Ingrid had to be carried out to the limousine. Thankfully, by the end of the wedding reception at Fort Lesley J. McNair, the rain had ended and the sky was clear.

On 25 November 1989, our youngest daughter Renee and Frank Strickland were married at the chapel at Fort Myer. We had lived at Fort Myer during Renee's last two years in high school, and she had always thought it would be pretty cool to get married there. I had another opportunity to wear my military dress uniform. Renee asked me to wear it because the Army had been such a huge part of her childhood, and it was still such a huge part of me. She wanted me to be my Army self at least one more time.

Renee and Frank met courtesy of the U.S. government. She was an Air Force captain stationed in Los Angeles, and he was working as a civilian for the Department of the Navy in Washington, D.C. They had been working long distance, over the telephone, on the same project.

Before she had a chance to see him, Renee expected Frank to be much like the rest of the men she was working with—several years her senior and a bit on the crusty side. So when she walked into the office at Cape Canaveral Air Station where they were to meet for the first time in person, she walked back out. The only person in the office was this young, very good-looking man. As it turned out, she says, she was in the right place, and he was the right man.

Renee and Frank did not have a hurricane for their wedding. They had snow instead. Luckily, everyone was still able to move around.

We had a champagne breakfast for Renee the morning of her wedding at our home. Louise noticed that Renee was a bit on the nervous side, and knew exactly what to do. She fixed Renee a mimosa, partly to calm her nerves and partly because of her long-standing love of champagne, which began when we were stationed in France.

As I was getting ready to walk her down the aisle, Renee was shaking like a leaf. I asked, "Are you sure you want to do this?" Nearly twenty years later, I know she is still glad she said yes.

After I had left FEMA, Republican congressman Thomas Ridge of Pennsylvania—the same Tom Ridge who became the first secretary of the U.S. Department of Homeland Security when it was established after 9/11—wrote an article quite critical of FEMA. I felt obligated to respond, and I did so in a letter to the editor.**

Essentially, I explained that FEMA did not have authority over all those who respond to disasters, that it was merely the federal coordinating agent for a wide range of emergency management activities, and that its roughly 2,500 employees had jurisdiction over 130 separate programs and activities. "It is clear to me that if there were no FEMA, someone would have to invent one," I wrote. It would still need to be independent, I continued, but if we were inventing it today, I would suggest some changes. Among those I listed were that I would get rid of the political appointees, and "I would enhance the agency's ability to provide emergency public information to disaster victims so that the real victims of disasters receive accurate guidance in obtaining assistance uncluttered by the debate of politicians and others that create false expectations and confusion." I conceded that FEMA could have done some things better, citing as examples the responses to Hurricane Hugo and the Loma Prieta earthquake near San Francisco, California, which had both occurred in late 1989. But the finger-pointing that ensued had been off base, I wrote, noting, "The professionals at FEMA deserve better than they have been receiving."

Ridge's article was not the last critique of FEMA that irritated me. In 1993 the U.S. General Accounting Office (GAO) issued a report that bothered me no end. Some in Congress had asked GAO to "examine the adequacy of the federal strategy for responding to catastrophic disasters and to develop solutions for improving it." I found the report biased from the opening paragraph on, and I was not surprised. Many of those who had requested the report had crossed swords with FEMA in the past. I was invited to appear before the GAO officials hearing the review of the report in early 1993, and in my remarks, I pointedly asked if they wanted to go back to 1979, when the functions performed by FEMA were dispersed through five or more agencies.[8]

** *Washington Post*, 17 November 1989.

Despite the unfairness of the report, it was quite clear to me that the FEMA I left in 1989 was not the FEMA that is now fighting for its life. With all due respect to the series of acting directors and directors who succeeded me, the allegations on the table would not have been made during my tenure. The most basic leadership has long been missing at the agency. And since those at the top of the organization have not been taking charge, the agency has foundered.

That brings us to the FEMA of 2005 and the federal response to Hurricanes Katrina and Rita. Turning on the television and seeing the faces of New Orleanians trying to seek higher ground as the city flooded reminded me of so much I had seen elsewhere, including the despair of Ethiopians ravaged by starvation during the 1985 drought and the terror of Vietnamese civilians caught in free-fire zones in 1968.

I was in Houston, Texas, on Friday, 2 September 2005, to attend the annual Prairie View—Texas Southern football classic. I made a reconnaissance from my hotel to the Astrodome and Reliant Stadium to check out the route I would take to the game. That is when I heard on the radio that Katrina victims were being transported from the Superdome in New Orleans to the Houston Astrodome. I saw buses arriving at the Astrodome. Curious to see how things were going, I hung around to see for myself.

What I saw was very close to chaos. After passengers were unloaded, they did not seem to know where to go, and no one else seemed to know how to help. There did not appear to be anyone in charge. Local citizens who had brought donations to the Astrodome were leaving the supplies in the parking lot helter-skelter.

More than mildly disturbed, I called FEMA headquarters in Washington, D.C., on my cell phone and asked to speak to whomever was in charge. I ended up talking to someone who identified himself as the deputy director. "I am Julius Becton calling from the Astrodome in Houston," I said. "I used to be. . . ." He interrupted, saying, "I know who you are!" I then described what I was observing and asked him to tell Mike Brown, who was then FEMA director, that I was here and prepared to help in any way. That was the last thing I heard from FEMA. My call was never acknowledged. When I returned to Virginia I told the secretary of state and Nebraska senator Chuck Hagel's office what had happened and offered to help if there was a public investigation.

I realize that there have been major changes in FEMA's mission and structure since my days at the agency. During the Clinton days, FEMA lost its national security responsibilities and many of its ancillary activities and became primarily an agency that dealt with natural disasters, specializing in preparedness, mitigation, response, search, rescue, and recovery.

So what happened? I think I have more than a clue. When the Department of Homeland Security was being set up, I was asked to spend some time with various congressional staff members. I cautioned them about the pitfalls of creating a bureaucracy—added layers between FEMA and the White House—that would impede FEMA's ability to accomplish its mission. During my directorship I had a direct link to the president and vice president. Mike Brown did not. In addition, FEMA had lost key professional personnel since the late 1980s.

When the magnitude of Katrina became known, it seems to me there was only one place for the FEMA director to be, and that was at the point of greatest need. It is true that local and state governments are responsible for their own people. But when it became obvious that they were incapable of doing so because they were ill prepared and overwhelmed or incompetent, that is when Mike Brown should have done what Lt. Gen. Russel L. Honoré, who was in charge of the military response, actually did. Honoré arrived in the area of the worst devastation and immediately took charge. As New Orleans mayor Ray Nagin said of Honoré during a radio interview, "He came off that doggone chopper and started cussing and people started moving."[9]

By the way, although I never did speak with any FEMA folks after 2 September, I talked with Russ Honoré at least three times during his tour of the area. I congratulated him on the job he was doing, and we talked about the FEMA representation on the Army staff and how it differed from my days as FEMA director.

During his remarks at Coretta Scott King's funeral on 7 February 2006, former president Jimmy Carter suggested that if the Katrina victims in New Orleans had not been overwhelmingly black, the response would have been entirely different. Could that be true? Possibly. Would it have taken days to relocate these citizens? I think not. After all, OFDA had personnel on the scene in Mexico City within hours after the earthquake of 1985.[10]

Jimmy Carter had the courage to speak aloud what other people had thought but were too polite, or too politic, to say.

★ ★ ★

CHAPTER SEVENTEEN

Prairie View

W hen I joined ACI I informed the company president that I was engaged in conversations about a job as president of PVAMU. I thought I was a real long shot, in part because I did not think PVAMU was ready for a leader with a background in the military.

The first inkling I had that I was a serious contender for the position was in September 1989, when I received a series of questions from the search committee. In follow-up, I was invited to meet with selected members of the Texas A&M University System Board of Regents and Dr. John B. Coleman, who had been the first black member of the board. Interestingly, every member of the board was an Army officer of one type or another. After a second meeting with the regents, I went to PVAMU for an interview with an eighteen-member panel that represented the students, faculty, and community leaders.

I found out later that Henry Ponder, president of Fisk University, was the other finalist for the PVAMU position. As it happened, my military background worked to my advantage. PVAMU had been having serious financial problems and was on the brink of being thrown into receivership. The regents' and the university panel's desire for someone to come in and "kick butt" outweighed their desire for an academician to head the university.

I looked forward to being president of Prairie View. I had been there as an ROTC instructor in 1957 and had earned my undergraduate degree from the school in 1960. I wanted to leave my mark on the institution, to make it better for the students already enrolled and for those who would attend in the future. "The Hill," as the university is affectionately known, had done well by me.

The PVAMU Web site describes the university's history this way:

Prairie View A&M University, the second oldest public institution of higher education in Texas, originated in the Texas Constitution of 1876. On August 14, 1876, the Texas Legislature established the "Agricultural and Mechanical College of Texas for Colored Youths" and placed responsibility for its management with the Board of Directors of the Agricultural and Mechanical College at Bryan. The A&M College of Texas for Colored Youths opened at Prairie View, Texas, on March 11, 1878.

The university's original curriculum was designated by the Texas Legislature in 1879 to be that of a "normal school" for the preparation and training of teachers. This curriculum was expanded to include the arts and sciences, home economics, agriculture, mechanical arts, and nursing after the university was established as a branch of the Agricultural Experiment Station (Hatch Act, 1887) and as a land grant college (Morrill Act, 1890). Thus began the tradition of agricultural research and community service, which continues today.[1]

PVAMU is one of the nation's top producers of black engineers and has graduated more African American three-star generals/flag officers than any other institution in the country. Its College of Nursing, based in Houston, is one of the state's largest sources of African American registered nurses.

Located in eastern Texas, forty-five miles northwest of Houston, PVAMU's physical terrain belies it name. Instead of treeless grasslands, the campus has large oaks and maples, and the lawn areas are a rich green. When I attended, the university had almost 3,000 students. The student body numbered more than 5,000 when I became president, and enrollment had grown to 7,262 by the fall of 2002.[2]

Our move to Prairie View in December 1989 marked the thirty-seventh time Louise and I had moved since we had been married. It was old hat to us. This time, however, the move was very different. Mom Thornton had died, and all of our children had left home. It was just Louise and me.

The PVAMU president's house had not been used as such for quite some time, and it had to be renovated for us. Because it would not be ready until the spring, Louise and I spent our first two weeks in Prairie View with Walter and Audrey Redd. I had first met the Texas-born and -bred Walt in 1953, when we both attended infantry courses at Fort Benning. In the summer of 1955 Walt was assigned to the 42nd Armored Infantry Battalion in Mainz, Germany, assuming command of headquarters and headquarters company.

I was already the commander of that battalion's Company D. Three years later, when I left Prairie View's ROTC department to become a full-time student, Captain Redd replaced me. After he was separated from the Army, Walt went to work in the bursar's office.

After we left the Redds', Louise and I moved into a house we had rented from a former PVAMU faculty member. The house needed a thorough cleaning because it had been unoccupied for quite some time. Irene Wallace, who we hired to do that job, did it so well that Louise was mightily impressed. When we moved into the president's house Irene applied to become house-keeper, and Louise was sure Irene was right for the job. In addition to her housekeeping skills, Irene was from a small town near Prairie View and knew the community and the culture of the area. She kept the house immaculate. More important, she was loyal and discreet. She also had a good sense of humor, and we shared many laughs.

We arrived at Prairie View in December on the day Christmas recess began. We were shocked at what we found. The students were gone, and the campus looked like a garbage pit. Instead of taking their trash to the trash containers, students had gotten into the habit of throwing their trash out of their dormitory windows onto the ground.

So my first task as president was literally housekeeping. I had the university groundskeepers clear the yards and get the dormitories cleaned up. I vowed that this would never happen again, at least on my dime, and the solution was easy. Students were notified that littering the grounds could lead to expulsion. I have no idea how many students we threw out of school that first semester, but there were quite a few. The word spread like wildfire that the new president was crazy or something, but also that he meant business.

I held my first annual meeting with the entire student body at the William J. "Billy" Nicks Fieldhouse shortly after the Christmas recess. It was my intention to use the meeting in the building nicknamed the "Baby Dome" as a forum to introduce myself and deliver a state-of-the-university address in which I updated students on new policies and informed them about what was going well and what was not. Of course, attendance was voluntary, and only a few hundred students showed up for the first meeting. I quickly got the point. All other campus activities were curtailed during future all-campus meetings, and entertainment such as having the marching band play or the Concert Choir sing was offered. The audience subsequently grew to several thousand.

As another way to communicate, I started a biweekly radio talk show on KPVU, the university radio station. Devonya Smith, a senior communications major, acted as emcee. She took call-in questions and also solicited comments on campus, and it turned out to be a very candid thirty-minute program that reached beyond the campus boundaries.

I also held monthly meetings in the administration building to entertain questions from the students. These "Chats with the President" demonstrated the administration's commitment to making Prairie View an open community and our willingness to listen to student concerns. The usual participants were those with problems, concerns, or axes to grind. Students with no problems did not normally attend these meetings.

To keep up-to-date with what was happening, I also formed a Student Advisory Council made up of student leaders, which met monthly in my office. I routinely ate lunch at the dining hall, either with students or faculty. And I commandeered a golf cart from the maintenance department to facilitate my movement about the sprawling campus. Traveling by golf cart was a great way to give visitors a tour, and it also made it easier for me to make unannounced inspections and visits (some called them "sneak attacks") when I saw the need to do so. Finally, as I had in previous jobs, I maintained an open-door policy, letting it be known that anyone could schedule an appointment to see me.

I knew that it would be an uphill battle to win over the students and faculty. My military background did not endear me to some factions. Rumors circulated that the university would have reveille in the morning when the flag was raised and that students would be required to wear uniforms, march to class, and salute their professors.

Faculty reactions to my appointment were more troubling. Approximately 20 percent of the current faculty had also been at PVAMU in 1957 when I was an assistant professor of military science and tactics. This group of long-serving faculty constituted my core support. Another 60 percent had open minds about my appointment as president. But the remaining one-fifth wanted nothing to do with me. They were either antimilitary, or they harbored big-time resentment because I did not have an earned doctorate. Some of my detractors fell into both groups.

Shortly after my arrival, the campus police informed me that there was a drug problem in one of the dormitories. I was hardly surprised; the same thing was happening at colleges and universities throughout the country. At

PVAMU, however, it was not just a matter of students using drugs. Students in the dormitory were actually producing crack. There was no way I would tolerate that.

With my support, the campus police contacted the proper law enforcement authorities and secured their cooperation. A mutual decision was then made to plant an undercover police officer from another community in the dormitory. Posing as a student, the officer moved in, and in very short order we resolved the problem. But even though the deterrent impact of the sting was tremendous, I was not satisfied with just shutting down the crack operation. I knew that if the students did not purchase their drugs on campus, they would buy them elsewhere. Since my philosophy on illegal drug use is zero tolerance, I felt we needed to keep the heat up.

Enter the drug-sniffing dogs. Periodic, unannounced inspections of all male and female dormitories were initiated and the first was fairly successful in uncovering hidden stashes. The second and third inspections were not as successful because word spread from dorm to dorm that a raid was under way. This gave offenders time to dispose of their drugs. The fourth inspection had a different modus operandi: The dogs were used to sniff automobiles in the parking lots first.

By the end of my second year as president, the need for inspections had decreased dramatically. My administration took the harshest action that could be taken against student drug offenders. No exceptions.

Just as the drug problem was not unique to PVAMU, neither was premarital sex. I regularly saw female students leaving male dormitories while I was out for my early morning runs. Perhaps because I have four daughters and seven granddaughters, I wanted to discourage this behavior. Sure, they may have been consenting adults, but that was not the issue. I did not think parents had sent their children to school to cohabit. They sent them to PVAMU to get an education, and I do not think sex education was what they had in mind.

A complaint from a female student focused my attention on this problem. She was sick and tired of being kicked out of her room when her roommate's boyfriend came over. Think about it. Why should she have had to inconvenience herself for their pleasure?

I could not stop the students from having sex, but I could certainly frustrate their ability to do it on campus, particularly because PVAMU had no coeducational dorms. Although there had always been restrictions on the times male and female students could be in each other's dorms, the restrictions were not being enforced when I became president. I set out to enforce them. The policy regarding dorm visiting hours for individuals of the opposite sex was prominently disclosed in literature sent to students, and I personally discussed it at freshman orientation and all other student assemblies. Dorm monitors also made spot inspections. A student was given a warning for a first offense. For a second, he or she was expelled.

Some might argue that I was on shaky legal ground. To me, that argument has no merit. A student had no vested right to be in any dormitory other than the one he or she was assigned to. I am pleased to report that I heard few complaints once the crackdown on visiting hours began.

A larger potential problem when I took over at PVAMU was that access to the campus was totally unrestricted. This did not sit too well with me. I felt that a gatehouse was needed to achieve the appearance of control on campus. When the gatehouse first went up, some students complained that its real purpose was to lock them in. After a couple of weeks, however, the buzz died down.

I also ordered the installation of blue-light phones with a direct line to campus security across the campus, and I encouraged female students to walk in pairs after nightfall.

I had heard that the university might have a problem with guns. That was believable; after all, we were in Texas, where gun-toting is a state tradition. Tradition notwithstanding, I found it intolerable that students might have guns and other weapons on campus. My idea to solve the problem was one of my less-brilliant ones, however. I had the campus police put out an amnesty box, where students could turn in their weapons, no questions asked. We may have gotten a few rusty knives, but that was all.

There was also a rash of false fire alarms, particularly in the women's dormitories. I publicized a $100 reward program for information leading to identification of the person or people who were pulling the alarms. Disciplinary options for when the perpetrator was caught ranged from restricting the student to his or her classes and dorm room to expulsion.

I only had to pay the reward one time because members of the Student Government Association and the student disciplinary board were more than willing to help police the campus. Students grew weary of having to leave their dormitories at all hours of the night, and they started speaking up.

One of the primary reasons I had been selected as PVAMU president was to restore fiscal integrity at the university. Under my predecessor, Dr. Percy

Pierre, PVAMU had fared well academically. But Percy apparently failed to pay attention to a host of administrative details, and over time they ballooned into big problems. By the time I arrived, the Board of Regents had stripped Percy of his powers over purchasing and procurement and his authority to bind the university in external matters. The school was on the brink of being thrown into receivership.

My goal was to regain control. From just a glimpse I knew that I had my work cut out for me. There were serious fiscal irregularities. The athletic program was picking up funds from elsewhere to support its activities. Although there was a cap on the number of out-of-state students who could receive scholarships at in-state rates, that cap was being ignored. Certain vendors were unwilling to provide needed products and services until outstanding bills were paid.

It was a long time before I learned the true extent of the complex web of woes that was the university's finances. The simplest explanation for why the trouble started was that during the early 1980s the university did not have an adequate automated accounting system. The purchasing process was manual, and it took weeks, if not months, to order supplies and materials. To make matters worse, the Pierre administration brought in a new fiscal staff and removed many of the people who knew the existing systems.

During much of the 1980s, in order to meet the immediate purchasing needs of the staff and faculty, the controller allowed orders up to $250 to be placed verbally, with the paperwork sent to his staff later. This inevitably led to disaster. If a faculty member needed $1,000 worth of a product, a staffer in purchasing would place four orders of $250 each, thus meeting the letter, if not the spirit, of the controller's policy. And staffers in purchasing generally did not send the orders to accounts payable, so when that department received invoices, it was often unable to determine which account to charge. On at least two occasions the controller instructed accounts payable to simply pay all bills, which led to numerous vendors being paid several times.

After years of operating this way the university ran out of funds and had several hundred thousand dollars worth of invoices due. To cover costs it could not put off, the university began drawing on local scholarship and endowment funds that were deposited in local banks and were not supposed to be used for general expenses. Eventually, the PVAMU was so broke that it was forced to borrow $1 million from Texas A&M University. State auditors reported that Prairie View's accounting records were so poor and inaccurate that it would not be a good idea to automate them anyway. This led to the threat by the state to place the university in receivership.

In the spring of 1989 Dr. Perry Adkisson, chancellor of the Texas A&M University System (TAMUS), focused on the particularly troublesome topic of PVAMU's athletic programs. In a memo to the interim PVAMU president Dr. Milton Bryant, Dr. Adkisson noted that the athletic program had been operating at a sizeable deficit for several years and suggested the formation of a task force to recommend a plan to eliminate the deficit.

As I learned later the projected athletics budget deficit for fiscal year 1989–90—my first as PVAMU president—was $804,679. The only way to significantly reduce it and keep the athletic program going would be to cut the number of scholarships awarded to athletes. The task force charged with studying the problem had asked whether PVAMU could operate its athletic program without scholarships and answered its own question in the negative in a memorandum circulated to university leaders. The task force also concluded, "Prairie View A&M University will not be able to carry out its essential auxiliary needs and functions in housing, dining hall repairs and renovation, and health services if it continues to support the deficit in athletics at its present level."

Within my first three weeks on the job, I asked the Texas Rangers to conduct an audit. I suspected that some felonies had been committed. It was also necessary to get up to speed quickly on how the university was funded, so I could better understand what had happened, see the pitfalls to avoid, and chart the fiscal recovery of PVAMU.

The sergeant who led the audit was a white man who was about five feet, eleven inches tall. The other ranger was a black man who stood at about six feet, two inches. Both commanded respect. Since I wanted people on campus to know the extent of the problems that we faced, I had the Rangers appear at one of my monthly meetings with the students. They garnered plenty of attention. It did not hurt matters any that they were armed and wore their Ranger cowboy boots and big white Stetsons both outside and indoors. And ultimately, the Rangers confirmed my suspicions. They did find instances of improper use of funds.

In April 1990 PVAMU was scheduled for accreditation by the Southern Association of Colleges and Schools. I would have preferred more time to prepare, but that was not in the cards. Fortunately, Dr. E. Joahanne Thomas-Smith, who was the chair of the university's English Department, headed the accreditation team. We passed the review.

After the accreditation I held an offsite retreat for the PVAMU deans and vice presidents to discuss the challenges we faced. Harold Bonner, vice president for administration, gave a presentation on the university's fiscal situation. Judging from their reactions, this was the first time the management team had heard just how bad things were. For example, housing and dining were supposed to be self-sustaining. They were not and never would be until the university stopped permitting money generated from these accounts to be used for other purposes.

After much agonizing I made the decision to suspend nine of the eleven intercollegiate athletic sports programs. Athletic scholarships were a major financial drain, and the university simply could not afford them. I discussed the matter with Calvin Rolark, who was president of the PVAMU National Alumni Association, to give him a heads-up and to explain my thinking, but I did not win him over. Calvin was adamantly opposed to the suspension of the athletic programs.

My office contacted the media and told them there was going to be a very important announcement at PVAMU pertaining to athletics. All three major networks covered the press conference on 26 May 1990. They smelled bad news. I announced that all but two of the university's intercollegiate athletic programs were suspended, even basketball and football. I retained cross-country and track because our women's coach, Barbara Jacket, had already been named the head coach for the U.S. women's track team for the 1992 Olympics in Barcelona, Spain. There was no way would I harm her program!

My decision to suspend the athletics programs caused a firestorm. In early June a group of alumni invited me to Houston to discuss what I had done.

I could have talked until I was blue in the face and it would not have made a lick of difference. The alumni either did not understand or did not want to hear my explanation that the university could no longer afford to channel funds to athletics from other areas that screamed for attention. I told the alumni that the dormitories were in dire need of repairs. There were fire code violations galore, and the Texas fire marshal had threatened to close PVAMU's dorms if they were not brought into compliance. We also had an asbestos problem in five of the dormitories, including the largest, which housed some 750 female students.

Another perspective of the controversy. (Reprinted with permission of "Tank McNamara")

I had naively thought the alumni would support my decision, or at least come to see that it was necessary. I was wrong. Even though what I described made for a pretty sorry mess, they felt my decision to suspend the athletic programs was grossly unjustified.

By mid-July, almost coincidental with the national PVAMU alumni association convention in Detroit, ten of the eleven sports programs had been reinstated. All except football had found alternative means of financing from a variety of sources, including private individuals, businesses, and fraternal organizations.[3] Alumni athletes who were members of the National Basketball Association and Major League Baseball were obvious targets of the fund-raising efforts.

But none of this changed the way the alumni felt about me. The June meeting with alumni was a cakewalk compared with the reception I received at the July convention in Detroit. They wanted to hang me in effigy. They were soliciting signatures on a declaration of no confidence and carrying placards and wearing pins and buttons that carried the same message. I felt like I was being impeached.

TAMUS Chancellor Perry Adkisson was routinely invited to address the alumni at the annual PVAMU conventions. After the president of the alumni association introduced him, Perry went to the podium. He gazed out over the audience for a long moment, and then he spoke. The first thing out of his mouth caught everyone by surprise. He said, "You didn't elect President Becton and you can't fire him, so you might as well support him." Having dispensed with that preliminary matter, Perry went on to discuss TAMUS and how Prairie View fit into it. Then he answered a few innocuous questions and went on his way. Later that afternoon there was a vote on the "no confidence" resolution. The results were overwhelmingly in support of me.

I still feel I made the right decision in suspending the athletic programs. However, the opposition was understandable. It was Texas, after all, where football is king. When I was commander at Fort Hood, I remember gazing out of the window on Friday night flights back to the base and being able to track the towns across the state by the football fields that were lit. And although PVAMU had not had a winning football season since 1964, many of the more vocal alumni had been at the university when the football team was enjoying its best years.

Interestingly, the beginning of the decline of PVAMU football coincided with the enactment of the federal Civil Rights Act of 1964. Integration offered choices to black athletes that were previously foreclosed, and many black athletes chose to further their education at majority white colleges and universities that enticed them with more attractive financial aid packages. PVAMU and other HBCUs could not compete against large state schools and rich private ones for star black athletes.

I cannot say that the administration that preceded mine closed its eyes and fed the PVAMU football program. There was simply a lack of fiscal oversight, which enabled the athletic director to have funds channeled from other areas to football. Although the athletic director was eventually indicted by a grand jury, neither he nor any other members of the administration were ever accused of embezzlement. They were definitely guilty of using funds for improper purposes, however. The endowment is a case in point. Although it was rumored that PVAMU's endowment was worth as much as $18 million at one time, it had been completely depleted when I took over as university president. All the money had been used for administrative and operational purposes.

The university leadership took a wide range of actions to restore PVAMU's fiscal integrity in the early 1990s. We established a team to make sure the accounting system was automated within a specified time frame. We drew up an operating budget that was consistent with the funds available to the university, and we demanded accountability for those involved in spending. We eliminated purchasing violations and got rid of nonessential personnel. We saved money by contracting out many of the service operations. Travel and other unnecessary expenditures were reduced, and we lobbied for an increased share of funding from TAMUS and the state legislature. Finally, we initiated and followed sound fiscal policies and procedures.

My inauguration as president was scheduled for the fall of 1990, and it was decided early on to hold the ceremonies in conjunction with Homecoming. Since no funds were budgeted for the inauguration, frugality was the operative word.

My first decision, who would be the keynote speaker, was easy. Shortly after I arrived on campus I asked Colin Powell, who was by this time chairman of the Joint Chiefs of Staff, to visit as soon as possible. The inauguration seemed an appropriate occasion, and he agreed to come as long as world events did not get in the way. As the fall arrived, Colin's office advised that he was committed to three activities in October and November: 1) visiting the forces gathering in the Middle East as a run-up to the first Gulf War; 2) escorting his Russian counterpart through the United States; and 3) visiting PVAMU. Needless to say, we felt very good about the company we were keeping.

For Colin's presentation, the inauguration planning committee settled on a day devoted to the military. Army cadets and Navy midshipmen would be on parade, and a firing battery from Fort Hood would render the proper salute. I was authorized by the Board of Regents to present an honorary doctor of law degree to Colin Powell; it was only the second such degree ever awarded by PVAMU. In addition, there would be a fashion show, an open house, and a black-tie dinner at the Baby Dome, to which the public was invited.

I was a little disappointed in the lack of participation by students and alumni. I suspect that many used the occasion to show their lingering displeasure over my football decision. But the bulk of PVAMU faculty attended, along with the traditional assortment of academic dignitaries and a contingent of military personnel from Fort Hood and other Texas-based facilities who were responsible for creating the largest collection of helicopters ever on campus.

Although the faculty's commitment to the students was unquestionable, it was impossible not to notice that, as an institution of higher learning, PVAMU was failing its students in some respects. The students were not being well served in terms of housing and facilities in particular. And they were often given the back-of-the hand treatment by staff. Somewhere along the way, some of the staff and even the faculty lost sight of the fact that the students were the reason that they were employed by PVAMU. To improve attitudes I arranged quite a few seminars for key administration and clerical staff on how to deal with the public, which in this case meant the students. I let my managers know in no uncertain terms that I would not tolerate shabby treatment of the students.

Management of the dormitories was one of my first concerns. The littering and vandalism had been the fault of students. But I strongly suspected that for the situation to have deteriorated to the point it had reached when I arrived on campus, the management of the dorms by physical plant personnel had to be lacking. I put new people in many positions.

Of course, there are always some outstanding people in place. Adam Barnett, who managed the freshman dormitory, was one of those gems. The guy was a genius in working with the students. He created a family environment, and he put his money where his mouth was, more than occasionally reaching into his own pocket to help the students.

Using Adam Barnett as a base, the university leadership set out to implement an excellent idea Louise came up with to assign houseparents to each dorm to enhance the living environment. We recruited retired faculty and other people in the community to help the young resident advisers, who were students themselves and not particularly experienced in managing people.

At about the same time, Louise started to hold birthday parties in the president's house for all the students born in a given month. We started off by having cake and ice cream, but soon expanded that into a much heavier meal with punch. Initially, we ordered the cakes from the caterer who ran the campus dining facility. But those cakes were not nearly as good as the cakes Louise baked herself, and they were much more expensive, so we provided our own. Presents were awarded to students who drew their names out of a hat. The presents were well received, but we soon learned that the students preferred money to, say, instant cameras. Seldom did anyone leave without winning something.

To this day, I am still moved by the reaction of one senior. After her name was drawn and she saw that she had won a camera, she started crying. I asked, "What's wrong with her? What have we done?" One of her friends went over to her and came back and said, "You're not going to believe this, but this is the first present she ever got for her birthday." After talking with the student, Louise learned that even her mother did not call or send a card on her birthday, and she had never had a birthday party. And she was not the only one. Too many of our students came to college from broken homes, having only one parent or none at all.

Too many of PVAMU's students came to the university with academic handicaps, as well. Reading skills in particular were horrible. I had seen the test scores. Think about how poor reading skills get translated in the classroom. If a student cannot read, he or she usually will not understand the spoken word either. And imagine what goes on in a chemistry class or a math class if students do not understand the lecture or the lab instructions. But PVAMU's faculty did a tremendous job in bringing their students up to par. Despite their academic deficits when they came out of high school, PVAMU students I knew almost all got up to speed in the classroom, graduated, and went on to secure decent jobs.

English teachers faced the greatest challenge. I will give just one case in point. The College of Agriculture sent Louise and me a smoked turkey from its farm one Thanksgiving. It was huge, and there was no way we could eat all of it by ourselves. Adam Barnett had identified some students who would not be going home for the holiday, and he was trying to pull together a Thanksgiving meal for them. Louise said we would be glad to give him half of our turkey. When classes resumed after the holiday, an English teacher asked her students to write an essay about their vacation. The teacher sent me one of the papers, in part to let me know how the student appreciated our contribution to the Thanksgiving meal Adam had put together, but also in part to let me see what she faced in the classroom. It was so poorly written that I sent the essay back to the teacher with the comment, "Thank you for the note, but I can also appreciate the challenge you face."

I would love to say that all of the students PVAMU enrolled came to campus with SAT scores of 1,000 and ACT scores of 22, but I would be lying. The university has an open-admissions policy, allowing anyone with a high school diploma or a general educational development, or GED, diploma to earn provisional admission.

This is not an indictment against the students. It is an indictment of the U.S. public education system, which fails to adequately prepare so many students for college. Far too often secondary schools just pass students on to the next grade without seriously considering their level of achievement.

I personally discovered an example of how the "pass-on, push-out" approach was taken with student athletes in particular. One fall day I bumped into a good-looking, large young man on campus. I did not remember this student, who stood nearly six and a half feet tall and weighed probably 245, being on our football team, so I asked one of the football coaches about him. "I'm sorry; he's not eligible," the coach replied. Incredulous, I asked why. The answer floored me: "Well, he played football at a major institution in the Southwestern Conference for five years, and then he transferred to Prairie View with seventy-eight semester hours. He has dyslexia. And no one paid attention to the lack of progress he was making in school until his eligibility ran out, and then they said, 'You're out.'" This was one of the problems PVAMU faced, and I was not too sure how to lick it.

A large number of the university's students were failing. That was to be expected because they had not been equipped to perform in a college environment. Sure, I would have liked to go back to the students' secondary schools and say, "Hey, you didn't prepare these students." That approach might work fine to improve the academic performance of the future cadres of students, but it would do nothing for those already at PVAMU. The faculty, administration, and staff had to get our current students over the hurdle. We had to shore up their fundamental skills so they could succeed in their intended majors.

In 1989 it was decreed that all Texas high school graduates must take the Texas Academic Skill Proficiency test. If a student did not pass the reading, writing, or mathematics portions, PVAMU required him or her to complete remedial work in any area of substandard performance before going beyond thirty semester hours of college coursework. The state said sixty, but we limited it to thirty.

Many students who entered the university on a provisional basis became juniors and seniors—serious students doing well. It is a rare student at PVAMU who earns his or her degree in four years. Four and a half years is more typical, and almost all the engineers take more than five years to complete the program. We adopted the hare-and-tortoise philosophy. It

might take a longer time, but we got them there. When our students graduated, they had a quality degree that they could take anywhere.

In 1993 Wes was a captain in the Army and commander of the U.S. 3rd
Infantry Regiment, the "Old Guard." The Army drill team, assigned to his
company, had been invited to Houston for a performance, and Wes had also
arranged for the team to perform at halftime of a basketball game between
PVAMU and Texas Southern. One of Wes' buddies who was also a captain
in the Old Guard, Rich Ward, came along on the trip.

After an outstanding performance, the drill team returned to Houston.
Wes and Rich remained with Louise and me at Prairie View and were
shooting the breeze in our kitchen when Rich noticed that some guys were
urinating in the driveway. Wes went outside to see what was going on, and
one of the guys told him, in unprintable terms, what he could do with
himself. Rich, who is about the same size as Wes (six feet, two inches tall
and about 240 pounds) and also an airborne ranger, came outside, and one
of the guys pushed him. Wes went back into the house to tell his mother to
call campus security.

When Wes stepped back outside one of the guys sucker punched him.
Wes' lip exploded, and he went down on one knee. All of this happened
at the most inopportune time. Louise and I were having dinner with Bill
Harris, the president of Texas Southern University, and his wife Wanda. I
could not help but hear the commotion, so I rushed outside. Wes and Rich
were taking care of four of the guys. I put the fifth fellow on the ground, and
stood with my foot on his neck until the campus police arrived.

The police got out of the car with their shotguns drawn. Louise very
aggressively convinced them not to point the guns at Wes because he was her
son. When he took the battered people away, campus police chief Rayford
Stephens remarked to Louise, "For once they can't blame the police."

When it was all said and done, two of the guys went to the hospital and
later to jail. I drove Wes to the nearest hospital, which was in Tomball. Since
PVAMU's medical clinic was not equipped to handle the situation, they had
called ahead and I was pleasantly surprised to find a plastic surgeon on duty
in the emergency room. While Wes carries the scar today, the surgeon did
a fine job.

It was rather embarrassing for Wes to get on the plane the next day
with several stitches in his fat lip and to have to explain to his soldiers what
happened. About two years later Wes received a call from a Texas state

Queen Elizabeth II, President Bush, and me. (Courtesy of the White House)

attorney, who informed him that one of the guys had been placed on probation and if he chose to press charges, the guy would go to jail for a while.
Luckily for him, Wes wanted to give the knucklehead a second chance and
chose not to press charges.

Although Louise and I spent nearly five years at Prairie View, I maintained
strong ties to Washington, D.C., and these connections occasionally
produced some real surprises. In the early spring of 1991 I received a call
from the White House. Would Louise and I be available to attend a state
dinner in honor of Queen Elizabeth II? Although Louise was not bursting
with enthusiasm ("We just left Washington last week!" she protested), I, of
course, said yes to the White House. Shortly thereafter we received the official invitation.

The closer it got to the 14 May 1991 dinner, the more excited I felt.
Louise and I had been invited to the White House quite a few times, but
this would be our first state dinner. According to press coverage of the event,

there would be 132 invited guests, including Gen. Colin Powell and Gen. Norman Schwarzkopf.[4]

Louise was seated next to George W. Bush, the president's son, who was then president of the Texas Rangers baseball team and would later become the forty-third president of the United States. My dinner partner was Nancy Sununu, wife of the White House chief of staff. Considering my past relationship with John Sununu, I was flabbergasted at being seated next to his wife, but we had a very pleasant dinner conversation.

However, it was the receiving line before the dinner that was most exciting part of the evening. It was not every day that we were able to meet and greet the president of the United States and the queen of England! Louise and I were definitely standing in "high cotton." Almost matching that thrill was when, at the end of the evening, the billionaire philanthropist and diplomat Walter Annenberg offered us a ride back to Philadelphia with him and his wife. We declined, as we were waiting on the delivery of our own car. Arnold Palmer then asked me how my golf game was coming along. I guess he assumed that all retired generals played golf. Later, Dick Thornburgh, former governor of Pennsylvania, inquired as to my car and driver, likely thinking back to when I was an Army general and did have a car and driver. I told him I was the driver, and the car was rented.

I am not sure why we were invited to that state dinner. If I were to guess, I think it might have related to the last-minute change of heart about my becoming the first secretary of the Department of Veterans Affairs. The invitation to dine with the queen may well have been President Bush's way of making amends. It may have also been the result of my relationship with President Bush while he was vice president and I was director of FEMA. We met quite a few times and established such a good relationship that when he was president-elect and the Texas coast was threatened by a late-season hurricane, he called to ask whether he should visit the FEMA operations center in the San Antonio area. VIP visits tend to disrupt FEMA operations, so I candidly advised him to wait and told him why. He said, "Thanks Julius," and took my advice. When I retired from PVAMU, President Bush even made a sizeable contribution to the university's scholarship fund.

Whatever the reason for that invitation, our visit to the White House did considerable good back at PVAMU, as it chipped away at the negative views of those folks who believed that I should not be president of the university.

I cannot say the same for the next visit I made to the nation's capital. In mid-August 1991, Connie Newman, who was then the director of the federal Office of Personnel Management, called and asked if I would be willing to testify on behalf of President Bush's nomination of Clarence Thomas to the U.S. Supreme Court during Thomas' confirmation hearing before the Senate Judiciary Committee.

I was indebted to Connie Newman because she had recommended me to ACI after my tour at FEMA and also because she had agreed to speak at PVAMU's 1990 Honors Convocation, which was a celebration for students who excelled academically. My past interactions with Thomas had been very limited, dating back to when I was FEMA director and he headed the Equal Employment Opportunity Commission. But I had no reason not to testify on his behalf. He seemed to me to be a decent person, and he had been recommended by the president, whom I considered a friend. Since I owed Connie, I agreed to testify on Thomas' behalf.

Of course, I knew nothing about his relationship to Anita Hill or her allegations about his sexual behavior. My prepared remarks dealt only with the public record of Thomas' work at the EEOC and our limited personal interactions at informal gatherings of the Republican Party clan, which, quite candidly, included very few folks of color. I testified on 19 September 1991, rather late in the day and for fewer than ten minutes. Because I had less than thirty minutes to catch my plane back to Texas, I was excused with no questions. Two other presidents of HBCUs were also at the hearing to support Thomas. They were Talbert Shaw from Shaw University, which was my brother Joe's alma mater, and Jimmy Jenkins from Elizabeth City State University.

But earlier testimony by black Democratic House members John Conyers of Michigan, Louis Stokes of Ohio, Major Owens of New York, and Craig Washington of Texas had been very critical of Thomas. As a matter of fact, Craig Washington was quite distressed that I was there in support of the nomination, particularly since he was a graduate of PVAMU and an outspoken supporter of the university.

He was not alone in criticizing me for supporting Thomas. All hell broke loose when I returned to Prairie View. There was a lot of righteous indignation that I, as a university official, had testified for Thomas because he was opposed to the principle of affirmative action. This anger was vented in various ways, including irate calls to my radio show and posters on campus that expressed outrage. Barbara Jones, dean of the business college, was one of the more outspoken critics. Although we consider ourselves friends to this date, I honestly doubt that Barbara has completely forgiven me.

I have had little contact with Justice Thomas subsequent to the hearing. I have been told that he showed his appreciation to those who supported him by hosting a reception in his home. I have no proof of this, since I have never been invited to his home. And since he has been on the Supreme Court, I have seen little bearing his name with which I agree. Without a doubt, this is one of the things that I would have done differently if I had a chance to do it all over again.

But the Clarence Thomas incident did lead to another Becton encounter with John Sununu—one that gave me a good laugh. Following Thomas' confirmation on 15 October 1991, President Bush sponsored a reception in the Rose Garden. I was invited, but unable to attend. Our son Wes was permitted to represent me.

As Wes tells the story, after the ceremony was over, he had an opportunity to meet some of the dignitaries and celebrities who were there. Sylvester Stallone of *Rocky* fame sat right in front of him. And Wes soon spotted John Sununu. He knew that Sununu and I had been at odds over the nuclear power plant in New Hampshire and that I was not one of Sununu's favorite people.

Wes made a beeline to the White House chief of staff and asked him for his autograph. Sununu was very kind and gracious until Wes asked, "Do you know my father, Julius Becton?" Without a further word, Sununu quickly handed back the program he had autographed and excused himself. Wes said Sununu might have felt a bit intimidated since he is not a tall man and Wes is. I wish I had been there to see Sununu hurrying away!

By 1994 we were tired. Louise and I had given the university our best, but it was time to go back east to our home in Springfield, Virginia. We had moved so often that we yearned to enjoy a home that was ours on more than a temporary basis.

The decision to leave Prairie View was not difficult because I was proud of my record of accomplishment as university president. I felt that I had left my mark on the institution and made it better. That is what I had set out to do. Even though my strong right arm, Dr. Flossie Byrd, whom I had appointed provost, had also announced her intention to retire, I was comfortable in the knowledge that we were leaving a superb team of professionals in place who could continue what we had started.

So in a January 1994 letter to the university I announced that I would retire as president, effective 31 August. A 9 January article in the *Houston Post* offered a very positive review of my time as president, noting that PVAMU's student athlete graduation rate had averaged between 57 percent and 64 percent during my tenure, placing it among the highest in the state. The lead of the article summed up the many changes that had occurred:

> When Prairie View A&M University President Julius Becton takes his 5:30 AM daily walk around campus these days, the view is quite different from when he arrived there four years ago.

- The graffiti [are] gone, and the campus is clean and orderly.
- The mood of the campus also is different.
- Chaos has been replaced with order. Credibility has been restored, morale is up, and the administration, faculty, staff, and students are more unified.

Much of the credit for those changes, according to many people on and off campus, goes to Becton.[5]

While Louise and I were anxious to return to Springfield, we also wanted to make sure that we would be comfortable with whomever was selected to follow us. In addition, Ross Margraves, the chairman of the TAMUS Board of Regents, made it clear that he expected me to approve my replacement. Since I had advised the TAMUS chancellor that I would stay on until my replacement was named, I was eager to expedite the search process.

When the search committee produced a slate of three finalists, I was not particularly impressed. At about the same time that the TAMUS Board of Regents was interviewing the three finalists, I received a call from Bob Nabors, one of my aides in VII Corps who had gone on to become a major general. He had bumped into Chuck Hines and mentioned to him that PVAMU was looking for a new president. Apparently, Chuck was interested.

I first met Chuck Hines when he was a colonel on staff at the Army War College. He held a Ph.D. in sociology and was highly regarded by the war college community. After several years serving as an expert on women in combat, doing a stint at the Enlisted Personnel Directorate of the Office of Personnel Operations, and finally serving as commander of the U.S. Army Military Police School at Fort Gordon, Georgia, he retired as a major general and eventually became director of security at the Smithsonian Institution. It was there that Chuck came to my attention again.

I mentioned to Ross Margraves that I might have another name for the regents to consider, but I would need some time to do some checking. He gave me the okay, and I hurriedly started contacting everyone I knew who could vouch for Chuck's potential to lead the PVAMU. Only one person—a retired general officer, university graduate, and someone I held in very high esteem—cautioned against Chuck's selection based upon his past experience; this individual particularly criticized Chuck's interpersonal skills. By contrast, several of Chuck's former bosses gave him a clear "thumbs up" and MPs with whom he had worked either praised him or made noncommittal comments. His current boss, Connie Newman, who had become undersecretary of the Smithsonian, gave him high praise.

Ultimately, I asked Ross Margraves to add Chuck to the short list. Over the objection of the president of the PVAMU National Alumni Association, who was concerned about an MP taking over the university, and one regent who had similar concerns, Ross and I were able to delay any final decision until Chuck could appear for an interview. He did well before the board. And during his visit to the campus I thought Chuck was eloquent and persuasive, although a couple of the senior members of my staff were visibly uncomfortable with Chuck's mannerisms. I made it a point to persuade them not to jump to conclusions. The bottom line: Maj. Gen. Charles Hines, USA (Ret.), became the sixth president of PVAMU.

Satisfied that the university would be in good hands, Louise and I rushed to head home, sure that the climate and programs we had championed would flourish.

Nothing, it turned out, could be further from the truth. After Chuck Hines took over at PVAMU, everything began to change. Over the next few years, favored programs were terminated, unnecessary lawsuits became the rule, morale among the faculty and senior administrators headed south, and the president's suite became a fortress, complete with security locks.

When I first started receiving negative reports, I was leery of getting involved. Chuck Hines was the president, and any new president would be expected to make changes. But when a dean I had gone out of my way to recruit was fired for what appeared to me to be a frivolous reason, I went ballistic. I wrote to Hines asking him for his reasons for the firing. He returned my letter with marginal notations that he had made a "command decision." I then wrote to the new TAMUS chancellor, another retired Army general, who basically advised me that Hines was in charge, and he was sure it would work out.

Not long thereafter I visited the campus during the annual alumni convention. I was disturbed to see that the president's house, which had been refurbished at a cost of nearly $200,000 for occupancy by Louise and myself, had been demolished. I was denied access to the new science building for what seemed to me to be a spurious reason. And following this visit, I received word that as far as the university president was concerned, I had become persona non grata on campus.

There was no way to get around it: I had made a gross error in judgment. I did not understand how I could have been so wrong about Chuck Hines since I had based my support for his presidency upon what I had been told by his references. I went back to my sources to find out how I could have been so far off base, and when I challenged them, my "friends" responded, "Well, you didn't ask me specifically. . . ." In my follow-up conversation with Connie Newman, I discovered that Chuck was about to be fired by the Smithsonian when I made my first inquiries. When I asked why she had not told me about that, her eyes answered, "We wanted to see him gone."

Finally, in the spring of 2002, the TAMUS Board of Regents decided that it was time for Chuck to leave. I suspect that the board had not taken action before then because Hines was black, and it wanted to avoid negative criticism from the state legislature's black caucus. The board was also convinced by now that sufficient talent was in place on campus to operate a high-quality university without a domineering president.

So on Thursday, 16 May 2002, Chuck Hines submitted his resignation to the chancellor and was given a generous severance package. By contrast, I had had to pay half the cost of moving our household goods when I left PVAMU. Also in contrast with how I left the president's office, Chuck was told to be completely off the campus by no later than the weekend after his resignation was tendered.

Willie Tempton, who had been vice president for finance and administration under Chuck Hines and also one of my students back in the 1950s, became the interim president. I had brought Willie to the campus after his retirement from the Army. Once again, I was welcome back on the Hill.

CHAPTER EIGHTEEN

★ ★ ★

An Improbable Journey

At the 1995 annual meeting of the Association of the United States Army (AUSA), out of the clear blue sky, Harvey Gough suggested a trip to Kursk, site of a World War II battle between the Russians and the Germans–"the largest armored engagement of all time."[1] Harvey had first approached Lewis Stephens, who was a good friend and the former commander of the 49th Armored Division, Texas National Guard, with the idea. Lewis said if I would go, he would also.

It was not difficult making up my mind to go. I had never been to Russia before, and our trip would coincide with the 1996 elections in that country. It would give me an opportunity to drive the very same route the Soviet forces would have taken if they had attacked while I was VII Corps commander. Finally, I had only traveled to East Berlin once before, by train and at night, before the unification of Germany. Now I would have a chance to see the former East Germany countryside.

Harvey set about making the trip happen. He attacked the problem with the zeal of a Patton or Rommel. No stone was left unturned. Estimates of the situations in each country we would pass through were prepared; warning orders were issued; rosters of participants were prepared, revised, reordered, and scrubbed; a preliminary itinerary was prepared; and initial cost estimates were worked up. Harvey was in his element. As early as the second week in November, e-mails and faxes began to flow. Harvey reported that on a trip to Germany, he had met a German lieutenant colonel who was interested in Kursk and willing to work the German archives.

By the latter part of November Harvey was negotiating for rental cars. Of course, we had to be sure that we could take the cars through the old Communist Bloc, so Harvey's initial request made it clear that we would like to be able to drive in Hungary, Poland, Romania, Bulgaria, Czech Republic,

Slovakia, Slovenia, Croatia, and Ukraine. As of 11 December 1995 there were ten names on Harvey's travelers' list. A week later, Harvey received a letter from David Glantz, who wrote a 1985 paper titled "Soviet Defensive Tactics at Kursk" when he was with the Center for Land Warfare at the U.S. Army War College. In his letter, Glantz described the source materials necessary for conducting a Kursk battlefield tour. He also suggested two persons who might be useful to us as we planned our trip. In March 1996 a few of us participated in a briefing by Chris Lawrence and the Dupuy Institute about the Kursk battle. This was the first time we met Chris and his wife Tanya, who was a Russian citizen from Moscow.

Also, while on a visit to the University of North Carolina at Chapel Hill, I had met a Ph.D. from Russia. Since natives can always share helpful insights to foreigners, I took the opportunity to write her and ask, "Are there any pitfalls or problems that we might run into, keeping in mind that two of us are black Americans? Any recommendations as to hotels and/or places to see? Will we see any monuments to the war or the specific battle? Keeping in mind that the Russian election will occur during our visit, should we anticipate any problems with the folks in and around Kursk? Finally, do you have any recommendations in general that would either increase the effectiveness of our trip or make it more enjoyable?"

I received the following response:

> Travel with at least one other person at all times; even if you are only going across the street, don't go alone. Don't buy food from kiosks, along the street; buy food from restaurants or at local grocery stores. Dress in older, casual clothes so you will not stand out as foreigners. Close and lock your suitcases when you leave your hotel room. If your suitcase can take extra locks, it would be wise to put one on. There is a museum in Kursk. If you have to change money, do it at a bank, not at one of the many shops that advertise "exchange." From those places one is likely to get counterfeit, in addition, criminals watch for foreigners at those places and rob them. Bring small, inexpensive things for gifts, things American, even postcards with photos of DC, for example. Beware of vodka! Pretend to drink it, whenever you can get away with it. Be sure to take a full supply of any medicines you need. If your stomach is not too fond of odd food, bring plenty of medicine for that. The food tends to be rich and fatty. Be sure to drink bottled water.

By departure time, the travelers' roster included Maj. Bill St. Amour, myself, Harvey Dickerson (hereafter Harvey D), Harvey Gough (Harvey

G), Chris and Tanya Lawrence, Lewis Stephens, and Mike Shaler. Also accompanying us was Jeff Greene, a television producer with the Military Channel, INC, who had been referred to us by my old friend, the journalist Joe Galloway. We would meet the German members of our delegation when we got to Krakow, Poland.

On 7 June 1996 Harvey D and I boarded Icelandair Flight 642 at the Baltimore airport en route to Reykjavik. We arrived in Iceland early on 8 June, clearly inappropriately dressed in shorts for the near 50-degree weather. Luckily we did not have to leave the terminal. After a bit of coffee and some shivering, we boarded a flight to Frankfurt.

Saturday, we joined the rest of the Kursk-bound Americans at the home of Lt. Gen. John Abrams, who was the commander of V Corps. Dinner was delightful, and General Abrams talked more than anyone had heard him do in recent memory, mostly about "down range" and "in the box." Those phrases are jargon for, respectively, Hungary and the American military units in the former Yugoslavia. Abrams was full of praise for our troops.

"D-day" finally arrived. We topped off our four Opel Omegas with gasoline, put CB antennas in place and posed for group pictures, then rolled out about twenty minutes later than we had planned. Of course, with Harvey G in the lead vehicle, we knew we could make up the lost time. Bill St. Amour, who joined our party at the last minute, rode with Harvey G. He had no visa for Russia, but had been told he could pick that up at the border. The Lawrences rode with Lewis Stephens. Mike Shaler had Jeff Greene, and Harvey D and I rode together.

As we approached Hof, my mind raced back to those days when American troops were defending the real estate leading into what was then West Germany. As had been surmised then, the terrain was ideal tank territory.

As we drove on, it soon became apparent that we had crossed into the former East Germany. The roads were not nearly as good as those we were leaving behind. Overall, there were fewer signs of affluence, and it was clear that this part of Germany was ten to fifteen years behind the area that had been West Germany.

The original plan was to visit Auschwitz during the afternoon of June 11, but we arrived in Krakow entirely too late. Harvey G had failed to figure the inordinate amount of time required to cross the border with Poland into our itinerary. As we approached the border, we removed our antennas and drove our four-car convoy bumper to bumper. Harvey G, in the lead vehicle, bypassed all the other vehicles waiting to cross. When he finally reached some official who might stop him, he would scream, "AMERICANS, AMERICANS! FOUR MACHINES! AMERICANS!" After the officials checked our passports, international driver's licenses, and authorization to drive rental cars east, we were on our way.

We arrived at the Hotel Continental in Krakow at about 2030 hours and went to Harvey G's favorite restaurant. There, we met the European colleagues who were joining us for the remainder of the trip. I excused myself immediately after dinner and left the restaurant. The square had been very crowded when we first went in, but now it was almost deserted, and the words of my Russian adviser came rushing back: "Don't go out alone." With some trepidation, I found a taxi. My knowledge of the Polish language and Poland's currency was nonexistent, so I am convinced the taxi driver charged me twice the fare. But who is counting now?

The next morning we Americans set off for Auschwitz and Birkenau, the notorious World War II concentration camps used by the Nazis to commit unspeakable atrocities against Jews and others deemed "inferior." The Germans wanted no part of that visit, so they headed east along with Chris and Tanya.

We arrived at Auschwitz at about 1020 hours. Some of the buildings had been restored to their World War II appearance. We viewed a brief film depicting life at the camps and then walked through Auschwitz and the larger Birkenau. The cold evil I felt walking around these camps almost defies description. They are something every citizen should see regardless of nationality because, in my judgment, given the "right" circumstances, the Holocaust could happen again.

We Americans, trailing our European compatriots, reached the border between Poland and Ukraine at about 2000 hours. Harvey G again did his thing, but it took us two hours to get through the checkpoints this time. Part of the problem was the fact that Bill St. Amour did not have a Russian visa. The Ukrainians were not about to permit him to cross into their territory without the proper papers. Since Bill spoke the language, or at least one they understood—probably Russian—we were eventually permitted to continue on after paying about $165.

When we rolled into Lviv at about 2330 hours, the streets were deserted. Harvey G and Bill were able to talk a Ukrainian citizen into leading us to the Hotel Royal, but our guide disappeared when we hit our first police roadblock and our convoy was stopped by a young police officer. Bill did the

Refueling in Ukraine from Ukrainian army gas truck. (Author collection)

talking. After he explained who we were and why we were roaming around his city this late, the police officer finally permitted us to leave, but only after paying a fine of about $1.60. We reached the hotel at about midnight, parked some distance away, and paid someone to watch the cars. Then we called home at a cost of about $7.00 each before at last hitting the sack.

The next day, after a quick breakfast, we were on the road at about 0930 hours. We had decided that we would drive as far as we could on this leg of the trip. Our biggest problem was the police checkpoints, where we were stopped five or six times. We passed through Kiev at around 1830 hours and finally reached the Ukrainian-Russian border about 0200 hours on 14 June.

As usual, Harvey G "negotiated" his way to the front of the long line of stopped vehicles. But this time, his ploy did not work so well. An irate citizen approached the border guard supervisor and complained that our convoy had driven by his parked vehicle. That citizen's complaint added about forty-five minutes to our stay. We got to the Russian side a little after 0300.

Realizing that Bill St. Amour's missing visa would be bothersome, Harvey G and crew concocted the story that it had been lost as we traveled from the western Ukraine border toward Russia. That started a long series of discussions, telephone calls (including one to Tanya, who had already reached the hotel we would be staying in near Kursk), miniconferences, and more calls. We were finally permitted to depart the crossing site at about 0545 hours.

It was daylight when we arrived at the Hotel Yuzhanya in Belgorod. The large hotel lobby was dingy, dark, and foreboding. The hotel clerk was located behind what appeared to be a bulletproof glass shield. The elevator was inoperable because the elevator operator would not arrive until 0800 hours. The rooms were small and the furnishings were Spartan to say the least, with a thin mattress on the bed, a black-and-white TV, a small table, and three lights of which only two worked. The bathtub rested on three-inch stilts, and the water faucet served both the tub and the washbasin. Despite these less than inviting accommodations, I was asleep as soon as I hit the bed.

I awoke at around 0930 hours. All I wanted was to have breakfast and start in on the briefings scheduled for that afternoon. But when I got downstairs I was told that our group leader—presumably Harvey G—Bill St. Amour, and Jeff Greene had been "requested" to report to the office of the minister of interior to "explain why Bill had no visa and why Jeff had no stamp on his visa."

Realizing just how serious this could be, I spent about ten minutes with Harvey G, explaining that this was not the time to pull any stunts. In my judgment, if the occasion permitted, he should explain that we realized we were in the wrong and do his best to convince the authorities that we had no sinister agenda. I urged Harvey G to explain that Bill was in Russia without a visa because, as an active duty Army officer, he would have found it almost impossible to get one. He was accompanying us for the express purpose of being our interpreter, and we would be on our way out of the country on Monday.

Harvey G did not have the opportunity to say anything, however. According to him, the female colonel wanted nothing to do with him, and she made that abundantly clear. Ultimately, Bill was expelled, Jeff was required to return to the border station for the purpose of getting his visa stamped, and Harvey G was sent back to the hotel.

Bill took Harvey G's Opel. He was to drive back to Charkov, Ukraine, and wait for us there. Jeff and Mikhail, our Russian guide, rode with Bill to the border crossing, accompanied by a Russian official in a separate car. At the border Jeff obtained the red stamp, and Bill continued into Ukraine. The Russian official who escorted them to the border refused to bring Jeff and Mikhail back, explaining that "foreigners are not permitted to ride in their cars."

The border guard supervisor was much more accommodating. He stopped a Russian in a rather large sedan and put Jeff and Mikhail in the car, instructing the driver to deliver them to Belgorod, no questions asked. When Bill reached the Ukrainian side of the border and they discovered that he had been kicked out of Russia, they wanted no part of him either and expelled him from Ukraine.

There were several mysteries surrounding this episode. Why had the interior officials not simply stamped Jeff's visa in Belgorod? Why did the female colonel have a photocopied picture of Jeff, which he spotted while he was in her office? How did Jeff happen, that very afternoon, to meet the striking blonde who latched onto the group for much of our visit? On our last morning in Belgorod, Harvey D was up early for his usual morning stroll and saw that same blonde getting out of an official-looking black Renault with several antennas. When the driver saw Harvey, he sped away.

Despite the morning's visa drama, we started our briefings and tour of the battlefield on schedule. Three Russian colonels joined us, two of whom were retirees. One of the retirees was from a museum in Moscow and was an expert on the Kursk battle; the other was a veteran who had actually fought at Kursk. The active-duty colonel was the son of one of the Russian commanders in the battle. Two Russian women also came along—one allegedly from the Moscow museum, and the other supposedly from a travel agency. Our German friends were convinced that at least one of the two women was KGB (or Federal Security Service, as it is now called). Additionally, we had a TV camera crew from Moscow, hired by Jeff Greene.

Most of us rode in an air-conditioned Mercedes bus that was fairly new, and we had a police escort. Harvey G opted to drive his own car. During the bus ride, Chris briefed us about the area, what we were about to see, and the significance of the battle. And there was no longer any pretense that this was a low-profile trip. The police escort drove at breakneck speed with the siren blasting, chasing everyone out of our way, and our kamikaze bus driver followed right on the escort's tail. Even Harvey G was concerned!

That night, Harvey G, Mike, Lewis, and I went to the local telephone office to call home. In order to place a call, we had to give the attendant some money and received a wooden marker with a booth number. The office had only one booth designated for international calls. Once in the booth, we dialed the number we wanted to call, and then we had to punch a button on the phone in order to be heard when the called party answered. Punching the button also started the clock. A two-minute call to my home cost about $7.00. Later when we compared notes on our calls to Steamboat Springs, Dallas, and Washington, it was clear that there was no rhyme or reason for the cost.

We continued our tour of the battlefield on Saturday, 15 June. At one location we met a woman whose mother had been hanged by the Germans. Needless to say, this made our German colleagues a bit uneasy.

During the tour of the battlefield Jeff Greene's camera crew interviewed each of us. A mighty strange thing happened as one of these interviews was being conducted. One of the Russian colonels told the crew that he had been sent to Kursk by the Russian authorities to "revise" history. Specifically, he said, he was told to inflate the numbers of German casualties (which he admitted had already been inflated) and to reduce the recorded number of Russian casualties.

But the Germans traveling with us were involved in a bit of revisionist history, too. Major General Dieter Brand's story was that the Germans really won the battle but were pulled out at a critical point by Hitler so that the Third Reich would be able to repel the Allied invasion of Sicily. Throughout the tour the Germans held tutorial sessions in which they would compare notes and discuss their "facts" in relation to those presented by the terrain, Chris Lawrence, and the Russian historian.

In the search for the "truth" I turned to an article by Col. Frederick C. Turner, USA (Ret.), in the May–June 1993 *Armor Magazine*. Turner concluded by comparing the Battle of Kursk to the encounter between the *Monitor* and the *Merrimac* during the U.S. Civil War. He wrote, "Neither side was defeated in the battle, which had been practically a stand-off. Both sides had sought decisive results, but had ended up doing little more than stopping the enemy attack."[2]

After the Saturday tour I was asked by General Brand whether a Russian woman whose family had saved and befriended a German soldier during the war could join us for dinner. It turned out that the woman, a Ph.D. in chemistry, was five years old when her family saved the German officer. In 1992 she had tracked the officer down, and they had become good friends. She joined the dinner party and obviously enjoyed herself. After dinner I made presentations (V Corps commanding general coins, paperweights, and some other knickknacks) to our Russian guests. For my gesture I received a great big bear hug and kiss from the senior retired Russian colonel.

When we started our tour on Sunday, the 16th, I asked to visit a polling place, since it was a momentous day in Russia. I found out later that one of the cameramen predicted that it would be the last day of democracy in Russia. About mid-afternoon the bus pulled up to a schoolhouse in a very small village. The building turned out to be a polling place.

We entered through what turned out to be the exit for the voting area, and we saw several people filling out paper ballots and depositing them into a large box. But the person in charge told us to go back out and around to the entrance. There, we saw a person checking the voters' identification, a large poster with pictures of the thirteen primary candidates, and a man who appeared to be in charge. The man refused to allow us back in. We created quite a stir, but to outward appearances, at least, the voting that day in Russia looked very similar to what one could find in any small farming village in the United States.

That Sunday evening, Harvey G, Harvey D, Mike, Lewis, and I decided to eat out. We had been served the same meal of breaded chicken, sliced cucumber, and tomato twice at the hotel. We also wanted a drink, and there was no alcohol available in the hotel.

Mike had developed an ingenious way to communicate with Russian waiters. He had a 3 x 5 card that had English, Russian, and German words for beef, chicken, fish, and pork written on one side. The other bore a hand-drawn picture of a coffee cup, ice cream, and cake. That evening, we had a much better meal than what we had gotten at the hotel.

We were up fairly early the next day to head west in our convoy that was reduced to three cars because Bill St. Amour had taken the fourth. We got no farther than a quarter of a mile from our hotel before we were stopped for speeding. We were permitted to continue after an incoherent discussion between Harvey G and the police, and we reached the Ukrainian border within the hour. We had no problems exiting Russia. As a matter of fact, some of us suspected that the Russians were happy to see us go.

I came away from Belgorod with many impressions. One had to do with our physical surroundings. Almost everything appeared to be hopelessly broken or in serious need of repair. The accommodations were primitive and dirty, and there were potholes everywhere both in the city and out in the countryside. There was absolutely no drainage anywhere. In addition, it was clear that the people of Belgorod, like those throughout Ukraine, were not used to seeing black folks. Everyone seemed to stare at us. No one was abrasive or overbearing. They were just inquisitive. Moscow may have its tourist face for foreigners, but Belgorod was not ready.

We definitely encountered a police-state mentality. The interrogation of Bill St. Amour sounded a great deal like something that would have happened under the old Soviet regime. We all had the nagging sense that the KGB (or FSS—again, if it walks like a duck) was present wherever we went. And few Russians accepted the simple truth about why we were in the country. I was asked time and again, "We know why the Germans and the Russians are here, but why are you Americans here?" My answer, "We are professional soldiers and we wanted to see and evaluate for ourselves," was just not accepted.

My final lasting impression of my tour was that I was very interested in the attitudes of the three Russian colonels. The two retired old-timers were both talkative, particularly after a couple of drinks. However, the active-duty officer seldom entered into any conversation with us.

While we had no problems getting out of Russia, we had a big problem getting back into Ukraine. Apparently, our visas authorized only one transit through Ukraine, and we had used that one when we were heading east. How the Ukrainians expected us to get out of Russia by car without going through their country is a mystery. Our German friends passed through without much fuss, but it took us almost two hours to reenter Ukraine. Once there, we were stopped several times by the local police and quasi-military soldiers. We were fined only once—about $10—when Mike Shaler passed a farm tractor in a no-passing zone.

We arrived in Lviv at about 2230 hours and checked into the same hotel we had stayed at before, even though we had no reservations. Once again I called home, using the same telephone I had used four days earlier. This time the three minutes cost $36, more than five times what it had earlier.

We headed west for Hungary on 18 June. The closer we came to the Hungarian border, the more prosperous the area appeared. We crossed the border at Chop, Ukraine, where there was about a mile backup of cars and more than a two-mile backup of trucks waiting to cross into Hungary. Harvey G pulled his usual trick of driving to the front of the line screaming, "AMERICANS, AMERICANS—THREE MACHINES!" We were delayed about ninety minutes at customs—again because of our one-time visa for transit through Ukraine. But we were released with a "good riddance" look from the customs officials after being hassled.

Compared with what we had seen of Eastern Europe, Hungary was a great improvement. It was cleaner and brighter and it had well-marked modern service stations. Also, it lacked checkpoints manned by the military or local gendarmes. We arrived at Taszar at about 2100 hours and went to see General Abrams in his V Corps tactical operations center (TOC), which far exceeded anything I had ever considered when I was in VII Corps.

As we were departing the area, I experienced an ego deflator. I stopped to talk to a couple of young officers, one of whom was a black female captain. After a few minutes she asked, "Who are you?" When I told her that I used to command VII Corps, she had not heard of that unit either. Apparently, she did not believe anything I told her until a brigadier general wanted to talk with me.

On the next day, 19 June, we received a series of briefings and were taken on a tour of the airfield with its base hospital. We were on the road by about 1220 hours, heading back to Germany via Austria. It was during this stretch that Harvey G finally got stopped for speeding. As we drove by him arguing with the police, Mike Shaler took a picture of him doing his arm-waving drill. Would you believe it? He talked his way out of a fine.

The rest of our travels were fairly uneventful. Looking back on it, I was glad I had made that trip. Auschwitz, where the extremes of man's inhumanity to man are clearly in evidence, is something everyone should see. Russia was fascinating, and I am glad to say that I think the KGB/FSS was probably more confused after we left than it was before we arrived. I would be happy to fly back to Russia for another visit. However, I have no intention of driving there from Germany again, and I certainly have no desire to return to Ukraine.

I was most impressed with our visit to General Abrams' TOC in Hungary. The U.S. forces were well taken care of by the Hungarians and had a mission they understood. There was clearly a high order of professionalism. I was told that signal facilities and capabilities there were probably the best ever. Every soldier had access to telephones and e-mail. And I was pleased to see a high level of black Americans in the TOC.

★ ★ ★

CHAPTER NINETEEN

My Toughest Challenge

A few months later, when I was safely back home in Virginia, I received a phone call from Connie Newman. Connie was now a member of the D.C. Financial Control Board (formally, the D.C. Financial Responsibility and Management Assistant Authority*), as well as the number-two official at the Smithsonian Institution. Dr. Andrew Brimmer, chairman of the Control Board, had asked her to call to see whether I would "give us a hand in brainstorming a certain matter." I knew that the five-member board had been set up by Congress in 1995, after the District of Columbia's debt reached more than $700 million and its elected officials seemed incapable of managing the crisis or of providing efficient services to citizens. Without asking for further clarification, I told Connie I would help, and she said Dr. Brimmer would contact me. Thirty minutes later Brimmer called. He asked me to come to a meeting the next morning, and I agreed.

When I walked into the suite of offices occupied by the Control Board, I was ushered into a conference room, where Brimmer introduced me to board member Joyce Ladner and board executive director John Hill. After some brief small talk, Brimmer started telling me how bad things were in the D.C. school system. He described the academic status of the students as a near disaster. The physical plant was almost in complete collapse, and employee morale was at rock bottom. Brimmer went on to say that the Control Board was going to remove Dr. Franklin Smith, the superintendent of schools, and appoint a CEO to run the schools. Further, the board planned to considerably reduce the authority of the elected school board by appointing an Emergency Transitional Education Board of Trustees (ETEBT) that would set policy for the system.

---

*Board Membership: Andrew Brimmer—Chair, Connie Newman—Vice Chair, Joyce Ladner, Ed Singletary, and Steve Harlan.

As I listened, I decided that they wanted me to be one of the trustees and thought, "Serving pro bono on one more board won't hurt." Then Joyce Ladner, who had been the interim president of Howard University, said, "The first thing you have to do is . . ." I realized the Control Board did not want me as a trustee; they intended for me to become the new schools superintendent.

The Control Board members described a similar school system take-over in Chicago, where the CEO used a business approach, hiring the staff required to perform the jobs that needed to be done and firing those who did not measure up. They said the superintendent of the D.C. Public Schools (DCPS) would be one of the nine emergency trustees and would report directly to the Control Board. The D.C. City Council and the mayor would have no control over the school system, and the unions would be co-opted if need be.

I said I would have to think about it. And that is exactly what I did for the next couple of weeks. I agonized over the decision, and I discussed the offer with many friends, including Bill Tidball, who had been my chief of staff at FEMA. I told Bill that if I had someone like him to help me, it would make my decision much easier. He had decided to take an early-out from FEMA and was planning to move to Kansas City, where his wife Ann had been reassigned by her employer. The morning after I spoke with Bill about the school board, Ann called. She said Bill would probably say yes if I asked him to join me and that he could commute from D.C. to Kansas City on weekends. This was music to my ears.

The other shot in the arm came from my son Wes. I could easily reject the offer, he said, because I had done enough public service and by then had no kids in D.C. schools, although at one time all five of my children had been D.C. public school students. Then he asked a discomfiting question: "How would you feel, however, if at some future date you had a grandchild in the system and knew that you had turned down an opportunity to do something about it?"

No one said, "Don't do it," but the late Maj. Gen. Fred Davison, a native-born Washingtonian, did question my sanity. He said that dealing with those folks in the District was impossible, that I would be getting myself into a no-win situation. By contrast, Norman Augustine, CEO and chairman of Lockheed Martin, was enthusiastic about my accepting the challenge, and he said he and his company would support the school system if I took the position. When I asked Norm why they had not supported it in the past, his answer was simple: "We didn't trust those people in charge!"

On the Sunday after my meeting with the Control Board, Chaplain Ed Maney was the guest preacher at the Fort Myer Memorial Chapel, where Louise and I attend church services. His sermon dealt with Moses and the lesson that one is never too old to accept certain challenges. When I told him about the job offer, he beamed and replied, "I sure am glad you were in the congregation this morning."

During this period of indecision I read and reread the Control Board's *Children in Crisis: A Report on the Failure of D.C.'s Public Schools*. The report was based on a thorough audit conducted with the help of KPMG, the giant business services firm. Its conclusion was haunting: "The deplorable record of the District's public schools by every important educational and manage- ment measure has left one of the city's most important public responsibilities in a state of crisis, creating an emergency which can no longer be ignored or excused. The DCPS is failing in its mission to educate the children of the District of Columbia. In virtually every area, and for every grade level, the system has failed to provide our children with a quality education and safe environment in which to learn."[1]

The report contained nothing but bad news. It noted that on major examinations that test student competence and achievement, District students consistently lagged behind the national averages and the averages of comparable urban school districts. The test results of students in the poorer wards of the city were lower than those of students in more affluent areas, which was no surprise. But the disparity, the report noted, was growing steadily worse.

I was absolutely appalled at the high school dropout rate. The statistics were staggering—"criminal" might have been a better word. In 1995 only 53 percent of the students who had entered D.C. high schools in ninth grade actually graduated four years later. Just two years earlier, the graduation rate had been ten points higher.

What was causing this hemorrhage of students from the system? I was certain that the home life of students influenced their decision to leave school. However, I was equally sure that the students dropping out felt there was nothing for them at school. The promise that they would get the educa- tion they deserved had been broken too many times, so they gave up. In short, the system had failed them.

It seemed that everything was now broken, and the state of the D.C. public schools was a far cry from when my and Louise's children had attended them. Louise and I never had a serious complaint about the caliber of the education our children received. As I read the various assessments of the state of public education in the District, I wondered what in the world had happened.

At about this time I started thinking maybe I really could help. I knew how good the schools could be because my children had attended them, and I was optimistic that they could be restored. I believed there were people in the DCPS administration who were dedicated public servants who wanted only the best for the students.

Still, my mind was not completely made up. The scales were finally tipped in favor of my accepting the position when Bill Tidball and my old friend Harvey Dickerson, who had retired from the Army as a colonel, said they would help. After Bill and Harvey pledged their support, I told Dr. Brimmer I would accept the superintendent position.

There was much to be done as head of DCPS. For one thing, I needed to meet with Franklin Smith, the outgoing superintendent. The sooner we got together, the smoother I could make the transition. As I hoped he would, Smith gave me some useful advice about the people I would be dealing with, especially concerning those whom I could trust and those of whom I should be leery.

Having been burned in the past, I also wanted to find a qualified media person as soon as possible. Loretta Hardge, who was on the staff of the GWU, was highly recommended, so I called the university's president, Dr. Steve Trachtenberg. I told him without any fanfare who I was and what I wanted, and Dr. Trachtenberg told me I could have Loretta "on loan." He wished me well, then asked, "Have you checked with your shrink lately?" Steve has been a good friend ever since.

I also met with Bruce MacLaury, who had just retired as CEO of the Brookings Institution and been appointed chairman of the ETEBT. A Control Board member arranged the meeting to see how well we would get along. Bruce and I quickly recognized that we would have no problem working together.

The next decision point dealt with money. Dr. Brimmer and I settled on a total compensation package of $125,000, $90,000 of which was salary and $35,000 of which were unspecified benefits. We memorialized the deal with a handshake. I knew the Control Board's tenure was three years, and I did not want to be bound by a contract that would force me to stay on as schools superintendent if a new board turned out to be less compatible.

At that time the annual salary for members of the elected D.C. school board was $35,000, which made them the highest paid school board in the country. DCPS spent more than $1.4 million on the school board in fiscal year 1995, which was more than three times the sum spent by neighboring Fairfax County, Virginia, and Montgomery County, Maryland. DCPS even outspent the Chicago school board by more than $200,000, despite the fact that the Chicago board was responsible for a school system with four hundred thousand students, or five times as many as were in the DCPS system.

The Control Board decided that the D.C. school board would regain its original responsibilities upon the termination of the ETEBT on 30 June 2000. In the interim the school board would continue to oversee charter schools in the District, and its members would serve as advisers to the unpaid emergency trustees and the superintendent/CEO. Some Control Board members wanted to do away with school board members' salaries altogether and reimburse them only for expenses. I strongly disagreed, arguing that such an action would be considered vindictive. I suggested that we pay school board members $15,000 to $17,500, and the Control Board selected $15,000. If I had known then the problems I would have with the school board members, I would have been in the forefront advocating that they be paid expenses only.

When all these planned changes became public knowledge, the school board promptly filed a lawsuit, arguing that the Control Board did not have the authority to reduce their authority.

The media also went to work once word leaked that I was going to be the new DCPS superintendent/CEO, a title borrowed from Chicago Public Schools. Reporters looked at every document available. They talked to my colleagues, friends, and former subordinates at FEMA, AID, and PVAMU. And, of course, they contacted folks in the Army. One TV crew even ambushed me one evening as I was getting out of my car at my home in Springfield.

On Friday, 15 November 1996, the Control Board held a public meeting and a press conference in the Luther Place Methodist Church. Despite the gravity of the measures on its agenda and its declaration of "a state of emergency in the District of Columbia public school system," the mood of Control Board members was rather upbeat.[2] They were trying to project hope for the city. The Control Board officially voted on the removal of Franklin Smith, the appointment of the new superintendent/CEO, the reduced authority of the elected school board, and the appointment of the ETEBT.[3]

Dr. Brimmer introduced me as the new superintendent/CEO and gave me an opportunity to say a few words. I stressed that my priority would always be "children first." I outlined the challenges facing the DCPS, including resolving health and safety issues and getting for teachers the tools they needed. And I made a promise that the ETEBT and I would "be diligent in our effort to create an optimal learning environment that is stimulating and challenging for students and teachers alike. Our goal is to build an environment that fosters success. Remember . . . children first—and failure is not an option."

The in-depth assessment of the District school system had recommended that we follow the model that had been set in Chicago. There, city schools had reached such a sorry state that in 1995 the Illinois governor and the state legislature gave Chicago Mayor Richard M. Daly sweeping authority to take over the school system and run it.

Mayor Daly abolished all of the regional school boards and established a single, citywide five-member school board. He appointed his chief of staff as the new board's chairman and made his comptroller CEO of the system. Daly then instructed all the city agencies that their first mission was to do the jobs they had and their second mission was to support the school system. This mandate, in and of itself, gave the school system unbelievable support. The mayor then increased the school system's budget and granted a pay raise to teachers.

Within his first few weeks on the job, the new CEO of the Chicago Public Schools balanced the budget, a move that led to the elimination of a $1.3 billion deficit over four years. The CEO also ended labor unrest, improved facilities, and created new education programs designed to root out waste, fraud, and abuse. The city created an educational program that encompassed all grade levels. Focusing on a practice that had compounded the problem of poor literacy among students and graduates, the city also discontinued social promotions.[4]

There were some significant differences in what appeared possible in the District of Columbia, however. The D.C. mayor, city council, and elected school board were all opposed to the Control Board and the ETEBT being there in the first place. And while the powers of the school board had been reduced, its members could still raise all kinds of hell by going out to the schools and trying to intimidate principals into doing what they wanted done. In addition, we had no authority to lean on the police department, fire department, public works department, or any other District agency to do anything in support of the schools. Finally, the District of Columbia labors under a particular burden that no other jurisdiction in the country bears: Since the city is the headquarters of the federal government, both the U.S. Congress and the Executive Branch have a great interest in District affairs, and neither is at all shy about interfering.

Notwithstanding our obvious constraints, the ETEBT tried to emulate the Chicago model. We established a hotline operated by two full-time professionals to give parents and school system employees a formal mechanism for voicing complaints and concerns. We also set about establishing a skilled administrative team that would report to the superintendent/CEO.

Herb Tillery, a native Washingtonian whom I had met when I was the VII Corps commander and he was an MP in Germany, came on board as the chief security officer for DCPS. Charles Williams, a no-nonsense engineer who had retired from the Army as a major general, joined us as the chief operating officer (COO), which made him responsible for all DCPS physical facilities operations. I also established the position of chief academic officer (CAO) and set about searching for the right person for the job.

The DCPS was based on the neighborhood school concept. Each high school had so many elementary, middle, and junior high schools that fed into it based on neighborhood location, and these clusters of schools were administered pretty much independently. On the whole, I think the neighborhood school concept is a great idea. But it can be too insular. For example, if an elementary school in Cluster One in the northeast section of the city was having great success with some new policy, there was no guarantee that the idea would be shared with other schools throughout the city. So when someone recommended getting rid of the clusters and establishing a system in which individual assistant superintendents were responsible for administrating each of the three levels of schools, I immediately saw the wisdom in the idea. It would tighten up management and ensure the free flow of good ideas and information.

In choosing the assistant superintendents, I relied heavily upon the recommendations of Dr. Mildred Musgrove, who had served as Franklin

Bill Garner's views on a course of action. (Reprinted with permission of the *Washington Times*)

Smith's chief of staff. And shortly thereafter I moved Mildred herself into the CAO position.

I selected Helena Jones to be assistant superintendent for middle schools and junior high schools because of the great reputation she had earned as the principal at Roper Middle School. I chose Ralph Neal to be assistant superintendent for the senior high schools. As principal at Eastern Senior High School he had proven that he was willing to take risks for the good of the students. When he asked why I wanted him to take the job, I said, "Because you have tried every conceivable way to beat the system. You know all the answers, so now you can deal with all the other high school principals." And for assistant superintendent for elementary schools, I selected Kenneth Whitted, whom Mildred Musgrove recommended because he was a successful elementary school principal.

I had known going into this job that the DCPS personnel system was in disarray. The human resources people we brought in discovered just how bad things were and uncovered a total disaster. All personnel records for the approximately ten thousand DCPS employees were contained in boxes scattered all over the office. A random review of the files that could be found showed that they were largely incomplete. I then started hearing rumors that we were paying people who no longer worked for DCPS. Sure enough, we eventually found out that eight people on the payroll were dead. Yet the checks that had been sent out in the deceaseds' names had been cashed.

I tried hard to convince the Control Board that DCPS should have a pay system separate from that of the city, which was designed for a twelve-month year. School system employees were paid on three different pay periods, which added to the chaos. Teachers had a ten-month pay year and were paid on the first and fifteenth of the month. Principals were paid semimonthly for a total of twenty-four pay periods, and nonteaching employees were paid every two weeks year-round.

In its criticism of the DCPS, the Control Board had noted that there was a serious misalignment in the allocation of the school system's personnel resources. For example, the board found two executive assistants working in the superintendent's office who were listed in the personnel records as being assigned to elementary education. Such "error-prone information" made it impossible for the board to determine the number of personnel who actually directly served the District's students, but the board concluded that hundreds of DCPS personnel did not.[5]

A person with a strong financial background was desperately needed to help straighten out this mess. Dr. Abdusalam Omer became the first DCPS chief financial officer (CFO), and he was replaced in April 1997 by Edward Stephenson, who had worked with the Control Board since its start. Stephenson later wrote this devastating description of the situation in an internal DCPS memo: "Payroll records were in a shambles, there was no effective budgeting, accountability for expenditures was nonexistent, and contracts management was abysmal. As a result, DCPS had no idea how many employees they had, where they were located, which contracts were in effect, how much was owed on outstanding invoices, what ongoing monthly expenditures were taking place, what federal grant money was available and how it was being used. . . . Several vendors would not do business with DCPS, including some critical textbook suppliers. Numerous staff members, including hundreds of teachers, did not receive paychecks each pay period."

Getting a handle on the DCPS finances was a true cause of heartburn. Funding for the schools was based on X number of students and Y number of employees. Not only did the system have no idea how many people were employed by DCPS, but the exact number of students was indeterminate, as well. As of November 1996, our best count was 78,648 students; a January audit supported that figure.

But providing special education was even more complicated than it seemed. The DCPS special education program was in receivership, having been placed there for being out of compliance with federal law. Shortly after I became superintendent/CEO, Jerome Miller, who had been appointed general receiver by the federal district court, briefed me on the situation. In the process I discovered that the DCPS had paid millions of dollars for special education, foster care, and related matters. Some of the expenditures should have been reimbursed from the city-controlled Medicare fund, but this did not always occur. The U.S. Department of Education was withholding some $3 million because DCPS had not complied with federal policies in the placement of some special education students in private schools. The federal government also owed us $5.8 million for transportation. As Miller explained it to me, in some cases the special education program was no more than a parking place for students, due in large part to legal requirements. For DCPS, the bottom line financially was that, in effect, one-third of the budget was being spent for less than 10 percent of our students.

Chuck Williams, our COO, found similar trouble on his beat. His first two challenges involved ridding the system of some questionable contracts. In 1993 DCPS had contracted with ServiceMaster Company to provide maintenance throughout the system. The cost for that first year had been $105,000. But just three years later it had ballooned to $17 million, and there were serious questions about why the system was outsourcing maintenance. There were clearly no savings, and the quality of the work ServiceMaster was doing was questionable. There was also a suspect contract with a security company called MVM, Inc., that was run by a former agent of the Secret Service. We later found out that the school system was not getting all the services specified in the contract because it had never actually come forward with the necessary funds.

I decided early on to devote my first ninety days on the job to learning everything I could about the DCPS system. But there were some substantive actions that needed to be taken before those ninety days were over, and before my entire leadership and management team was even in place. One of those actions created the first major controversy I faced as DCPS superintendent/CEO.

Two DCPS middle schools, Kelley-Miller and Evans, were only nine blocks away from each other, and the enrollments in both were less than 30 percent of what they should have been. Kelley-Miller was the older of the two schools and had many fire code violations. It made perfectly good business sense to merge the two student bodies in the newer Evans facility, and I announced the plan to do so in early December 1996.

The first inkling of trouble was a visit by Terry Hairston, the elected school board's representative from the city ward in which Kelley-Miller and Evans were located. I had told my staff that although the school board members no longer ran the school system, we would afford them the courtesy of listening to their suggestions and concerns because they were still the elected representatives of the people. So I listened as Hairston railed against the decision to merge the schools. He pleaded and cajoled. He even threatened that there would be blood in the streets if the merger went ahead because the students did not like each other. (In threatening this, Hairston was, of course, ignoring the fact that Kelley-Miller and Evans students would eventually be put together when they moved on to high school.) He went on and on and finally stormed out of my office.

The merger was to take place at the start of the New Year, and the ETEBT scheduled two town meetings to seek the support of students, parents, teachers, and community leaders. The first town meeting gave me a glimpse of how illogical, and even vicious, such meetings could become. But when the combined school opened its doors in January, there were no rabble-rousers, placard carriers, or demonstrators. The merger was very peaceful, and there were immediate tangible benefits for students from each school, particularly an appreciable decline in the student-teacher ratio.

Nonetheless, the incident gave me my first taste of the kinds of opposition my team and I would encounter as we forged ahead with efforts to improve the DCPS system. It would get a lot worse.

A particular thorn in my side was a group called Parents United for D.C. Public Schools, an organization formed in 1981 to fight cuts in the school system's budget. In 1994 when the city council did not appropriate sufficient funding for maintenance of the physical plant, the group filed suit. The suit was clearly on point, because when the ETEBT assumed control there were at least 1,400 fire code violations in the school system. But it also ended up causing major headaches for those of us brought in to correct just such problems. The case ended up in the hands of Superior Court Judge Kaye Christian, who turned out to be overzealous, to put it mildly. Christian took it upon herself to close "unsafe" schools, which she defined as any school where repairs were being made.

As part of my discovery period, I held separate meetings with all principals, teachers, and staff. I also attended a breakfast meeting with Parents United. During our discussion the six or seven Parents United members in attendance said they would use the meeting as an opportunity to "educate" me on their organization. They boasted of an organizational membership of seven thousand across the District's eight wards, and they considered themselves the eyes and ears or the community. They listed a litany of concerns and issues, from school security and budgeting to student-teacher ratios and school closings. They further demanded that I meet with them regularly and that I consult them on every action dealing with the school maintenance system. I refused, of course.

About a week after my meeting with Parents United, I attended an orientation session for the elected school board. I felt obliged to engage the board, which would regain control of the school system come June 2000. At that orientation, I discussed a number of issues that faced the system, including budgeting and personnel problems. I expressed my willingness to have an open dialogue, and I stressed once again that the days of micromanaging by the board were over.

I also consulted interested parties outside the DCPS system. Several members of Congress had useful advice. Republican Rep. Tom Davis of Virginia recommended that I compile a list of accomplishments during the first three months the DCPS was under my helm. Newt Gingrich, the Georgia Republican then serving as Speaker of the House, urged greater use of technology in the schools and directed his staff to send letters to the Smithsonian and the Wolf Trap Foundation for the Performing Arts encouraging these organizations to get involved with the system. U.S. Department of Education Secretary Richard Riley assured me that his department would work with us. And D.C. Councilwoman Kathy Patterson promised that she would provide the DCPS with "behind the scenes support." It was not long after making that pledge, however, that she declared "war" on the system and publicly denounced the DCPS leadership. Patterson frequently said, "Those two generals must go!" She meant, of course, me and Chuck Williams.

Vermont's then–Republican senator Jim Jeffords was a major force in helping me, and he arranged a visit for me to Chicago that December so I could get a firsthand look at its reforms. I met with school officials, and we discussed in depth how they handled a myriad of issues, such as standardized tests, homeless students, truancy, and the media. Repeatedly, the Chicago school officials emphasized the need to measure progress in reaching ten strict quantifiable goals. I learned that the Chicago system had reestablished strict accountability. It published school test scores and required that parents pick up report cards and attend parent-teacher conferences. What made all this possible was the fact that the Illinois legislature had authorized the mayor's takeover of the Chicago school system, and the mayor, in turn, appointed his own people to run it.

Back in Washington, D.C., I continued my whirlwind schedule, meeting with Librarian of Congress Dr. James Billington to discuss how the Library could help the schools. We went back more than forty years, having both attended Lower Merion High School. Ray Smith, CEO of Bell-Atlantic NYNEX, also attended that meeting and offered to provide note-book computers to all the DCPS school principals. I also saw U.S. Attorney General Janet Reno, who was interested in initiating a conflict resolution project in the schools and who, starting in March 1997, took to visiting schools at least once a month.

Several of the people I consulted, including economist Alice Rivlin, a director of the Federal Reserve who later replaced Andy Brimmer as chair of the Control Board, got me thinking about the importance of having a true academician serve as CAO, working to develop and strengthen academic standards. That CAO, in effect, would run the schoolhouse while the super-intendent/CEO acted as the firewall between those in charge of academics and the rest of the world.

Meanwhile, the ETEBT met every week. Its unpaid members were truly dedicated, sincere citizens, but came very close to micromanaging from time to time. The typical agenda included my weekly update, followed by presentations from key DCPS staff—Chuck Williams on operational issues; Cecilia Wirtz, our general counsel, on legal problems; Abdusalam Omer on the budget; Lewis Norman on personnel difficulties; and Mildred Musgrove on academic challenges.

The ETEBT meetings usually lasted two and a half to three hours. Members went off on tangents, prolonging the meetings with discussions of things that were not germane to the agenda. Don Reeves, who had been newly elected president of the school board, was an ex officio of the ETEBT, and he turned out to be very disruptive at the meetings. He also constantly leaked the emergency board's deliberations and decisions to the press.

In mid-January, a retreat was held for ETEBT members.** Two new members of the board, Nate Howard and Emily Washington, needed to be brought up to date, and we had a rich, full agenda. Among other things, we discussed giving a heads-up to certain folks concerning the proposed DCPS budget for 1998 and decided to conduct a closed session for the full elected school board. We set 30 June as our target date for completing both our operations plan and our education plan. And shortly afterward, the decision was made to replace Mildred Musgrove as CAO.

Six months after taking over the DCPS, I was generally optimistic. At a media briefing, I and my DCPS management team discussed accomplishments in a number of areas but acknowledged that many improvements would not be evident until school resumed in the fall. DCPS had every intention of opening all of our schools fully stocked and on time. The buildings would be clean, safe, and in working order. Principals would be qualified, and teachers would be held accountable. We acknowledged that the areas with the most room for improvement included better maintenance—"massive repairs and extensive funding were still needed"; adequate supplies and personnel; and an honest budget for each school, to be completed in June. We knew how many people worked for the schools, although there were still questions about where they all worked and which payroll they were on. I was still committed to identifying and firing ineffective principals. When pressed by the media to grade my performance, I gave myself a C+.

The 11 May 1997 edition of the *Washington Post Magazine* carried my picture on the cover and featured an article by Peter Perl and Debbi Wilgoren titled "Basic Training."[6] The article's opening statement describes better than any other that I have read how I was brought into a system that "had been failing for years, a system in which administrators diverted money from schools to a bloated central office, principals had been pressured to hire cronies and relatives of school board members and other city officials, and teachers had faced no more accountability than the students to whom they had given unearned promotions." The article continues, "Rebuilding such a system would take time: For each of the headline-making displacements and replacements, there would have to be countless incremental changes in the way the schools operated, changes that added up to nothing less than a cultural revolution."

** Members: Bruce R. MacLaury—Chair; Maudine Cooper—Vice Chair; Peter Gallager; Elliott Hall; Nathaniel Howard; Charito Kruvant; Don Reeves; Emily Washington; and me.

The article suggests that one of my fundamental problems was "being a strong leader, answerable only to the U.S. Congress and the D.C. Financial Control Board. . . . The dilemma is that, although some stakeholders in the D.C. school system wanted change, others—those with a vested interest in the current system—did not, and many resented that General Becton was not answerable to locally elected officials." I was accused of making decisions behind closed doors without appearing to sufficiently involve or consult the community, which is quite correct. I was hired to exercise strong leadership, and, as the article stated, I was "castigated for doing exactly that." The article suggested that many members of the community either had given up on the school system or expected me to work instantaneous miracles.

When D.C. mayor Marion Barry was privately asked his views on how well Becton had done his response was basically that he had not seen any improvements. But that response must be taken in the context that Mayor Barry had been opposed to the entire concept of the Control Board and the DCPS takeover from the very beginning. When the same reporter who had spoken to Barry asked me what I thought about his comments, I simply replied, "No comment!" I had learned years earlier that fighting a public official in the press is a no-win situation.

The next time I saw the mayor one-on-one, I reminded him that I had been in the city in the 1960s when he first ran for the school board and that he had been involved in the city and school affairs ever since. I said, "You have had more than thirty years, and I have had six months." He changed the subject.

As the 1997 school year ended, I tried to attend as many of the high school graduation exercises as I could. I could not help but wonder how many of the graduates had made it to the podium on merit rather than by benefit of social promotion. I renewed my commitment to eliminate the latter as soon as possible. Also in early June I began working with my team to develop a plan to handle the small percentage of students with severe behavior problems by placing them in an alternative educational program out of the mainstream.

In July I had my first real confrontation with the ETEBT. I prepared a memo to each trustee in which I expressed my frustrations with leaks from the board to the news media and informed the trustees that I no longer intended to share sensitive personnel information with them prior to release to the public. Of course, even that memo was leaked to the press. I received a predictable response from Don Reeves, the president of the elected school board, who, by the way, admitted to being the "leaker." Reeves sanctimoniously explained his actions by saying, "Reform of our schools is a public matter."

The press supported Reeves, calling my memo a "silly declaration." But in my judgment DCPS leadership was dealing with the sensitive issue of prematurely alerting current employers of potential employees that individuals were being considered for positions with DCPS. For example, Sheila Graves, the leading candidate for chief of human resources, worked for the secretary of defense. Arlene Ackerman, the leading candidate for CAO, worked in the Seattle public school system.

The ETEBT later censured Don Reeves for revealing confidential information, but this did not reduce the criticism from parents and others who felt that they had not been privy to the trustees' deliberations. One parent and Parent-Teacher Association president said, "We need to know what the trustees are thinking about and what they're intending to do. The parents and the kids are not the people who broke the system. Therefore we're not the people who should be kept in the dark."[7] I could have screamed in reply that my team and the ETEBT board members also were not the ones who broke the system, nor did we stand by and do nothing when it was being busted. But I did not.

The next firestorm I ran into involved holding principals more accountable for their performance. To help weed out poor performers and incompetents, I proposed appointing all principals to one-year, rather than three-year, terms. I believed that the shorter terms were necessary to allow more rapid elimination of principals who did not make the grade. The proposal for shorter terms was immediately attacked from almost all sides within the school system. Parents and D.C. council members also attacked the proposal. The critics saw no reason to reduce job security for good principals and felt that such a draconian policy demonstrated a lack of confidence in all principals.

On 14 August my office named eight principals who were being fired and thirty-one others who were being appointed or reappointed. I used this occasion to reaffirm my confidence in most of the D.C. public school principals. The action was accompanied with the following statement: "The principals being fired are not qualified in my judgment. They have not met the standards that are the minimum standards to be a principal in the D.C. school system. We expect principals not to be just the lead teacher but to run things in their buildings." I further stated that some other principals were "on probation" and would be carefully watched and supported when possible. Once again, the critics attacked. Some complained that I had moved too rapidly to fire the principals. Others complained that I had not fired more.

Meanwhile, ETEBT had long been conducting hearings on federally mandated school closings. We had to close at least six schools, and Chuck Williams used the following criteria to identify those that should not survive:

- Underutilization
- Physical condition and cost of repair
- Composition of student population, including number of out-of-boundary students
- Educational and other programs
- Proximity to other schools
- Projected demographics
- Public transportation
- Potential value if sold or leased
- Age and major modernization
- Compliance with the Americans with Disabilities Act

We conducted citywide workshops to explain our criteria, and we publicized the names of eighteen schools that had been selected for potential closure. Everyone realized that the DCPS had a large amount of underutilized space and a runaway deferred maintenance challenge. In fact, the General Services Administration estimated the total cost of immediately needed repairs to D.C. schools to be in excess of $2 billion.[8] Even so, we encountered the "not in my backyard" response. No one wanted his or her neighborhood school to be closed.

After our third open hearing, some people tried to intimidate me. I was personally threatened with statements such as, "We know where you live." After one incident, Al Gurley, my security guard/driver, physically removed several attendees who were out of control.

The trustees finally voted in public to close thirteen schools, two of which would be completely gutted and rebuilt. The public clamor continued. ETEBT hearings were interrupted by organized demonstrations of parents and students. And we were vilified. *Washington Post* columnist Colbert I. King told me personally that he was devastated that we would even consider

The first lady, the president, the first lady's chief of staff, and me. (Courtesy of the White House)

"closing" the school his grandparents, parents, and he and his siblings attended. That school, Thaddeus Stevens Elementary School, was one of the two slated to be gutted and rebuilt in a way that preserved its outward appearance because it was the first school black Americans attended back before the turn of the twentieth century.

But if the principal and school closing debacles were serious, the roof repair issue was a showstopper. On 21 July 1997 I ordered the start of repair work on the roofs of forty-three schools. This brought DCPS directly in the sights of Judge Christian, keeper of the Parents United lawsuit against the school system.

The judge had ruled that no one could be in any school while repairs were under way, even though expert roofers and school officials said the work posed no danger to building occupants. (As an aside, I was amused that while visiting one of our elementary schools, First Lady Hillary Rodham Clinton was videotaped remarking that the White House was undergoing roof repair, but they continue to occupy the building.)

DCPS expected that repairs to twenty-three schools would be completed by the scheduled first day of school, 2 September, but work on the other twenty would require more time. I considered delaying the opening of some schools by a week if necessary so repairs could be completed, but I expected that temporary relocation of students would probably be sufficient.

The roofing work was slow to start because time-consuming District purchasing and contracting procedures had to be followed, there were delays in obtaining permits, and we had to explain ourselves to all sorts of interested parties. Almost anything we wanted to do required the approval of the D.C. City Council, the Control Board, and Congress. We were frustrated by the lack of support we were receiving from elected officials, who were quick to criticize but unwilling to help solve problems.

Things had gotten worse by 9 August. The roof repairs were not proceeding quickly enough to be completed by 2 September, so I decided to delay the opening of all schools for three weeks. I issued a public state-ment explaining the delays in obtaining necessary funds, the slow receipt of bids from contractors who were reluctant to undertake work from the District because of past problems getting paid, and the slow pace of getting contracts written and approved. I also blamed the Parents United lawsuit, which was still pending despite the fact that we had resolved the fire code violations within the schools. Clearly, as long as the lawsuit was in place, Judge Christian would be involved in any efforts to improve the physical plant. I hoped to bring public pressure on the judge to acknowledge and correct the fallacy in her ruling that school buildings could not be occupied while structural work was ongoing. My scheme did not work.

The delayed school opening ignited a firestorm of criticism. Some people accused me of treating the parents of the District of Columbia as if they were my inferiors in the military. Some parents threatened to bring their kids to our offices for "babysitting" while they went to work. Other parents demanded to know what they were expected to do with their children. My unspoken thoughts included the question, "Whose kids are they, anyhow?"

It was reported that I viewed the delay in school opening as an "incon-venience." Quite frankly, I do not recall ever saying that, but reports that I did generated an angry response from D.C. City Council member Kevin Chavous, who told me, "Inconveniencing seventy thousand–plus kids is a crisis. . . . There has got to be some accountability for what is a massive plan-ning failure."

According to the media, the trustees and I were in a finger-pointing fight with Parents United, with each side accusing the other of being responsible for the delayed school openings. Although DCPS and Parents United eventually agreed to cooperate in asking Judge Christian to set aside her ruling preventing occupancy of any school building while roof repair work was ongoing, it was assumed that bad blood between the school officials and the parents group remained. In my judgment, that was a major understatement.

In late August I met with the school principals to introduce Arlene Ackerman as the new CAO and to build support for the changes DCPS was implementing in the system. I also wanted to make sure the principals understood that they would be held more accountable than in the past. My team received praise from some principals for our focus on academics and the lack of a "political" agenda in all of our discussions.

But even though I had been on the job for only nine months, other stakeholders characterized my status as DCPS superintendent/CEO as "shaky" at best. The chairman of the House subcommittee charged with overseeing District affairs noted that while the DCPS was moving in the right direction, the jury was still out on me as superintendent/CEO.

The media reported that the one recurring theme to emerge from an analysis of my performance was that my leadership style was tantamount to "decide and announce," without soliciting public consultation or debate.

The comment of a D.C. City Council member embodied this sentiment: "Becton would gain credibility if he spoke more openly. He sometimes comes off with the air of, 'I don't have to deal with you all.' And that flies in the face of what meaningful reform is all about. General Becton's public image was of a military leader who is used to giving orders and having them obeyed, who didn't see any particular need to consult with elected officials or parents prior to making a decision, and who didn't even see the need to explain his action to anyone other than the Congress and the D.C. Control Board to whom he reported." (*Washington Post*, 20 October 1997, B-3.)

My supporters knew better and made their views known. But in spite of my efforts to increase the flow of information to the public by establishing forums such as weekly public briefings, the image of me as an autocrat who reached decisions arbitrarily and unilaterally persisted.

In mid-September my son Wes got fed up after reading about a particularly vicious verbal attack on me and wrote a letter to the editor of the

Washington Post asking everyone to "Give General Becton a Chance." He asked why any seventy-one-year-old man in his right mind would leave retirement and take on the monumental job of trying to fix the DCPS. He concluded remarks by writing, "He cares about the future of the District's children and was disgusted by what he saw. . . . It's because he cares more about the children and getting the job done than about himself."[9] I could not have been more proud.

In late October problems with school repairs surfaced again, this time over boiler replacements. The media called it "a contest of wills" between Judge Christian and me.[10] I believed boiler repairs were badly needed in some schools and authorized repair work. Judge Christian ordered the repairs halted, stating that any repairs required her specific approval before commencement. She repeated her belief that her mandate resulting from the Parents United lawsuit meant that she had final authority to approve all repairs. I believed that I had the authority and the responsibility to order the repairs started. Here is how an editorial in the *Washington Times* described the situation:

> How ridiculous have things become? This ridiculous: If workers need to hammer a hole in the wall to install wiring and cable for Internet access, the work creates a fire code violation. If janitors move furniture into a hallway to clean and buff the floors in a classroom, the work creates a fire code violation. . . . If new boilers are installed in the bowels of the basement, or new roofs put on, or classrooms are reconfigured to meet parents' satisfaction, or windows are weatherstripped, or water pipes soldered, or escalators repaired, or outside stairwells roped off for repair, or puckered floor boards replaced, or new backboards installed in the gymnasium . . . once any of these things happens, once the issue is brought to the court's attention, once Parents United for D.C. Public Schools sneezes, the vicious cycle of disruption kicks in.
>
> What then? If Judge Kaye Christian, who oversees the case, issues an order to shut down a school, officials must comply.[11]

Still, by the end of my first year on the job I was convinced that we were gaining ground, and I was determined to make the DCPS exemplary by 2000, when authority for the school system would be returned to the elected school board.

Judge Kaye Christian keeps a problem child after school to teach him a lesson. (Reprinted with permission of Joe Azar of the *Legal Times*)

Critics, however, continued to focus on the school system's problems. Lack of progress on improving the academic programs and the ten months it took to hire a new CAO were particular sore points. There were also complaints that I had failed to get rid of more substandard employees. One Control Board member put it this way: "The problem with keeping people around is they become entrenched, and they can undermine you. One of General Becton's characteristics is that he is cursed with being a very decent person. . . . He probably would have gained additional support had he gone in and shaken up the place."[12]

On 20 November, in an editorial, the *Washington Post* declared, "If the past 12 months have taught anything, it is the simple lesson that reforming a 77,000-student school system in deep crisis and with an entrenched, change-resistant bureaucracy is almost too big a job for one person to handle. Yet even with the handicaps of an agreeable but largely feckless board of appointed trustees, and long neglected personnel, financial and building maintenance problems, Lt. Gen. Becton appears to have laid the groundwork for achieving the kind of progress that the DC Financial Control Board had in mind when it hired him out of retirement last year."[13] The editorial went on to suggest that more poorly performing principals and teachers needed to be fired. And it concluded, "It's time the trustees began to take the public into its confidence. Year two must achieve major breakthroughs."

The New Year started with release of the results of an audit the Control Board had conducted on the school repairs done in 1997. The auditors determined that the DCPS leadership was overwhelmed and willing to cut corners. Bruce MacLaury, chairman of the ETEBT, and I challenged the findings, asserting that the audit was ordered too early for us to get our files in order. Bruce believed the audit's timing was politically motivated.

At about the same time, Virginia representative Tom Davis, D.C.'s Democratic congressional delegate Eleanor Holmes Norton, and the congressional subcommittee that was our watchdog conducted a hearing. They credited us with making some progress, but I was faulted for underestimating the negative public reaction to the delay in starting the school year.

Then the U.S. Court of Appeals for the District of Columbia ruled that the Control Board had acted illegally in creating the ETEBT, thereby invalidating any authority it had over the school system. That presented an immediate dilemma. To whom, if anyone, was I supposed to report? I had long ignored the elected school board, and the Control Board had the rest of the city to run. The ETEBT members rejected the suggestion that they remain on as voluntary advisors. That seemed to leave me to operate as a "lone ranger," which, frankly, suited me just fine.

Chuck Williams resigned on 24 February 1998. I had refused to accept his resignation several weeks earlier, but this time, it was a fait accompli. He had had it with the lack of support from those who should have been most interested in the success of the DCPS system. He was, he told me, tired of "being beaten up and embarrassed" by the public, and particularly by Judge Christian.

It was not too long afterward that Tony Williams, the District's CFO, fired my CFO Ed Stephenson. Technically, Ed, like all city agency CFOs, was under Williams' control. Nonetheless, I blew up. As Bruce MacLaury said, "If some were trying to derail General Becton's school reform efforts, they could hardly have found a more effective tactic. To have Stephenson yanked out of the office at the very moment of critical budget hearings is incomprehensible!"[14]

During this series of personnel changes, I started reassessing my own tenure. I had originally planned on being around until the return of the school system to the control of the elected school board. But with Chuck and Ed gone, I began having second thoughts. Then in mid-March Dr. Andy Brimmer, Chairman of the Control Board, announced that he would leave in June after the end of this term. So I announced that I would also make my own departure in June.

I did not even last that long, however. In April I was accused of misleading the Control Board on a matter concerning personnel, and I felt that my integrity had been impugned. At a hastily called press conference, I pleaded "physical, emotional, and mental exhaustion," adding, "It was no longer fun to get up in the morning and go to work."[15]

Clearly, I wanted to leave on my own volition before being forced out. Another reason for my departure was closer to home: Louise and our daughters were tired of the abuse I was receiving. But not all of the reviews of my tenure were bad by any means. After I announced my resignation I was gratified to receive a number of very kind comments from quite a few people, including Donald Graham, publisher of the *Washington Post*. Graham's handwritten letter is included as Appendix 5 to this book.

Looking back I realize that in running DCPS, I failed to carry out one of the basic tenets of leadership. I had failed to communicate, to talk and listen to my constituents. The truth is that when I took the job, I was of the opinion that the community could not care less what was happening to the schools. Because the schools were in such disarray, I unwisely and unfairly concluded that the parents were lethargic and just plain unconcerned. This belief led me to comment to the press, "If I had one silver bullet, it would be greater parental and community involvement. I did not go out to generate, to develop, as much community and parental involvement as I should have, clearly."[16]

Ever since I left the DCPS people have asked whether I think there is any hope for District public schools. My standard answer is, "Yes . . . but." If the person asking is someone with the clout to make a difference, I openly speak my mind. I tell him or her that as long as the Congress permits every politician in the District to have an impact on the schools (today, the superintendent must respond to more than twenty folks), there will be no significant improvement. I tell them to duplicate what happened in Chicago. That the schools must be removed from local politicians' control and that a state of emergency must be declared. Then, the city's mayor must appoint a "czar" and a five- to seven-member board of education, determine a meaningful funding stream, and start with an accurate physical plant assessment to bring all antiquated schools up to par. Finally, tell everybody else, "KEEP YOUR HANDS OFF!"

Some suggest a different approach, with the first step being "Elect a white mayor and a majority white city council. Then, appoint a five-member board of education that has complete control of the superintendent as well as the entire charter school system; enforce all applicable DCPS policies, including those concerning truancy, teacher certification, and special education; improve the teacher pay; and offer incentives for parents to get involved."

That approach suggests a belief that the problems with the DCPS system have resulted largely from the fact that most of the individuals in charge have been black. I disagree with such thinking. In my judgment, the DCPS system has collapsed because the individuals in charge have lacked sufficient economic and political power.

I argue that the DCPS should be among the top public school systems in the nation. Yet, how many members of Congress who live in the District of Columbia have entrusted the education of their own children to the DCPS? I would wager, from considerable experience, that the number is very small.

When I met President Bill Clinton for the first time in December 1996, shortly after I had been named the DCPS superintendent/CEO, Clinton asked, "General, what is your goal or vision for the school system?" I replied, "To create a school system in which you and your vice president would have enough confidence to send your own children."

Clearly, that has not happened.

CHAPTER TWENTY

★ ★ ★

Retirement at Last

I did not set out to find another job after leaving the DCPS. Just in case I was inclined to do so, Louise issued one of the rare ultimatums of our marriage. If I took another job like that one, she warned, we probably would not be together to celebrate another wedding anniversary. These were pretty strong words, and I heard them loud and clear.

Still, I have never been a couch potato. Back when I was president of PVAMU, someone compiled a list of the various regional, state, and national organizations in which I served and came up with no fewer than seventeen boards and advisory committees. In retirement, I was determined to be as active as ever and to continue my involvement in some areas that had long been of interest to me. One of these was equality of opportunity and affirmative action.

While I was PVAMU president I received a visit from Bryce Jordan, president emeritus of Pennsylvania State University, who wanted me to serve as an expert witness in the federal case *Knight v. Alabama*. Jordan, two other university presidents emeriti, Harold Enarson of Ohio State University and Robin Fleming of the University of Michigan, and Robert Anderson, vice provost at Iowa State University, were already on board, and they and the court had identified the need for someone to represent an HBCU. Jordan wanted me to become that person, and I was happy to accept the challenge.

Knight involved desegregation and equalization of funding and facilities among historically white and black state schools in Alabama.[1] To say that the litigation had been protracted is an understatement. The case had been filed in 1981 and was the result of a 1978 review of public higher education in Alabama by the Office for Civil Rights in the U.S. Department of Health, Education, and Welfare. In 1991, U.S. District Court Judge Harold

L. Murphy had issued a remedial decree ordering the changes necessary to expand black student enrollment and black faculty employment in Alabama's predominately white institutions. The state had appealed, and the appellate court remanded the case to Judge Murphy in the U.S. District Court for the Northern District of Alabama. In preparation for retrying the case, Murphy decided to appoint five expert witnesses, and I would be one of them.

As part of my research I paid many visits to the two historically black institutions in the state, Alabama State University and Alabama A&M University. The new trial itself took six weeks. And Judge Murphy issued another remedial decree on 1 August 1995. A procedural history of the case written by court-appointed official monitor Carlos Gonzalez, describes the decree as comprehensive in nature and as encompassing such matters as fund-raising, establishing new academic programs, capital construction projects, the recruitment of white students to black universities, and the unification of the land grant systems of Auburn University and Alabama A&M University.

After Judge Murphy issued the 1995 decree, he asked me and the three former university presidents to serve on a long-term planning and oversight committee that would periodically report to him and also provide whatever assistance we deemed appropriate to the institutions involved in the litigation.

Jim Blackshear, the attorney who filed the suit that started the case in 1981, was quoted in a 2005 *Birmingham News* article as saying, "Nobody really contends that we have reached the end of the road when it comes to ending vestiges of segregation."[2] He is right. However, I cannot help but be encouraged by the results that have been achieved. Alabama is the same state, after all, in which Gov. George C. Wallace stood in the doorway in 1963 to prevent the admission of two black students, Vivian J. Malone and James A. Hood, to the University of Alabama.

Interestingly, in 1982, the year after the *Knight* case was filed, Governor Wallace recanted his segregationist views and admitted that he had been wrong. His onetime rallying cry of "segregation now, segregation tomorrow, segregation forever" has gone the way of the dinosaur. I am pleased to have played a role in lessening this barrier to civil rights in Alabama and in helping to enhance equal opportunity in public education and employment.

Testifying in the *Knight* case and advising on implementation of the settlement agreements was not my only chance to get involved in issues of equal educational opportunity. In late 2001 I received a call from Joe Reeder. Joe and I had met when he was the undersecretary of the Army and I was superintendent/CEO of the DCPS. He asked if I would take part in a friend-of-the-court brief in *Gratz v. Bollinger*. The U.S. Court of Appeals for the Sixth Circuit had ruled in that case that the University of Michigan's race-conscious admissions policy served a compelling interest in achieving a racially diverse student body. The U.S. Supreme Court had agreed to review the case. This *amicus* brief would support the lower court's decision.

Why would I be interested in the outcome of this case? The main reason was that I had firsthand experience of the problems a nondiverse officer corps could cause. I still remembered the indignity at Fort Benning when my white tactical officer asked to take a picture of me eating watermelon because he was sure that was what black people did. I vividly recalled the view of certain senior officers early in the Korean War that black soldiers could not be trusted in critical combat situations. I could never forget the racial tensions at Fort Hood, and the fear of bodily harm that inhibited freedom of movement within the barracks by members of certain racial groups.

The *amici* who joined in the brief sincerely believed that race-conscious admissions policies achieved a highly desirable outcome.[3] The reality is that disadvantaged members of American society are still playing catch-up, and achieving equal opportunity requires that consideration be given to that. In the words of the brief, "Based on decades of experience, *amici* have concluded that a highly qualified, racially diverse officer corps educated and trained to command our nation's racially diverse enlisted ranks is essential to the military's ability to fulfill its principal mission to provide national security."

In no way did I endorse a quota system, but I did subscribe to the military's attainment of the goal of a diverse officer corps that was representative of the total force. It was, and still is, my view that if the United States is to have an educated, well-trained, and effective military, the necessary educational, economic, and social opportunities must be made available to all young men and women. Whether admissions officers are selecting the next class of cadets at West Point or the next class of lawyers at Harvard, Yale, or Michigan, it is vital to consider race and ethnicity as one of many factors that will lead to the formation of a diverse student body and the proper training of tomorrow's leaders.

When America's young men and women in the military are called upon to defend our country, they do so today as a multiethnic, multiracial, male and female force. While today's military may not be a mirror reflection of the

U.S. population, it is close. This was not always the case, however. The battle to end discrimination in the armed forces took many years, but the results are obvious. As the recent wars in Iraq and Afghanistan have demonstrated, the United States has a highly trained and effective fighting force. That could not have been achieved so readily without the Army's equal opportunity/ affirmative action policy, which in my judgment is a combat multiplier.

Gratz involved the admissions policies of the University of Michigan's College of Literature, Science, and the Arts (LSA). Of particular interest was the LSA's practice, beginning with the 1998 academic year, "of awarding 20 points to applicants who were members of underrepresented racial or ethnic minority groups—i.e., African-Americans, Hispanics, and Native Americans."[4] The petitioners, both white, had been denied admission to the LSA and had subsequently filed a class action lawsuit alleging racial discrimination and violations of constitutional equal protection rights guaranteed by the Fourteenth Amendment.

In a 6–3 ruling issued on 23 June 2003, the Supreme Court invalidated LSA's admissions policies. Particularly objectionable to the Court was the automatic awarding of twenty points to applicants only because they were members of specified racial or ethnic groups. But that very same day, the high court reached a different decision in a case challenging the admissions policies of the University of Michigan Law School.[5] The petitioner in *Grutter v. Bollinger* was a white Michigan resident who alleged the same constitutional and statutory violations as the petitioners in *Gratz* and argued that the law school used race as a "predominant factor" in its admissions decisions.

The court, again ruling 6–3, found the *Grutter* facts distinguishable from those of *Gratz* because the law school's admissions policies were narrowly tailored to further the compelling governmental interest in the educational benefits that flow from a diverse student body. Therefore, the court ruled, the law school policy did not violate constitutional and statutory provisions relating to equal treatment. Also, the *Grutter* facts withstood constitutional and statutory scrutiny because the University of Michigan Law School gave individualized consideration to each applicant.

While the Supreme Court did not find our *amicus* argument persuasive in *Gratz*, it acknowledged our position in *Grutter*, writing in an opinion penned by Justice Sandra Day O'Connor, "High-ranking retired officers and civilian leaders of the United States military assert that, '[b]ased on [their] decades of experience,' a 'highly qualified, racially diverse officer corps . . .

is essential to the military's ability to fulfill its principle mission to provide national security.'"

Has the *Gratz* decision impeded the ability of the military service academies to recruit and enroll members of underrepresented groups? I have not done extensive research on the subject, but it is telling that the United States Military Academy at West Point did not have to change its admissions policy based on the decision. The case merely reaffirmed what it had been doing for years.

Even though I officially retired in 1998, I still had at least one big trip left in me. Bill and Ann Tidball planted the seeds for it not longer after I left DCPS. They lived in Hong Kong at the time; Ann was a vice president of Allied Signal for the Far East region, and Bill was a homemaker and part-time manager of construction for an orphanage in China. They invited Louise and me to visit them some time in the following year, and after much discussion, we set the date for March. I would make the trip by myself. Louise has a history of stomach problems with exotic food, and she has never loved flying. So it was best that she remain at home.

I had always made it a practice not to return to areas where I had fought in combat. But Bill persuaded me that it made no sense for me to be so close to Vietnam and not visit that country in addition to China. A bit reluctantly, I agreed to do so.

There were three necessities for travel to China and Vietnam. First, I needed to get the appropriate vaccinations. Next, I had to secure the necessary visas, which meant separate visas for Hong Kong and the rest of China. Finally, I had to use frequent flyer miles to upgrade my seat to business class. For flights lasting upward of fourteen hours, those extra inches of seat space make all the difference in the world.

I departed Dulles Airport at 0825 on 8 March and arrived at the new Hong Kong International Airport on Chep Lap Kok at 1820 hours a day later. Bill Tidball was waiting for me. The passage through customs was a breeze, and the Airport Express to Hong Kong was probably the finest train on which I had ever ridden. Bill and Ann lived on the twenty-third floor of an apartment building, and their home was all anyone could ever ask for, particularly as it came with a view of the harbor that was simply gorgeous.

Bill thought the best way to get over jet lag was to get onto a golf course. And that is just where we started—at the Lotus Hill Golf Resort in Panyu, south of Guangdong, China. With all its water hazards and long fairway bunkers, the course is not easy, which is one reason this golfing paradise is so popular with its club members and guests from Hong Kong and Guangzhou's fast-growing golfing community. Bill was right. Three days at Lotus Hill was just the right prescription for jet lag.

We returned to Hong Kong on Friday, 12 March, and the next evening we attended the formal AmCham Ball, which is hosted each year by the American Chamber of Commerce in Hong Kong. The cocktails were generous, the dinner was scrumptious, the opulence of the table prizes was out of this world, and the entertainment—"Spotlight on Broadway"—was as good as it gets.

We were off again on Sunday morning to China. Lee, our guide from the China International Travel Service, suggested that we get started on our tour right away, and before I knew it, we were in Tiananmen Square. It was rather difficult to visualize exactly where that young man had been standing as he faced down the tank column in the famous protest photograph from ten years before, but I remembered the photo vividly.

Our first stop was the Palace Museum, which had previously been known as the Forbidden City. The complex served as China's imperial palace for more than five hundred years. Today, it houses a great variety of rare cultural relics and works of art. Sprawling over 720,000 square meters, it is the world's largest and most complete collection of ancient palatial structures. We were told that the Forbidden City survived the Red Guard fanaticism only because Premier Zhou Enlai sent his army to protect it.

We stayed at the Palace Hotel, where it was difficult to appreciate that we were in the capital of China. Most of the customers came from outside China, and from the languages I heard spoken, it was clear that many were from non-English-speaking countries. Meals were simply overwhelming, as were my continued attempts to master the use of chopsticks. I did quite well as long as I did not think about what I was doing.

We also visited the Great Wall (if I could have seen the top through the fog, I might never have started the climb!) and the Terra Cotta Museum outside Xian. Xian is about ninety minutes from Beijing, and it struck me as being more like the China I had imagined than what I had seen so far. There were many more bicycles and carts and oxen, and far fewer cars, in Xian than we had encountered elsewhere.

The Terra Cotta Museum is the site of the Mausoleum of Emperor Qin Shi Huang (259–210 BC), the first ruler of the Qin dynasty. At the time of my visit, three vaults had been excavated, and further excavations were under way. A total of six thousand lifelike terra cotta warriors and horses had been unearthed, carefully arranged in military formations, as they appear to reenact the grand spectacle of Emperor Qin Shi Huang leading a large number of troops to unify China. The terra cotta warriors and horses and the bronze chariots that have been unearthed are superb historical art treasures.

During our return from the museum we made an unplanned visit to a rural home. The purpose of the visit was to view one of the caves in which families lived in earlier days. When we visited the cave was used for cooking purposes by a family consisting of a husband and wife and seven or eight children who lived in a nearby house made of clay, brick, and mortar. The family's home had electricity, but they got their water from a well.

The head of the household was a small, bent-over man with a stringy beard and a long pipe. He was very pleased to escort us through his yard, which was hard clay. Through our guide, I asked one of the little girls about school. Translating her reply, our guide said the girl was thirteen and had dropped out of school. When I asked why, I was told she "was bored." She went on to say that she wanted to be a doctor and take care of people. When I asked how she expected to do this without an education, she just shrugged and went off to play with other kids who, I assume, had also dropped out of school. The adults did not appear to be bothered by either our questions or the child's answers.

We returned to Hong Kong on 18 March, and getting back to the Tidball apartment felt like coming home.

Just three days later, we were in Vietnam. Since I had not planned ever to return to that country, I was distinctly uncomfortable when we arrived in Hanoi. Here I was in a place that heretofore was truly enemy territory. During the Vietnam War the only Americans besides Jane Fonda and her ilk who went to Hanoi had been prisoners of war.

En route from the airport to the Vietnamese capital, we saw few cars on the roads, which were the poorest I had seen thus far in Asia. But downtown Hanoi was thriving. The city's unemployment rate was 30 percent out of a population of about 3.5 million, and it appeared that all the jobless people were out on the streets. The greetings were friendly wherever we went, even at the infamous "Hanoi Hilton."

The Hoa Loa Prison was the most depressing site we encountered on the entire trip. It was officially closed, but money opens doors around the world, and we were permitted to enter. The prison had been built by the French in the nineteenth century, and every occupying force from then on had used it to imprison the Vietnamese. So it was the site of choice when the North Vietnamese wanted to hold U.S. prisoners. The cold, hard stone and cement and the fixed wrist and leg irons were grim reminders of what had happened there. With toilet and wash facilities that seemed to contain the barest of necessities, the Hanoi Hilton must rank among the most primitive prisons in the world. I could not escape the disgusting notion that Fonda and company probably drove past this facility, knowing what it was but having not the slightest apparent concern for those inside.

The next day, 22 March, we visited Ho Chi Minh's mausoleum. Immediately behind the crypt is the home Ho Chi Minh allegedly occupied during the war. By Vietnamese standards, it's an ordinary house, built on stilts. I found it difficult to believe that the North Vietnamese leader had lived there without the U.S. government either knowing that or somehow terminating him.

Our flight from Hanoi to the former Saigon, now Ho Chi Minh City, was delayed several hours. When we arrived, I was unable to recognize anything. The old Saigon, which had been a thriving metropolis back in the 1960s, had, after thirty years of growth, become Vietnam's showplace.

The contrast between Hanoi and Ho Chi Minh City reminded me of that between Beijing and Hong Kong. In 1999 Ho Chi Minh City had five million residents and two and a half million registered motorbikes. It was bursting with energy, and there were no signs of any checks being placed on the city's explosive growth.

I found the War Remnants Museum deeply disheartening. U.S. tanks and other weapons systems were displayed inside and out, and the message was unmistakably clear: The U.S. military and the "puppet" South Vietnamese forces—the Army of the Republic of Vietnam (ARVN), who had been defeated, had been the villains during the Vietnamese conflict. The museum's brochure featured this quote by former U.S. Secretary of Defense Robert McNamara: "Yet we were wrong, terribly wrong. We owe it to future generations to explain why."

Pictures of the village of Son My, which is commonly known as My Lai in the United States, were prominently displayed, with all the gore of the dead women and children in the ditches seemingly highlighted. So was the infamous picture of the ARVN officer executing a VC guerrilla. Victims of fragmentation bombs, Agent Orange, and napalm were pictured, as was a man, presumably a VC guerrilla, being dragged to his death by an APC. Another picture showed a man being thrown to his death from a flying heli-

copter and bore a caption explaining that he had refused to answer interroga-
tors' questions. The photo on the page following the Son My scene depicted
four U.S. soldiers and the bodies of two guerillas. The caption suggested a
common and casual barbarity among the American troops: "After decapi-
tating some guerillas, a GI enjoyed being photographed with their heads in
his hands."

All major U.S. units and their areas of operation were depicted on a large
map. Humanitarian activities by U.S. forces were not shown at all. Simply
stated, no U.S. unit was portrayed in a favorable light.

As we rode away from the museum, all of us felt dejected. It was very
sobering to see American soldiers portrayed as a depraved people who
victimized the Vietnamese. Based upon the official distortions I had just
seen, I seriously doubted if future generations of Vietnamese would ever
learn the truth about the conflict.

We left Ho Chi Minh City to visit Cu Chi. That seventy-five-kilometer
drive was not for the faint at heart, primarily because there appeared to be no
traffic rules. Whoever had the biggest vehicle had the right of way. Motorbike
riders exhibited utterly no regard for cars. I had never seen such apparent
mass confusion. Yet even so, everything seemed to work out. Although we
saw literally hundreds of potential crashes during the hour-long drive, we
spotted signs of only two actual accidents.

As we neared our destination we passed a war memorial bearing the
names of more than forty-five thousand Vietnamese. Innocently, I asked
our guide whether it included the names of both ARVN and VC dead.
Indignant, he said it memorialized only the names of "revolutionary forces,"
not those of the traitors.

The tunnels of Cu Chi are now quite famous and a prime tourist
attraction in Vietnam. The immense complex consisted of three levels and
included headquarters, supply facilities, eating and sleeping areas, command,
control and communications. Hundreds of VC guerillas could be housed
there, hidden from sight and, particularly at the bottom level, well protected
from American bombs. We entered one tunnel in which Bill Tidball took a
very unflattering picture of my backside filling up the tunnel entrance. We
managed to get through, but it was not fun and I would not want to spend
my life crawling around that tunnel.

I had spent some time at Cu Chi in the summer of 1968, and I must
have driven, walked, or flown over some of the complex back then. But I
had no idea at the time that the tunnels were there. It was unsettling to see

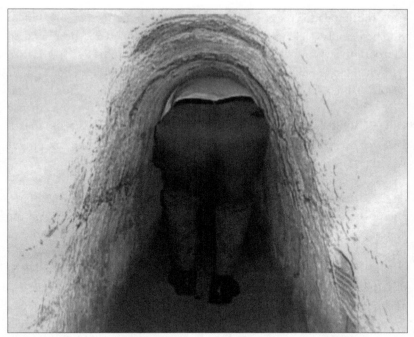

Me in the Cu Chi tunnel. (Author collection)

them now, all these years later. I, for one, was ready to get back to Ho Chi Minh City.

I am glad that I returned to Vietnam. The people were very friendly, the food was superb, and the prices were reasonable. And both the War Remnants Museum and the Cu Chi tunnels brought back memories I thought were long gone. Now I accept that they will always be a part of me.

I would encourage any GIs who venture back to Vietnam to leave the chip on the shoulder at home. The war is over. For all practical purposes, we lost. We know the good things we did, but they are not visible in Vietnam.

When I got back home to Virginia I resumed working on a range of projects. I have long been a member of the AUSA Council of Trustees. Over the years, I have served the private, nonprofit educational organization in a number of other capacities as well.

I have also long been associated with the George C. Marshall Foundation, which is devoted to teaching and promoting the ethical legacy left by its namesake, the great general once described as "one careful demon of integrity." The foundation presents an annual award to the person in public service who best emulates General Marshall. In October 2007, I am most honored to report, that award was presented to Julius W. Becton Jr.

When James Billington, Librarian of Congress, called me at home in the fall of 2001 to ask if I would be interested in being a member of the Five-Star Council, an advisory board to the Veterans History Project, I immediately said yes. While I wanted to oblige my old high school classmate and friend, I also felt excited about the chance to influence the direction the new project would take.

Congress unanimously voted the Veterans History Project into existence on 27 October 2000. Its mission is "to collect the memories, accounts, and documents of war veterans from World War I, World War II, and the Korean, Vietnam, and Persian Gulf Wars, and to preserve these stories of experience and service for future generations."[6]

The Five-Star Council's twenty-eight members represented a wide range of backgrounds and perspectives. Council members included former TV anchormen Walter Cronkite and Tom Brokaw, historian Stephen Ambrose, former Air Force Secretary Sheila Widnall, and then-current and former members of Congress such as Bob Dole, Daniel Inouye, and Max Cleland, each one a highly decorated veteran.

Billington convened the first meeting of the council on 8 November 2001. One of the first decisions we made related to the kinds of materials the Library would collect, such as books, maps, uniforms, and audiotapes. We expressed our preference for oral histories because we thought the uniqueness of each veteran's story would be better reflected if contributors were allowed to give their accounts in their own words. To collect these interviews, the project enlisted a wide variety of individuals and organizations, including Veterans Affairs volunteers, veterans service organizations, retirement communities, oral history societies, individual citizens dedicated to the project, and high school, college, and university students.

As of April 2007 the project had collected more than forty-five thousand interviews with veterans and individuals who directly supported the troops in time of war. More than 60 percent of the interviews are with World War II veterans, but the collection includes material from World War I and all the way through the current conflicts in Afghanistan and Iraq. The project also has amassed an extensive collection of photographs, journals, letters, and other documents. More than thirty-five hundred interviews have been digitized so that they are accessible to anyone through the Library of Congress

Web site.[7] To publicize the project, many Five-Star Council members have spoken publicly. I have done so myself when given the opportunity, including one appearance on the *Tavis Smiley Show*, during which I offered an abbreviated oral history of my own.[8] This account is included as Appendix 7.

In 2001 President George W. Bush appointed me to the American Battle Monuments Commission (ABMC). It is an understatement to say I was deeply honored. I could think of no better way I could pay homage to our fallen soldiers. The importance a soldier attributes to the decent burial of his fallen comrades is integral to the business of soldiering.

The commission's mission is to

- Design, construct, operate, and maintain permanent American military burial grounds in foreign countries.
- Establish and maintain memorials outside the United States where American armed forces have served since 6 April 1917, the date of U.S. entry into World War I, and within the U.S. when directed by law.
- Control the design and construction on foreign soil of U.S. military monuments and markers by other U.S. citizens and organizations, both public and private.
- Encourage U.S. government agencies and private individuals and organizations to adequately maintain monuments and markers erected by them on foreign soils.[9]

As a commissioner, I made two trips to the overseas cemeteries. I visited the smaller cemeteries because I wanted to demonstrate to the superintendents who managed them that the ABMC places great importance on their work. In March 2004 I visited Brookwood and Cambridge in England, Flander's Field in Belgium, and Oise-Aisne and Aisne-Marne in France. That November I visited Florence and Sicily-Rome in Italy and the North Africa American Cemetery in Tunisia.

But not all of my work as an ABMC commissioner was on foreign soil. During the Clinton administration, Congress had chartered the commission to build the National World War II Memorial on the National Mall. Once complete, it would be turned over to the National Park Service.

The dedication took place on Memorial Day, 29 May 2004, and I was fortunate enough to be there when it was officially opened to the public, as well

World War II Memorial under construction. (© Richard Latoff, 2007; reprinted with permission)

as to have had the privilege of being intimately involved in the construction of the memorial. I felt full looking out at the sea of people assembled for the dedication—young, old, and everything in between. I was particularly enthralled with the oldest veterans, many of them now infirm, who had taken great pains to be there. Why? Why would a wheelchair-bound eighty-two-year-old who had fought during World War II fly from San Francisco to Washington, D.C., to attend the dedication? The one-word answer is "pride." The veteran could finally see that his or her contribution to the war effort was being recognized by the entire nation. The National Mall was already home to a Korean War Memorial and a Vietnam Memorial, but until that moment, there had been no memorial for the granddaddy of them all.

That sense of pride was not felt only by veterans. The soldiers could not have fought as well as they did if the people back home had not been cranking out war munitions in factories, recycling, conserving rationed commodities, and doing everything else that needed to be done to win the war. All who made sacrifices for the war effort were proud of their contributions.

During World War II this country really lived up to its name as the United States of America. Everything that went into the war effort reminds me what a great country we have and makes me proud to be an American.

On the eve of the National World War II Memorial dedication, the ABMC members and members of the memorial advisory board had been invited to the White House for a reception. The two groups had dined the preceding night, enjoying our success, and several of us had commented on what the memorial meant to us personally. I had said that I could not help but marvel at how a janitor's son who joined a segregated Army could have turned out to be among the select group of people who had a direct hand in making the occasion possible.

At the White House reception, First Lady Laura Bush made her rounds of the guests, offering her congratulations. When she got to me, she repeated, almost verbatim, my remarks of the night before about my humble origins.

I was caught completely off guard. And I once again felt a tremendous sense of pride and accomplishment.

Epilogue

Louise and I have been truly blessed. We have five wonderful children and have been blessed with grandchildren and great-grandchildren. We have also been fortunate to meet some of the finest specimens of humankind we could ever hope to know.

We have tried to live decent, purposeful, and meaningful lives. Because I am human, I did not succeed at all times, but I always did try to do my best.

As I close, I share with you the thoughts of a soldier I met at VII Corps nearly three decades ago. Mario Mercado was the medical platoon sergeant of the 1st Battalion, 51st Infantry. Then a high school dropout, Mercado later went on to earn three master's degrees and a doctorate in education. As he wrote to me later:

> Sir, Douglas McArthur once said, "A true leader has the confidence to stand alone, the courage to make tough decisions, and the compassion to listen to the needs of others. He does not set out to be a leader, but becomes one by the equality of his actions and the integrity of his intent."
>
> As a young soldier, I realized that in motivating soldiers, you engaged their minds and their hearts. It didn't take me long to realize you were teaching other soldiers that it is good leadership to have a soldier feel part of the entire effort. . . . You motivated people by example–and by excitement, by having provocative ideas to make others feel involved. Thank you for the excitement, motivation, and for including me in the effort!
>
> Fixed Bayonets, Sir!

I was touched by his kind words, and I felt proud that I had a positive influence on his life. This is the kind of mark I wanted to leave. I sincerely hope there are others out there who were motivated by something I did or said to pursue their dreams and to try to be the best that they could be. When all is said and done, we live on this earth with billions of other people. Our lives are connected and interconnected, but in the final analysis, our lives are not all about us. Our lives are about Him and doing the work that He had for us to do.

Thank you, God, for your grace.

★ ★ ★

Executive Order 9981, 26 July 1948

Establishing the President's Committee on Equality of
Treatment and Opportunity in the Armed Services

WHEREAS it is essential that there be maintained in the armed services of
the United States the highest standards of democracy, with equality of treatment and opportunity for all those who served in our country's defense:

NOW, THEREFORE, by virtue of the authority invested in me as President
of the United States, and as Commander in Chief of the armed services, it
is hereby ordered as follows:

1. It is hereby declared to be the policy of the President that there
   shall be equality of treatment and opportunity for all persons in the
   armed services without regard to race, color, religion or national
   origin. This policy shall be put into effect as rapidly as possible,
   having due regard to the time required to effectuate any necessary
   changes without impairing efficiency or morale.
2. There shall be created in the National Military Establishment an
   advisory committee to be known as the President's Committee on
   Equality of Treatment and Opportunity in the Armed Services,
   which shall be composed of seven members to be designated by
   the President.
3. The Committee is authorized on behalf of the President to examine
   into the rules, procedures and practices of the armed services in
   order to determine in what respect such rules, procedures and practices may be altered or improved with a view to carrying out the
   policy of this order. The Committee shall confer and advise with
   the Secretary of Defense, the Secretary of the Army, the Secretary
   of the Navy, and Secretary of the Air Force, and shall make such

recommendations to the President and to said Secretaries as in the judgment of the Committee will effectuate the policy hereof.

4. All executive departments and agencies of the Federal Government are authorized and directed to cooperate with the Committee in its work, and to furnish the Committee such information or the services of such persons as the Committee may require in the performance of its duties.

5. When requested by the Committee to do so, persons in the armed services or in any of the executive departments and agencies of the Federal Government shall testify before the Committee and shall make available for use of the Committee such documents and other information as the Committee may require.

6. The Committee shall continue to exist until such time as the President shall terminate its existence by Executive Order.

Harry S. Truman
The White House
July 26, 1948

★ ★ ★

Selection Rates for Black Officers
to Brigadier General (ACC)

Year	Number Considered	Number Selected	Number of Black Officers Selected	Percentage Black
1970	4854	81	0	0%
1971	4577	80	3	3.75%
1972	4166	62	5	8.06%
1973	4012	62	3	4.83%
1974	3860	50	2	4%
1975	3498	56	2	3.57%
1976	3276	53	1	1.69%
1977	3400	50	2	4%
1978	3559	36	4	11.11%
1979	3282	59	5	8.47%
1980	3220	68	4	5.88%
1981	3110	63	4	6.35%
1982	2699	53	2	3.77%
1983	2650	60	4	6.66%
1984	2653	64	6	9.38%
1985	2762	63	2	3.17%
1986	2651	57	3	5.26%
1987	2618	56	3	5.36%
1988	2489	49	6	12.24%
1989	2210	46	3	6.52%
1990	2001	40	4	10%
1991	2203	37	3	8.10%
1992	1978	38	2	5.20%

Year	Number Considered	Number Selected	Number of Black Officers Selected	Percentage Black
1993	1745	38	2	5.20%
1994	1653	45	4	8.80%
1995	1749	45	8	17.80%
1996	1838	44	3	6.80%
1997	1815	46	3	6.50%
1998	1774	38	3	7.90%
1999	1725	40	4	10%
2000	1701	40	3	7.50%
2001	1615	40	4	10%
2002	1644	40	4	10%
2003	1661	40	4	10%
2004	1698	42	3	7.14%
2005	1712	32	2	6.25%
2006	1811	36	3	8.33%
2007	1878	38	4	10.53%

U.S. Army Center of Military History, Historical Resources Branch, Historical Resources Collection, Part II (HRC2—1984–2005), http://www.army.mil/CMH/reference/Finding Aids/HRC2.htm.

APPENDIX 3

★ ★ ★

Cold Reason

Opening Remarks by Commanding General,
VII Corps Tactical Seminar Cold Reason, 1–3 April 1981

I remind you that Cold Reason is not a test of the GDP [General Defense Plan] or of you, but rather a study in the decision making process facilitated by the use of known scenario. Let me conclude with my views on fighting the active defense, which is basically why I've requested that you brigade, regiment, and group commanders join with us.

It is important that you understand the need for awareness and decisions at the commander level. By awareness, I expect each commander to be familiar with his neighbor's terrain because he may well be called to fight his neighbor's ground. As I've said many times, ours is a battle of maneuver, and each commander must understand the total battle. He must "see" the big picture. We may not be able to talk to one another.

After awareness comes decisions, so let me talk about decision and the active defense. It's very difficult to make the transition from active defense theory to active defense practice on the battlefield. Whether this difficulty is because the theory is poorly stated or because the tasks related to the transition are difficult is judgmental. However, the execution of the active defense is very difficult. It is difficult because it demands a premium on the most difficult aspects of warfare:

- Knowledge (to "see" the battle)—awareness
- Quick, correct decisions based on limited information
- Fast, coordinated maneuver
- Exacting coordination of the combat multipliers.

In my opinion, few commanders and operators understand the complexity of decision making of the type required on the modern "active defense" battlefield. Obviously, my main stress here is on decisions. While we must encourage our subordinates to make decisions in their sectors, both they and we must recognize decision making that supports your plan and decision making that is unacceptable. I can't tell you what is unacceptable, but my experience tells me that too much independent decision making at company and battalion level will lead us into trouble.

In my opinion, commanders in the rank of colonel are the last people to conduct the active defense. Your battalions either attack, defend, or advance to contact independently about the battlefield. You, as colonels, are the ones who orchestrate this maneuver against the enemy. Frankly, if you are not in control of it, the fabric will unravel because I believe that no one lower than you will have the capability to see the battle from the vantage point necessary to keep it together. Someone must decide who gives up ground and who doesn't. Battalion commanders are going to be too busy fighting to make these decisions. They will earn their pay by killing and destroying enemy formations as efficiently as possible. We should look to them for efficient and violent execution of their assigned missions.

Rather than great decision making, we look to you, the colonels, as the key decision makers in combat. To be effective you must have the knowledge to "see" the battle, to be "aware," and make quick, proper decisions based on very limited information, sometimes by instinct.

Let me conclude with a few words directed specifically to colonels—commanders, brigade, group, regiment. All of our problems and challenges are resting and will continue to rest on your shoulders. You are the ones who must make it happen at brigade, group, or regiment. You have arrived and should be comfortable. You are the one who is the blockade between higher headquarters and the battalions. You are the one who must create the command climate in which our units are free to train. You must remember, tactically, lieutenant colonels fight. They are decisively engaged. You have already done that. Colonels orchestrate. Key decisions on the battlefield are made by the colonels. By your awareness of company battles within battalions, the colonel moves battalions in concert with the division/corps game plan.

The playbook: The colonel is aware of the impact of his decisions on the corps. The colonel is aware that a bad decision may cause the brigade rear boundary to be penetrated, which forces the division to commit its reserve. The colonel is aware that the corps must then swing its attention to that sector. Begin to move the corps reserve to back up the division that has committed its reserve, and then possibly ask for nuclear release.

The colonel must be aware that the movement of the corps reserve leaves the corps without freedom of action and necessitates the call for CENTAG [Central Army Group] or French reserves.

This brings us back to Cold Reason, a commander's exercise to demonstrate tactical decision relationships and criticality of timely decision making in order to fight he coherent corps battle. I say again, Cold Reason is not a test of the GDP, or of you as a commander.

★   ★   ★

Testimony before Homeland Security Subcommittee Staff, 5 May 2003: Gen. Julius W. Becton Jr., USA (Ret.)

I am here only because Doug Bobbitt invoked the name of my good friend P. X. Kelley, former commandant, USMC [U.S. Marine Corps].

While the term "homeland security" tends to conjure up all things to all people, I would argue that civil defense, as we practiced it during World War II would offer a close approximation as to what is needed. As you know, civil defense was (and maybe still is) a FEMA [Federal Emergency Management Agency] responsibility. I say that because national preparedness also used to be a FEMA responsibility.

In November 1985 I became the third director of FEMA, following Louis Giufridda, who had resigned under fire. As such I spent more time with Vice President Bush, National Security Advisor Colin Powell, and Attorney General Ed Meese than anyone else in the administration. Other than those three, I received very little guidance from the White House. I was invited to one Cabinet meeting and was never called to the White House by the chief of staff.

While I discovered that the term "civil defense" tended to turn people off, the "all hazards" aspect is really what's needed.

FEMA was formed from five different agencies:

- Defense Civil Preparedness Agency, Department of Defense
- Federal Disaster Assistance Administration, Department of Housing and Urban Development
- Federal Preparedness Agency, General Services Administration
- U.S. Fire Administration, Department of Commerce

• Federal Insurance Administration, Department of Housing and Urban Development.

This, in itself, presented real problems because each element brought its own PR, congressional liaison, general counsel, etc. As such, FEMA remained responsive to about twenty-five congressional subcommittees.

The external environment affecting us [FEMA] was dominated by four factors or trends:

• The federal budget deficit
• An eroding industrial base
• Growing foreign dependencies
• President Reagan's preference for emphasizing the states and localities and the private sector as service providers.

Some of my challenges:

• Giufridda departure two months before my arrival
• FEMA's budget was not approved, and I had to cut it by $13,800,000 in my first ten days
• Two grand juries were looking into alleged questionable practices in the agency
• More than thirty inspector general investigations were under way.
• There were no travel, recruitment, or training funds available for the prior ten months.

And, of course, my biggest problems were the low morale within the agency and its loss of credibility with everyone.

We published a new mission statement within six months: "Under the direction of the President, the mission of the Federal Emergency Management Agency is to plan for and coordinate the protection of the civilian population and resources of the Nation, to include planning for the continuity of constitutional government in time of emergency."

To accomplish its mission, FEMA acts as the focal point for all levels of government in developing a national emergency management capability that can deal effectively with any major emergency. . . .

During the mid-80s FEMA was concerned with the entire array of potential areas for which crisis management constructs would be required (i.e., attack preparedness, terrorism, disaster response, response to civil disobedience, overall federal coordination, etc.).

In order to accomplish those challenges, we had 135 different programs and activities. As we regained our credibility, we were given the overall responsibility for coordinating the development of a new National Security Emergency Plan. I considered my top priority to be protection of the civilian population and continuity of government.

Budgetary and political concerns slowly eroded many of those programs, and what resulted was an agency almost entirely devoted to disaster response. Even at the peak of our funding in 1987 dollars, in terms of civil defense per capita expenditure, we were in ninth place with an expenditures of $0.57, just ahead of France's $0.21 and well behind other countries: Switzerland—$42.96, Sweden—$18.02, USSR [Soviet Union]—$14.48, Denmark—$11.79, Finland—$10.27, Norway—$8.69, Germany (FRG)—$7.25, and Great Britain—$2.35.

The agency had always had approximately 2,600 full time employees. In the early 1980s only about 200 of these employees were disaster specialists.

Recently, I believe the agency's focus (and its 2,600 employees) has been almost totally disaster response. This is not a criticism of the disaster programs but an attempt to demonstrate how the programs have evolved.

As the new Homeland Security functions are developed, I would encourage that studies be undertaken of some other countries' emergency management programs that have been successful or have not been successful. England, Italy, and Sweden come immediately to mind. Also of interest would be the new programs in the Russian breakaway countries.

I believe that while it is of utmost importance to heavily involve state and local governments in civil preparedness, the federal role is essential to having the kind of programs the American citizens deserve. It should almost be a federalized program to succeed over the long term. Consistency is important to success, and the variety of political realities at the state and local levels have resulted in a whole array of programs in the past.

That being the case, however, you can be assured that several states will challenge the Homeland Security Department. Example: Both Oregon and Washington state were opposed to mandatory exercises involving terrorists with nuclear weapons. When we played hardball with the funding, they came around.

APPENDIX 5

The Washington Post

1150 15th STREET, N.W.
WASHINGTON, D.C. 20071
(202) 334-6000

DONALD E. GRAHAM
Publisher
(202) 334-7400

PRIVATE

Dear Gen. Becton,

Now that so many members of the Post staff have written editorials, columns, etc, about your tenure, I suppose even a publisher may be permitted a private word about my own reaction.

I think you're a remarkable man, and the city will be reaping the benefit of your tenure in the school system for years to come. I think your appointment represented a remarkable opportunity for DC to straighten out some long-standing problems. Many of those problems are now much improved.

Had a few more people been willing to give you a chance, I think we'd be even more clearly on the right track. But we're there, and while I don't think you'll ever get the credit you deserve, you have definitely got us started in the right direction. It will indeed take years to get where we're going, but we have a chance now.

Best,
Don.

APPENDIX 6

★ ★ ★

American Battle Monuments Commission Medal for Distinguished Service Award

The American Battle Monuments Commission [AMBC] Medal for Distinguished Service Award is awarded to Lt. Gen. Julius W. Becton Jr., U.S. Army (Ret), for his distinguished service from September 2001 to April 2005 as a commissioner of the American Battle Monuments Commission. Appointed by President George W. Bush, General Becton gave of his time freely in the interest of the commission's business. While traveling overseas to inspect the American memorial cemeteries and monuments, he provided sage advice to our employees and created good will among the people of the countries he visited. Through his personal contacts, he was highly instrumental in obtaining the support of government, business, and public sector constituencies for ABMC issues and priorities. General Becton helped establish policy and direction for this commission. His efforts on the commission helped complete and dedicate the long-awaited National World War II Memorial. As a member of the chairman's advisory goup, his wise counsel and strong leadership on policy issues and decision making contributed greatly to the American Battle Monument Commission's mission and reputation as one of the most efficient and productive executive agencies in the U.S. government. General Becton is a distinguished American who has worked diligently to ensure that our honored war dead, who paid for our freedom with their lives, will never be forgotten. General Becton's actions and commitment brought great credit upon himself, the American Battle Monuments Commission and the United States of America.

★ ★ ★

Veterans History Project Commentary from the *Tavis Smiley Show*

I have three young great-grandchildren. They know that their grandpop carried weapons and fought in three wars. But they don't know that when I first enlisted, black soldiers and white soldiers did not share the same barracks, or that after Vietnam, I was asked not to wear my uniform when speaking at a university because of antimilitary sentiments. They don't know much about my military career because, right now, they're too young to understand.

However, there may come a time when (for a school project or just because they're curious) they will want to learn about what I did as a soldier. But when this time comes, I may not be here to share my experience.

In 2000 Congress drafted and unanimously passed legislation to create the Veterans History Project so that my great-grandchildren and future generations will have access to my story, in addition to the stories of many thousands of America's veterans.

The Veterans History Project, led by the Library of Congress and supported by the AARP, is a call to action for all veterans of all wars and those who supported us, to submit audio and video recorded oral histories, along with letters, diaries, and other photographs. Once collected, these valuable materials will be made available to the public.

A few of us have shared our stories, but many of us have not. This is worrisome because we're running out of time to collect the stories of our older veterans. Of the nation's 19 million veterans, about 1,500 are dying each day, so there is an urgent need to gather their stories while they are still among us.

This is my story.

I liked the military. Why? As an African American soldier I was given an equal opportunity to succeed, but it did not happen overnight. It took a span over three wars for it to occur.

During my training in 1944, when I was in all all-black unit at MacDill Army Airfield, some of the service areas were run by Italian prisoners of war [POWs]. Black soldiers were given second-class treatment to them. I could walk into the shoe repair, and even though I had been the first in line, I would be the last person served because the fellow behind the counter, although he was a POW, he was white. I later served in the Pacific Theater of Operations in the all-black 93rd Infantry Division.

In 1948 President Truman issued Executive Order 9981, which basically declared an end to segregation in the military. Immediately after the order was issued, commanders were directed to read the order to their personnel. I was on reserve duty at Aberdeen Proving Ground when the post commander read the order, and then said, "As long as I am the commander here, there will be no change."

In effect, he was saying that officers' club number one and officers' club number two, noncommissioned officers' [NCO] club number one, and NCO club number two, swimming pool number one, and swimming pool number two would remain unchanged. Of course, white soldiers went to number one, and blacks to number two.

By the time we got to Korea in 1950, little had been done to end segregation. I was in an all-black battalion in a white division. However, when our regiment (two white and one black battalions) lost men and needed replacements, it didn't matter if the new soldiers were black or white. Our colonel said to put them where they were needed, and this led to the integration of the 9th Infantry Regiment. Black men, white men, yellow men . . . whatever their color/complexion had nothing to do with how well they could fight.

In Germany in 1955, as one of the first black company commanders in the 2nd Armored Division, my soldiers were not concerned about the color of my skin. Occasionally they found themselves defending theirs and my honor in off-duty locations where soldiers gathered.

In Vietnam I was the commander of an airborne cavalry squadron. I later commanded the 1st Cavalry Division in Fort Hood. And during the Cold War in Germany I had about eighty-eight thousand soldiers in my VII U.S. Corps command.

My story is different from the soldier who fought next to me in Korea. My story is different from the soldier I commanded in Vietnam. My story is different because no two stories are the same. But your wartime experience is just as important as mine.

The Veterans History Project wants to hear from you. Learn more about the Veterans History Project so you, too, can share your experience with future generations.

Chronology

29 June 1926	Julius Wesley Becton Jr. born in Bryn Mawr, Pennsylvania
1 March 1927	Louise Adelaide Thornton born in Chester Heights, Pennsylvania
September 1941–June 1944	Student at Lower Merion High School Ardmore, Pennsylvania
28 December 1943	Enlisted in the U.S. Army Air Corps Enlisted Reserves
21 July 1944	Entered active duty, private, Keesler Air Force Base (AFB), Miss., and MacDill AFB, Fla.
December 1944–August 1945	Officer Candidate School, Ft. Benning, Georgia
16 August 1945	Commissioned second lieutenant of infantry, Army of the United States (AUS)
October–December 1945	Platoon leader/executive officer, 369th Infantry Regiment, 93rd Infantry Division, Morotaii
January–November 1946	Platoon leader, 542nd Heavy Con-struction Company, Philippines, detailed to the Signal Corps (SC)
January 1947–October 1948	Promoted to first lieutenant AUS SC Student at Muhlenberg College, Allentown, Pennsylvania
29 January 1948	Married Louise A. Thornton
1 November 1948	Recalled to active duty as a second lieutenant, AUS SC, Fort Monmouth, New Jersey

5 December 1948	Shirley Inez Becton born in Philadelphia, Pennsylvania
December 1948–June 1949	Platoon leader, 29th Signal Construction Battalion, Fort Bliss, Texas, and Fort Bragg, North Carolina
11 May 1949	Promoted to first lieutenant AUS
June 1949–September 1949	Student, Infantry Officers Associate Basic Course, Fort Benning, Georgia
October 1949–July 1950	Platoon leader, K and L Companies, 9th Infantry Regiment, 2nd Infantry Division, Fort Lewis, Washington
July 1950–September 1950	Platoon leader, L Company, 9th Infantry Regiment, Korea
12 September 1950	Karen Louise Becton born in Philadelphia, Pennsylvania
19 September–15 November 1950	Medical channels: Korea and Japan
16–25 November 1950	Platoon leader and company executive officer, I Company, 9th Infantry Regiment, Korea
26 November 1950–5 March 1951	Medical channels: Korea and Japan
6 March 1951–4 May 1951	Commander, L Company, 9th Infantry Regiment, Korea
5 May 1951–August 1953	Platoon leader and instructor, Fort Dix, New Jersey, Camp Edwards, Massachusetts, and Indiantown Gap Military Reservation, Pennsylvania
1 November 1951	Integrated into Regular Army (U.S. Army [USA]), transferred from SC to infantry
12 June 1953	Promoted to captain AUS
September 1953–March 1954	Student, Infantry Officer Advanced Course, Fort Benning, Georgia

14 December 1953	Joyce Wesley Becton is born in Fort Benning, Georgia
March 1954–April 1957	Communications officer, company commander, and assistant operations officer (S-3), 2nd Armored Division, West Germany
29 October 1954	Promoted to captain, USA
5 February 1957	Transferred from infantry to armor
April 1957–January 1960	Assistant professor military of science and tactics, ROTC, Prairie View A&M College (PVAMC), Prairie View, Texas
February–May 1960	Student, PVAMC, BS in mathematics
28 February 1960	Renee Marie Becton is born in Hempstead, Texas
June 1960–June 1961	Student, USA Command and General Staff College, Fort Leavenworth, Kansas
7 February 1961	Promoted to major, AUS
August 1961–December 1963	Assistant G-3, 4th Logistical Command, Verdun, France
12 August 1962	Promoted to major, USA
February–June 1964	Student, Armed Forces Staff College, Norfolk, Virginia
June–July 1964	Airborne Course, Fort Benning, Georgia Qualified as a parachutist
July 1964–August 1965	Staff officer, Office of the Deputy Chief of Staff, Personnel (ODCSPER), Pentagon, Washington, D.C.
18 November 1964	Promoted to lieutenant colonel, AUS

August 1965–September 1966

Student, Institute for Defense Analyses and University of Maryland, MA in economics

20 October 1965

Julius Wesley Becton III is born in Washington, D.C.

October 1966–August 1967

Staff officer, Office of the Assistant Vice Chief of Staff of the Army (OAVCSA), Pentagon, Washington, D.C.

August–November 1967

Commander, 2nd Squadron, 17th Cavalry, 101st Airborne Division, Fort Campbell, Kentucky

December 1967–November 1968

Commanding officer, 2nd Squadron, 17th Cavalry, and deputy commanding officer, 3rd Brigade, 101st Airborne Division, Vietnam

December 1968–August 1969

Member, Deputy Chief of Staff, Personnel Special Review Board

31 July 1969

Promoted to colonel, AUS

12 August 1969

Promoted to lieutenant colonel, USA

August 1969–June 1970

Student, National War College

June 1970–January 1972

Commander, 2nd (St. Lo) Brigade, 2nd Armored Division, Fort Hood, Texas

January–August 1972

Chief, Armor Branch, Officer Personnel Directorate, Office of Personnel Operations, Department of the Army, Washington, D.C.

1 August 1972

Promoted to brigadier general, AUS

September 1972–January 1975

Deputy commander, USA Training Center, Fort Dix, New Jersey

12 August 1973

Promoted to colonel, USA

1 August 1974   Promoted to major general, AUS

January 1975–November 1976   Commanding general, 1st Cavalry
                                         Division, Fort Hood, Texas

3 June 1976   Promoted to brigadier general, USA

November 1976–October 1978   Commanding general, US Army
                                         Operational Test and Evaluation
                                         Agency, Office of the Chief of Staff
                                         of the Army, Falls Church, Virginia

1 May 1978   Promoted to major general, USA

1 November 1978   Promoted to lieutenant general, USA

October 1978–June 1981   Commanding general, VII US Corps,
                                         US Army Europe, Germany

June 1981–August 1983   Deputy commanding general,
                                         Training and Doctrine Command,
                                         and Army inspector of training, Fort
                                         Monroe, Virginia

23 August 1983   Retirement ceremony

January 1984–October 1985   Director, Office of Foreign Disaster
                                         Assistance, Agency for International
                                         Development, Washington, D.C.

October 1985–June 1989   Director, Federal Emergency
                                         Management Agency, Washington,
                                         D.C.

July–November 1989   Chief operating officer, American
                                         Coastal Industries, Arlington,
                                         Virginia

December 1989–November 1994   President, Prairie View A&M
                                         University, Prairie View, Texas

November 1996–May 1998   Superintendent/CEO, District
                                         of Columbia Public Schools,
                                         Washington, D.C.

Acronyms and Abbreviations

2/67 Armor	2nd Battalion, 67th Armor
ABMC	American Battle Monument Commission
ACI	American Coastal Industries
ADC	assistant division commander
AFSC	Armed Forces Staff College
AG	attorney general
AIT	advanced individual training
AMEDS	Army Medical Service
AO	area of operations
APC	armored personnel carrier
APFT	Army Physical Fitness Test
APFRI	Army Physical Fitness Research Institute
ARVN	Army of the Republic of Vietnam
AUSA	Association of the United States Army
BCT	brigade command team
CAO	chief academic officer
CAP	Civilian Air Patrol
CEO	chief executive officer
CFO	chief financial officer
CGSC	Command and General Staff College
CID	Criminal Investigation Division
CINC	commander in chief
CMMI	Command Maintenance and Management Inspection
COMMO	communications officer
COMZ	communications zone
COMUS	U.S. commander
CMACV	Commander, U.S. Military Assistance Command, Vietnam
CONARC	Continental Army Command
COO	chief operating officer
CPX	command post exercises
DCPS	District of Columbia Public Schools
DCSOPS	deputy chief of staff for operations and plans
DISCOM	division support command
DOD	Department of Defense
ETEBT	Emergency Transitional Education Board of Trustees

EMI	Emergency Management Institute
FBI	Federal Bureau of Investigation
FEMA	Federal Emergency Management Agency
FORSCOM	Forces Command
FPAO	Office of Force Planning and Analysis
FTX	field training exercises
G-1	personnel staff officer
G-3	operations officer
G-5	staff officer in charge of community affairs
GAO	U.S. General Accounting Office
GOMO	General Officer Management Office
GWU	George Washington University
HBCU	historically black colleges and universities
ICAF	Industrial College of the Armed Forces
IDA	Institute for Defense Analyses
IG	inspector general
IOAC	Infantry Officer Advanced Course
IOBC	Infantry Officer Basic Course
JSTARS	E-8C Joint Surveillance Target Attack Radar System
J-3	joint staff for operations
JSU	Jacksonville State University
LSA	University of Michigan College of Literature, Science, and the Arts
MARS	Military Affiliate Radio System
MP	military police
MSRC	Marine Spill Response Corporation
NATO	North Atlantic Treaty Organization
NCO	noncommissioned officer
NCOIC	noncommissioned Officer In Charge
NEO	noncombatant evacuation orders
NORAD	North American Air (now Aerospace) Defense Command
NVA	North Vietnamese Army
NWC	National War College
OAVCSA	Office of the Assistant Vice Chief of Staff of the Army
OCS	officer candidate school
OCSA	Office of the Chief of Staff, Army
ODCSPER	Office of the Deputy Chief of Staff, Personnel
OER	officer efficiency report
OFDA	Office of Foreign Disaster Assistance
OFPA	Office of Force Planning and Analysis
OML	Order of Merit List

OPD	Office of Personnel Directorate
OPTEVFOR	Operational Test and Evaluation Forces
ORSA	operations research/systems analysis
OSD	Office of the Secretary of Defense
OT	operational tester
OTEA	Operational Test and Evaluation Agency
PM	program manager
POW	prisoner of war
PVAMU	Prairie View A&M University
R&R	rest and recuperation
REFORGER	Return of U.S. Forces to Germany
ROTC	Reserve Officer Training Corps
S-3	operations officer
SCEPC	Senior Civil Emergency Preparedness Committee
SCLC	Southern Christian Leadership Conference
SGS	secretary of the General Staff
SRB	Special Review Board
SSC	Senior Service Colleges
STRAF	United States Strategic Army Forces
SWAC	Southwestern Athletic Conference
TAMUS	Texas A&M University System
TDY	temporary duty
TECOM	Test and Evaluation Command
TFAF	Task Force on the African Famine
TOC	tactical operations center
TRADOC	U.S. Army Training and Doctrine Command
TRICAP	triple capability
UN	United Nations
USAREUR	U.S. Army Europe
USAID	U.S. Agency for International Development
USAPFS	U.S. Army Physical Fitness School
VC	Viet Cong
VCSA	vice chief of staff of the Army
VFMA	Valley Forge Military Academy
WAC	Women's Army Corps
WO	warrant officer
WSAG	Weapons Systems Analysis Group

Notes

Acknowledgments

1. Harold G. Moore and Joseph L. Galloway, *We Were Soldiers Once . . . and Young: Ia Drang—The Battle That Changed the War in Vietnam* (New York: Presidio Press, 2004).

Chapter 1

1. *The Wall Street Journal Classroom Edition,* http://www.wsjclassroom edition.com/sponsor/honorroll.htm (accessed 21 October 2007).
2. The syndrome is named after William Lynch, a West Indies slave owner who purportedly taught American slave owners techniques for pitting African Americans against each other and thus keeping them in a perpetual slave mentality.

Chapter 2

1. One of my black classmates was John Rhinehardt, then a staff sergeant, who later became ambassador to St. John in the U.S. Virgin Islands and head of the U.S. Information Agency.
2. Fifty-five years later, on 28 September 2003, I was the church's centennial speaker.

Chapter 4

1. Clay Blair Jr., *The Forgotten War: America in Korea, 1950–1953* (Annapolis, Md.: Naval Institute Press, 1987)
2. Ibid., 430.
3. Ibid., 440.
4. S. L. A. Marshall, *The River and the Gauntlet* (New York: Time, 1962).
5. U.S. Army Service Forces, *Leadership and the Negro Soldier,* Army Service Manual M5 (Washington, D.C.: Government Printing Office, 1944).
6. Blair, *Forgotten War,* 150.

Chapter 5

1. For a fuller discussion of the 761st Tank Battalion, see Daniel K. Gibran et al., *The Exclusion of Black Soldiers from the Medal of Honor in World War II: The Study Commissioned by the United States Army to Investigate Racial Bias in the Awarding of the Nation's Highest Military Decoration,* ed. Elliott V. Converse III, with a foreword by Julius W. Becton Jr. (Jefferson, N.C.: McFarland & Company, 1997).

Chapter 7

1. For an excellent account of the Selma demonstrations, see David J. Garrow, *Protest at Selma: Martin Luther King, Jr. and the Voting Rights Act of 1965* (New Haven, Conn.: Yale University Press, 1978), 1–114.

Chapter 8

1. Bernard B. Fall, *Street without Joy: The French Debacle in Indochina*, rev. ed. (Mechanicsburg, Pa.: Stackpole Books, 1994).
2. The My Lai Massacre occurred on 16 March 1968. U.S. soldiers came into My Lai looking for Viet Cong (VC) troops. The villagers did not know or refused to say where the VC were. Convinced that the villagers could be a threat and also furious because fellow soldiers had been killed on previous occasions, some of the Americans killed between three hundred and five hundred unarmed Vietnamese civilians, women and children included. See Vietnam Online, http://www.pbs.org/wgbh/amex/vietnam/trenches/my_lai.html.

Chapter 9

1. There is a letter in my official file titled "Performance of Duty, Lieutenant Colonel Julius W. Becton, Jr. Armor" in which the lead paragraph reads, "The purpose of this letter is to inform you (President, Special Review Board) of the outstanding performance of duty by Lt Col JW Becton, Jr. while detailed from the Special Review Board during the period 1 April to 25 June to act as Chairman for the DCSPER Special Study of the Officer Efficiency Reporting System." It continues for three paragraphs discussing the study group performance.

Chapter 10

1. The fourth member, the senior Women's Army Corps representative, was not a graduate of a senior service college.

Chapter 11

1. Smithsonian National Air and Space Museum, "President Kennedy and the Moon Decision," *Apollo to the Moon*, National Air and Space Museum, http://www.nasm.si.edu/exhibitions/ATTM/md.html (accessed 22 September 2007).
2. Zelmo Beatty went on to play for the Utah Jazz and the New York Knicks. He was inducted into the Prairie View A&M Hall of Fame in 1998 and the SWAC in 1995.

Chapter 12

1. All Army testing was later put under the control of the Army Test and Evaluation Command, which is headquartered in Alexandria, Virginia.

Chapter 13

1. George Parada, "Erwin (Johannes Eugen) Rommel: The Desert Fox/Der Wustenfuchs (November 15, 1891–October 14, 1944)," Achtung Panzer! http://www.achtungpanzer.com/gen1.htm (accessed 11 October 2007).
2. Lee Ewing, "Corps Commander Says Abort or Get Out," *Army Times*, 29 June 1981.

Chapter 14

1. Colin Powell, *My American Journey: An Autobiography*, ed. Joseph E. Persico (New York: Random House, 1995), 269–73.

Chapter 15

1. U.S. Agency for International Development, Office of U.S. Foreign Disaster Assistance, *Office of U.S. Foreign Disaster Assistance: Annual Report FY1983* (Washington, D.C.: Agency for International Development, 1983), v.
2. U.S. Agency for International Development, Office of U.S. Foreign Disaster Assistance, *20 Years of Response: Office of U.S. Foreign Disaster Assistance: Annual Report FY1984* (Washington, D.C.: Agency for International Development, 1984), 72.
3. U.S. Agency for International Development, Office of U.S. Foreign Disaster Assistance, *Office of U.S. Foreign Disaster Assistance: Annual Report FY1985* (Washington, D.C.: Agency for International Development, 1985), ii.
4. Heidi Bommershine, *Heidi Redux* (Westerville, Ohio: Winterwolf Publishing, 2004), 109–10.
5. Chris Morris, "Band Aid," *Hollywood Reporter*, 13 July 2005, 3–4.
6. Ibid., 125.
7. Ibid., 125–7.

Chapter 16

1. Keith F. Mulrooney, *Emergency Management: A National Perspective III*, prepared under contract from the Federal Emergency Management Agency by Graham W. Watt & Associates, Fort Lauderdale, Florida, June 1989, 4.
2. The headquarters for the ten federal regions are as follows: I—Boston, Massachusetts; II—New York City, New York; III—Philadelphia, Pennsylvania; IV—Atlanta, Georgia; V—Chicago, Illinois; VI—Denton, Texas; VII—Kansas City, Kansas; VIII—Denver, Colorado; IX—San Francisco, California; and X—Seattle, Washington.
3. The bill was named after its U.S. Senate sponsors, who were Republican Phil Gramm of Texas, Republican Warren Rudman of New Hampshire, and Democrat Ernest Hollings of South Carolina.
4. Statement of Julius W. Becton Jr., before the Subcommittee on HUD-Independent Agencies, Committee on Appropriations, United States Senate, 5 March 1986. Also see Mulrooney, *Emergency Management*, 25–6.
5. According to the World Nuclear Association, "The April 1986 disaster at the Chernobyl nuclear power plant in the Ukraine was the product of a flawed Soviet reactor design coupled with serious mistakes made by the plant operators in the context of a system where training was minimal." See World Nuclear Association, "Chernobyl Accident," http://www.world-nuclear.org/info/chernobyl/inf07.html (accessed 22 September 2007).
6. Thule Foundation, "Mount Weather (The Shadow Government is Inside There Right Now)," excerpt from William Poundstone, *Bigger Secrets*, http://www.thule.org/weather.html (accessed 22 September 2007).

309 (13 June 1989): H 2474.

7. Tribute to Gen. Julius W. Becton Jr., 101st Cong., 1st sess., *Congressional Record*, 135 (13 June 1989): H 2474.

8. Government Accounting Organization, *Disaster Management: Recent Disasters Demonstrate the Need to Improve the Nation's Response Strategy*, GAO-93-46 (Washington, D.C.: 25 May 1993).

9. "Mayor to Feds: 'Get Off Your Asses,'" cnn.com, 2 September 2005, http://www.cnn.com/2005/US/09/02/nagin.transcript (accessed 21 October 2007).

10. Jimmy Carter, "Remarks by Former U.S. President Jimmy Carter at the Coretta Scott King Funeral," The Carter Center, http://www.cartercenter.org/news/documents/doc2295.html (accessed 17 October 2007.)

Chapter 17

1. Prairie View A&M University, "History of Prairie View A&M University," excerpt from "Prairie View, a Study in Public Conscience," a chapter in Henry C. Dethloff, *A Centennial History of Texas A&M University, 1876–1976*, Vol. II, ed. Frank D. Jackson, http://www.pvamu.edu/pages/605.asp (accessed 22 September 2007).

2. Prairie View A&M University Office of Institutional Effectiveness, Research and Analysis, *Prairie View A&M University 1999–2003 Fact Book* (Prairie View, Tex.: Prairie View A&M University, 2004), 74.

3. The football program was reinstated within a year, but there was a strict rule against awarding any scholarships.

4. "Guests at the State Dinner," *New York Times*, 15 May 1991.

5. *Houston Post*, 9 January 1994.

Chapter 18

1. Tim Spalding, The Battle of Kursk on the Web, http://www.isidore-of-seville.com/kursk (accessed 22 September 2007).

2. Frederick C. Turner, "Prokhorovka: The Great Russian Tank Encounter Battle with the Germans," *Armor Magazine*, May–June 1993.

Chapter 19

1. District of Columbia Financial Responsibility and Management Assistance Authority, *Children in Crisis: A Report on the Failure of D.C.'s Public Schools* (Washington, D.C., 1996).

2. District of Columbia Financial Responsibility and Management Assistance Authority, *Resolution, Order and Recommendation Concerning District of Columbia Public School System* (Washington, D.C., 15 November 1996), 5.

3. Ibid., 3.

4. District of Columbia Financial Responsibility and Management Assistance Authority, *Children in Crisis*, 50.

5. Ibid., 16.

6. Peter Perl and Debbi Wilgoren, "Basic Training," *Washington Post Magazine*, 11 May 1997.

7. Debbi Wilgoren, "D.C. School Trustees Ready to Act, Minutes Show," *Washington Post*, 11 March 1997.

8. District of Columbia Financial Responsibility and Management Assistance Authority, *Children in Crisis*.

9. Wesley Becton, "Give Becton a Chance," letter to the editor, *Washington Post*, 11 September 1997.

10. Debbi Wilgoren, "Battle Over Boilers Leaves D.C. Students Out in Cold," *Washington Post*, 28 October 1997.

11. Julius W. Becton Jr., "Mercy Please, Judge Christian," *Washington Times*, 27 October 1997.

12. Debbi Wilgoren, "One Year Later, Becton Still Struggling," *Washington Post*, 18 November 1997.

13. "D.C. School Reforms: Year One," editorial, *Washington Post*, 20 November 1997.

14. Debbi Wilgoren, "D.C. School Official Is Asked to Quit," *Washington Post*, 6 March 1998.

15. Debbi Wilgoren, "D.C. Schools Chief Hastens Departure," *Washington Post*, 16 April 1998.

16. Julius W. Becton Jr., "Our Children's Futures Are at Stake," *Washington Post*, 24 November 1996.

Chapter 20

1. Alabama Department of Postsecondary Education, *Functional Analysis & Records Disposition Authority* (Montgomery, 24 July 2002), 2–5.

2. "Desegregation Case Finally Pays off for Students in State: Black, Long-Neglected Universities Get Benefits of Courses, Resources," *Birmingham News*, 28 August 2005.

3. Myself, Adm. Dennis Blair, Maj. Gen. Charles Bolden, Hon. James M. Cannon, Lt. Gen. Daniel W. Christman, Gen. Wesley K. Clark, Sen. Max Cleland (D-Ga.), Adm. Archie Clemins, Hon. William Cohen, Adm. William J. Crowe, Gen. Ronald R. Gogleman, Lt. Gen. Howard D. Graves, Gen. Joseph P. Hoar, Sen. Robert J. Kerrey (D-Nebr.), Adm. Charles R. Larson, Sen. Carl Levin (D-Mich.), Hon. Robert "Bud" McFarlane, Gen. Carl E. Mundy Jr., Gen. Lloyd W. Newton, Hon. William J. Perry, Adm. Joseph W. Prueher, Sen. Jack Reed (D-R.I.), Hon. Joseph R. Reeder, Gen. H. Norman Schwarzkopf, Gen. John Shaliskashvili, Gen. Hugh Shelton, Gen. Gordon R. Sullivan, and Gen. Anthony Zinni.

4. *Gratz v. Bollinger*, 539 U.S. 244 (2003).

5. *Grutter v. Bollinger*, 539 U.S. 306 (2003).

6. Veteran's History Project: A Project of the American Folklife Center of the Library of Congress, (Washington, D.C.: Library of Congress, 2006).

7. The Web site of the Veterans History Project is http://www.loc.gov/vets.

8. The *Tavis Smiley Show*.

9. American Battle Monuments Commission, *Fiscal Year 2004 Annual Report* (Arlington, Va.: American Battle Monuments Commission, 2004).

Index

About the Author

Julius W. Becton Jr. was born on June 29, 1926, in Bryn Mawr, Pennsylvania, to Julius W. Becton Sr. and Rose Inez Becton. The eldest son of a janitor and a domestic worker, Becton enlisted in the then-segregated Army in 1943. Becton went on to serve his nation in three wars, receiving numerous awards for valor and meritorious service. During a military career that spanned nearly four decades, he rose to the rank of lieutenant general and commanded at every level in the Army, from platoon to the vaunted VII U.S. Corps, breaking countless racial barriers along the way.

Upon retirement from the Army in 1983, General Becton continued his life of public service. He served in the Reagan administration as director of the Office of Foreign Disaster Assistance and was subsequently appointed as the third director of the Federal Emergency Management Agency. In 1989 Becton was selected as the fifth president of his alma mater, Prairie View A&M University. After almost five years in that position, he returned home to Northern Virginia and was later asked to serve as superintendent and CEO of the District of Columbia public school system. Although officially "retired" since 1998, General Becton continues to serve his community and his country through his involvement in numerous pro bono boards. His sixty-year marriage to the former Louise Thornton has produced five successful children.